whistleblowers

Quentin Dempster

an
ABC
BOOK

Published by ABC Books for the
AUSTRALIAN BROADCASTING CORPORATION
GPO Box 9994 Sydney NSW 2001

First published May 1997

ISBN 0 7333 0504 0

Designed by Jim Shepherd
Set in 10.5/12 pt Riccione by
Midland Typesetters, Maryborough, Victoria
Printed and bound in Australia by
Australian Print Group, Maryborough, Victoria

Dedicated to those who have
the courage to put the truth first.

CONTENTS

Life is mostly froth and bubble
Two things stand like stone
Kindness in another's trouble
Courage in your own.

Adam Lindsay Gordon (1833–1870)
Bush Ballads and Galloping Rhymes

INTRODUCTION

WHISTLEBLOWERS ARE PEOPLE who alert the public to scandal, danger, malpractice or corruption. The people you meet in this book are ordinary Australians who decided to 'blow the whistle' and face the consequences. For many it became a personal ordeal requiring determination and courage.

We live in a corporate state. Corporate authority, public or private, exercises power for the good of the corporate entity. In the process, individuals sometimes become mangled and the truth is not confronted or it is covered up. Instead of being an asset to the corporate authority, those individuals in possession of unpopular truths can find themselves and their careers in jeopardy.

This is the moment when the individual must decide: to stand and fight or to withdraw and allow the corporate will to prevail. Some are backed into a corner where they have no choice but to fight, to survive the physical, intellectual, emotional or economic onslaught on their lives.

This book details the case histories of Australians who have faced moral and ethical dilemmas and, through a variety of circumstances, have become what is known as whistleblowers. Their stories are a guide, a warning and an inspiration to those of us who might have to face similar dilemmas.

One fact emerges: the failure of authority to recognise whistle-blowing as a positive and constructive force. Vested interests, be they political or economic or maintained for the pursuit of power alone, have little capacity to make concessions. In the conflicts which affect whistleblowers, vested interests can and have come off second best. But invariably it is the individual who suffers the most—from not being believed or trusted, from a shattering of self-esteem, from harassment, from intimidation, from being publicly discredited or abused. But whistleblowers are not victims or losers. They are winners. Through their personal courage, sacrifice and hardship it is we, the rest of society, who also win.

Whistleblowers around the world have established support groups to swing in behind anyone confronted with the dilemma of actually having to blow the whistle on corporate authority then sometimes face devastating personal consequences. For the manifest public benefit of their actions whistleblowers deserve recognition. Rarely, however, is it proffered. Sometimes it is lost in a thicket of claim and counter claim.

This book describes how some have fared through the conflict as well as the tactics and methods deployed against them, to defend the right to have the truth of a situation made public against sometimes overwhelmingly powerful forces.

Whistleblowers have a unique place in our history. On many occasions they have been agents for change—even if they did not know it at the time. This book cannot cover all those deserving cases but in recognising the few, we hope to acknowledge the existence of all other genuine whistleblowers.

The author wishes to thank Robyn Smith for her extensive research, editors Carolyn Beaumont and Nina Riemer for advice and support as the manuscript came together, ABC publishers John Kerr and Matthew Kelly for their support and encouragement and Judith Walker from the ABC's Legal and Copyright service. Acknowledgement and thanks are due to my ABC colleague Bruce Donald for his editorial, legal, trade practice and analytical skills in a number of investigations we worked on together as part of ABC TV's national investigative unit in 1995. Bruce Donald has been an unsung hero of ABC investigative journalism through the 1980s and early 1990s.

And the author wishes to emphasise that without the ABC, a national broadcaster committed to pursue its Charter objectives to inform the public of Australia, much of this work would not have been possible.

In the mid-section of this book is an analysis of the modern phenomenon known as whistleblowing. Reprinted with kind permission are extracts from William de Maria's critical analysis of whistleblowing legislation (*The Alternative Law Journal*, 1995) and John McMillan's writings on the international experience (*Corruption and Reform*, University of Queensland Press). Thanks are due to my wife, Elizabeth, a psychiatrist, for observations on the psycho-dynamics of the whistleblowers whose stories are told here.

Without the courage of the whistleblowers we would not be informed about what really goes on in our sometimes very uncivilised world.

Quentin Dempster
Sydney
March 1997

THE WESTPAC LETTERS

'The Bank and its employees stole money from its clients. Taking secret commissions and switching deals is stealing. And they tried to cover it up by trying to suppress the publication of those letters. I can think of no other worse case of corporate immorality.'—John McLennan, former internal efficiency auditor, Westpac Banking Corporation, to Australia's Parliamentary Banking Inquiry (1990–91).

JOHN ROSS MCLENNAN was born into a banker's family on 14 November 1946. At the time the McLennan family (elder sister Kaye, mother Vera Irene and father Alfred James or 'Fred' McLennan) was living in the township of Springsure west of Rockhampton in central Queensland.

Fred McLennan worked for the Bank of New South Wales and in the years of young John's early life the family had innumerable moves as the bank transferred the ever loyal Fred far and wide. John attended thirteen different schools before settling for the final four years of high school in Brisbane. The McLennans lived in transit accommodation in places are far removed as Chinchilla, Brisbane, Toowoomba and Sydney. They were staunch Presbyterians and regular church goers. The constant moves were unsettling for John but Fred's work ethic was a value anchor.

When the McLennans finally settled in Brisbane in 1961 John was enrolled at Brisbane Grammar School, a private school of good educational reputation. John was not academically brilliant. He struggled hard and achieved an average pass with just two As (as subjects were then graded), a few Bs and the rest Cs.

After leaving Brisbane Grammar in 1964 John McLennan particularly remembered the speech to the students from the school's then headmaster, Harry 'Shorty' Newell. (In the contrary style that is Australian humour, 'Shorty' was well over six feet tall.) Young

McLennan remembered Shorty intoning words to the effect: 'You've had years of education. If there's nothing else you take from this school, remember it's easy to go along with the mob, to do the popular thing. But you must stand back, think for yourself and make your own decisions in life—whether you're right or wrong—stand by your own judgment'. McLennan believed it was that sense of trusting your own judgment which stayed with him through his adult years. He had a fond memory of Shorty's speech echoing down the Great Hall at Brisbane Grammar School. It was Shorty's words and their influence on young John McLennan which years later would rock the Australian banking establishment to its foundations.

McLennan, funded by part-time work as a builder's labourer and his mother's job in a shoe shop, enrolled at Queensland University and studied science. He was strong in maths but that was about all. University life was something of a culture shock. He had moved into a flat in Brisbane while Fred and Vera lived in Surfers Paradise where Fred was the manager of the local branch of the Bank of New South Wales. And there were the distractions of girls. John soon fell in love with Chris, a fellow student. He and Chris wanted to get married. But Chris's parents objected. Because the legal age for marriage under Queensland law was twenty-one, underage 'children' had to have the consent of their parents. Chris's parents did not consent so John decided to challenge them with an application to a magistrate of the Children's Court. Chris's mother argued that Chris was not 'mature enough'. John thought it somewhat strange that at their age you could be sent to Vietnam to get your head blown off but you could not get married. He ran the case for himself and his sweetheart to get married. They lost. They were shattered.

John was not able to come to terms with university culture and wanted to get out. He'd been called up under the National Service Act and as an alternative to induction he had enlisted in the Citizen Military Forces for five years. When he quit university he also withdrew from the CMF, triggering the call-up. He was rejected on medical grounds—severe acne.

He had no strong political views about the conflict in Vietnam. In some ways he had been disappointed that he had not been able to embark on what many young men saw as an adventure. He did not have long hair, the almost mandatory fashion on campus in the 1960s. He was and remained a political conservative but with an inquisitive attitude.

Having thrown in university, a life of earning a living awaited him. Fred pressured John to join the bank, to 'give it a go for a couple of years'. John relented and applied for a job as a junior in the Bank of New South Wales—his father's bank.

It was a humiliating experience. He had to fill all the ink wells and change the blotting paper. He had to get a broom and sluice water dumped on the bank's pathways from a Brisbane storm. When he finally got to do counter work, his maths deserted him. It was Decimal Currency Day, 14 February 1966, the day Australia abandoned pounds shillings and pence. At the end of the day his counter deposits and withdrawals would not balance. There was a big deficiency. A customer rescued him from grave embarrassment. The customer, a local publican, walked up to the counter carrying a big wad of money. 'You've given me too much money,' the publican beamed. McLennan breathed a sigh of relief and thanked the customer for his honesty. The book was balanced.

McLennan soon hated counter work. He called it a 'nothing job'. By now he was a whiz at balancing the books. As a teller at the bank's Fortitude Valley branch he devised a structure to balance deposits and withdrawals through the day so that by knock off time, 2.50 pm, the entire branch's books could be balanced. Instead of having to stay back after the doors were closed, staff could leave almost immediately. This aptitude for devising new systems impressed the bank's middle management and McLennan was sent to the basement of the Fortitude Valley branch to work on accumulated months of books. He worked with speed and precision and soon finished the job—a cumulative balance of one of the bank's largest branches in Queensland.

Fred and Vera had moved again, this time to Sydney where Fred's own career was going well and he was appointed to the bank's central administration. Back in Brisbane John wanted out of the branch structure and he, too, went into administration where his job was to balance the books of all the bank's branches in the State of Queensland.

On 7 March 1970 John and Chris were married. Chris still had not turned twenty-one but her parents had relented and blessed the marriage. With a concessional staff mortgage from the bank they bought a house at Weller's Hill, a Brisbane suburb. Chris worked as a laboratory technician.

Such was the life of banking that they were soon on the move, to the nearby city of Toowoomba where John took a job as the manager's assistant for that branch's international department. The branch's biggest client was the Toowoomba Foundry, which had many international sales to the Middle East. He became interested in foreign currency transactions through this experience in international business and the buying and selling of currency.

From Toowoomba they moved to Darwin where the job of overseas officer was offered. McLennan was to manage a staff of five and handle transactions involving iron ore shipments, the export of prawns and the movement of travellers' cheques.

First Dilemma

IT was at this branch that John McLennan faced his first moral and ethical dilemma. He was not an active unionist. Most bank staff were members of the Bank Officers' Association as it was then called. While McLennan did not involve himself in any industrial politics he respected the right of the union to represent the staff in negotiations with the bank's management. One day he discovered that a senior Darwin officer had intercepted a message from the union's head office to its members in the Darwin branch to hold a stopwork meeting over an industrial issue. McLennan angrily confronted the officer and declared that he had no right to intercept the message. Affronted by this, the officer promptly suspended McLennan and sent him home. 'You're an arsehole,' he cursed as McLennan left the premises. At this time Chris was heavily pregnant and was terribly upset when John told her why he was home early. The officer later vowed to make sure that McLennan's career was finished. McLennan, back at work, responded by making sure his back was covered.

The bank officer, a heavy drinker, often attended a nearby pub for lunch. McLennan occasionally accompanied him. One day, when McLennan was expecting heavy paperwork in the afternoon, the manager pressured him to stay drinking at the pub after 1.30 pm. McLennan protested that he had to leave. 'When you come to lunch with me, you go when I say so,' the officer ordered. John McLennan turned on his heel and returned to work.

The McLennans' daughter, Kirsty, was born soon after in Darwin, but two months after the birth the family faced a crisis. John was stricken with blinding headaches and had to go home to bed. The headaches got worse. One Sunday night he collapsed and woke up in hospital. He was to remain there for more than four weeks while tests were done to try to discover what the problem was. Chris was struggling at home alone with the new baby while John's health problem remained undiagnosed. Doctors at one stage declared he had only weeks to live. Fred McLennan in Sydney was so concerned that he arranged for 'some strings to be pulled'. Special arrangements were made by the bank to fly the McLennan family urgently to Sydney.

Recovery was slow but young McLennan's health returned to normal. He was re-assigned to the bank's systems development area in central administration in Sydney with the job of computerising all international accounts. The bank's international accounting system was finally and successfully computerised in 1979. The success of the organisational and leadership effort was to earn McLennan many internal accolades including one from the then chief manager of the Bank's International Division, Mr Stuart Fowler. To McLennan's amazement Fowler wrote a letter saying that the bank would not be giving him a bonus for his work because he would be getting a promotion in due course. A bonus would be doubling up.

McLennan became a hotshot methods efficiency expert, designing new systems and procedures for the bank's entire domestic network. The cost of time was monitored to find out how much it took to write out a mortgage and do other routine chores in a search for speedier and more cost effective methods.

By the early 1980s Australian banking was changing. Management was to become focused on objectives and mission statements and performance indicators and market shares. Australian banks were no longer to be the providers of service but the sellers of 'product'. Banks became profit and product driven. In this process all forms of behaviour became justifiable provided profit was there. This cultural change would eventually rewrite the ethics of banking from service providers to product sellers.

During this process of change John McLennan was appointed manager of Personnel Administration in the Data Processing Division with 2000 specialist staff. The McLennans' second daughter, Fiona was born. Soon after, a son, Cameron, joined the family.

John McLennan, now in his mid-thirties, found a mentor within the bank. The chief manager of the Data Processing Division brought McLennan into the bank's executive group. In quiet, personal advice he told McLennan that it was 'okay to make a mistake—only don't make it twice'. After a career spent on making a bank's bureaucratic processes reach levels of control and precision, McLennan was being guided to change his mode of thinking from the old bureaucratic constraints to become more lateral.

Fred McLennan was now a senior ranked general manager, one of the bank's top ten executives. Young John had to cope with corridor talk that he had done well because of his father.

In 1983 Fred retired from the bank, which had been renamed Westpac to reflect a new competitive international image for what was by then Australia's largest bank. But he was soon back on temporary assignment to conduct an efficiency audit. In an unusual manoeuvre the bank appointed John McLennan to join his father's team. They became the bank's razor gang, moving through the administrations of the states, exposing shoddy management and upsetting many careers in the process. By 1986 the efficiency audit division was disbanded. John McLennan was advised that he had made too many enemies. He decided to leave Westpac.

Career Change

HE had an offer too good to refuse. It was a big career change with a downside. He would have to give up the bank's low mortgage interest rate for staff and substantial superannuation benefits. John McLennan went to work for car hire entrepreneur Bob Ansett's

Budget Rent-A-Car as manager of business development of the leasing division. The McLennans sold the family home in Sydney's St Ives and moved to a house at Terry Hills which they funded from John's superannuation payout. The banker's conservative image had to go as the job of developing a competitive business became the challenge. Bob Ansett, son of the legendary commercial aviation pioneer, Sir Reginald Ansett, was a master at marketing. He gave motivational speeches and attracted publicity wherever he went. Ansett was impressed with McLennan's work in business development but after eighteen months McLennan felt that his skills were wasted. He had developed some misgivings about the Budget group and its efficiency, but he found that walls went up whenever he tried to come to terms with the group's accounting methods and systems. While McLennan retained a soft spot for Bob Ansett he felt that the great entrepreneur and salesman was not being confronted with the truth.

McLennan left Budget before the group got into financial difficulties. The family moved to Port Macquarie on the New South Wales north coast to 'play farmers' on a property on the Hastings River. It was here that John McLennan met Port Macquarie solicitors John Garrett and Andrew Walmsley who, like him, were refugees from the big city. They asked him to do some part-time consulting work with local businesses including some that were in trouble financially. Others, although successful, needed directional advice. McLennan was introduced to some of the firm's clients including the husband and wife owners of a very successful Port Macquarie bus company, Sonters Pty Ltd. Reg and Thelma Sonter were past retirement age and Thelma was a paraplegic. The company owned and ran up to thirty buses mainly on local routes and for charter work. It had taken Reg and Thelma forty years to build up the company and now they were looking forward to retirement. They had some spare land which they wished to subdivide and sell to build a nest egg for that retirement. And they were proud that all the bus company's cash flow had gone into servicing the business which was virtually debt free.

Reg and Thelma had sought an investment loan from the local Westpac branch to fund the subdivision work in 1985. They had banked with Westpac for forty years and were obviously well regarded customers with such a large local business. Glenlauren Pty Ltd, Reg and Thelma's subsidiary company set up to handle the subdivision, was offered $1.1 million Australian dollars in the equivalent Swiss francs at a loan interest rate of 6.5 per cent—well below the 16 per cent to 18 per cent domestic investment interest rates then on offer in Australian finance markets. The original loan application by the Sonters was for only $500,000 but the bank told them the Swiss francs loan was such a good deal they should take their profits in advance and borrow $1.1 million. Reg and Thelma were talked into it.

But soon their investment loan went radically wrong.

John McLennan met the Sonters through a local accountant. He listened to their problems and introduced them to John Garrett. The Sonters by then were caught in a pincer of falling land prices and a debt over which they had no control. The falling Australian dollar continued to plunge them into financial crisis. The Sonters said the bank offered no help in managing their exposure and later refused a professional risk manager permission to manage it for them.

By the time John Garrett and John McLennan had a meeting with the Sonters on their property at Laurieton south of Port Macquarie in 1988 they were in desperate trouble. The now floating Australian dollar had nosedived in value compared with other currencies since 1985 and the Sonters' Swiss franc loan had quickly blown out to $2.5 million. The profit expected from the subdivision had been blown away with such overheads and they couldn't discharge such a loan even if they had achieved a good price for the subdivided land at sale. McLennan found the old couple in a state of distress as the bank had made its first threat to put their companies into receivership and sell all their assets.

McLennan invited John Garrett to attend a meeting with the Sonters and people he described as 'hit men' from Westpac's head office in Sydney. In the Sonters' house were Reg and Thelma and two of their three adult sons, staring increduously as the bankers spelt out the consequences of their indebted circumstances. McLennan recalled that he had never seen anything like it. The Sonters were confronted with a matter-of-fact statement that they should agree with what the bank proposed. The bankers wanted them to sign an agreement to sell their assets. And the proposal offered by the bank included a 'release' for the bank over any negligence claim. McLennan recalls them saying in effect: 'You had better sign this agreement or we'll sell you up and you'll have nothing'. Forty years of customer loyalty stood for nothing. McLennan did not speak during the meeting. He just observed.

'I sat watching the bankers as they cold bloodedly tried to coerce the Sonters by fear and intimidation into signing the agreement. I was horrified at what was unfolding. This was the bank I had worked for for twenty years. This was the bank my father worked for. This was the bank I had once considered as part of my family. In my naivety I had always believed that if the bank made a mistake, it would ensure the mistake was rectified. It was clear to me the bankers were following a well rehearsed "company line".'

At the end of the meeting, McLennan decided it was time he spoke. He told the bankers to 'go to hell'. He had long experience with the bank and he could say their behaviour towards their customers was completely out of order and he would be advising the Sonters to fight them. He said he had an intimate knowledge of foreign currency loans and the procedures to be adopted by the bank to hedge against currency fluctuations and protect the bank's customers from just such a situation as was confronting the Sonters. 'As I watched, my anger grew. I knew this was unjust. What I did not know was that this scene was being played out all over Australia. Many hard-working families were being put to the sword by banks desperate to cover up their incompetence and force the solution of their negligence on to their victims: the borrowers.'

When the bankers left without their signed agreement Garrett and McLennan set to work. Garrett and Walmsley started major commercial litigation against Westpac, filing a statement of claim setting out the facts as they knew them and seeking what is known as 'discovery' where Westpac would have to meet the reasonable demands of the plaintiff, the Sonters, to provide their documentary evidence in the loan arrangements, and more importantly the bank's internal policy documents which would demonstrate to the court the bank's negligence in marketing what was a 'defective loan product'.

John McLennan was moved to compassion and empathy for

Reg and Thelma who had worked so hard during their lives. He felt a growing outrage towards Westpac, his former employers. This sort of thing was just not done towards solid and loyal customers to the bank. The Sonter family was in a highly distressed state throughout the process of litigation with the prospect of losing everything if the action failed. To add to the distress one of Reg and Thelma's sons committed suicide. McLennan angrily blamed the bank. He became so enraged that on one occasion he rang the bank in Sydney and told one of its officers that as far as he was concerned the bank had killed Reg and Thelma's son. 'That's what you've done,' he shouted down the telephone. 'It was a huge emotional upheaval for me as well,' he recalled. 'It seemed to me the bank was treating the Sonters as "book entries" simply to be ruled off and was incapable of, or refused to see the impact their actions would have on the Sonters, their family and their employees.'

'Discovery'

GARRETT and Walmsley's demand for 'discovery' was opposed in almost every aspect by Westpac and its lawyers. The firm had to take the bank to court to contest every objection the bank put up to supplying documents. But the Port Macquarie lawyers won in court.

Such was McLennan's level of frustration that John Garrett asked him to take a back seat for a while and not be involved in the lawyer-to-lawyer negotiations in the discovery process. Eventually the documents came and the bank's methodology in marketing the foreign currency loans to customers with sound asset backing and the 'hedging' of the foreign loans the bank had committed itself to was exposed. A settlement favourable to the Sonters was eventually negotiated 'out of court'. It was a 'good' settlement, although the terms had to remain secret.

The documents 'discovered' through the process were substantial but in later litigation McLennan discovered the bank had withheld a large number of important policy documents on the grounds that they were 'not relevant'. The bank's tactics had become apparent. They argued that discovery demands were 'not reasonable', or 'relevant', or that they did not know if the specific documents requested actually existed or if they did exist whether they had been destroyed by the bank in the normal course of events. The tactic was to force the litigant to court to argue every objection. This in turn forced litigants with diminishing resources to decide if even more funds should be put at risk.

As a result of the Sonters settlement in September 1988 an article appeared in Sydney's *Sun-Herald* newspaper. McLennan's involvement in the case was publicised and over the following days he received telephone calls from other foreign currency borrowers in similar difficulties to the Sonters. McLennan was contacted by Ian Fisher, a farmer who had borrowed heavily. Trevor King, a Queensland property developer, was also on the phone. Such was the response from distressed investors wanting to know what they could learn from the Sonters' case that McLennan and Fisher decided to call a meeting. In all twelve foreign currency borrowers indicated they wanted desperately to attend. McLennan had listened to tales of financial woe. Some of the investors lost control and would cry over the phone of their embarrassment and desperation, of their humiliation at jeopardising their previously sound businesses, farms or personal savings.

The 'gang of thirteen' as it was later called (twelve investors plus John McLennan) met at the El Rancho Motel in Port Macquarie in December 1988. They decided to form the Foreign Currency Borrowers Association to seek comfort in their adversity, if nothing else, to coordinate their fight against the banks. McLennan was elected president from the floor. It had a dramatic effect on his life. There were no consultancy fees in this for him. The investors were already in a state of financial stress. For two days the group listened as one by one each investor stood up and recounted, sometimes in tears, the shame of financial ruin, the marital breakdown, the destruction of self-esteem and self-confidence.

'That's when they began to fight. They were not alone,' McLennan recalled. Up to this point the banks had quietly taken the borrowers down a dark alley and beaten them into submission. Now they would find a mob waiting for them.

McLennan spent most of the day and half the night on the telephone talking to association members. More members joined. At the height of its campaign membership reached 250 foreign currency borrowers. The pressure of being both a financial consultant with intimate knowledge of the banks' inner workings as well as a personal counsellor was enormous and draining. McLennan knew that the only way he could fight the banks was to expose them in the media. He mounted a personal campaign through the media and with the fearless reporting of a number of prominent journalists (most notably Anne Lampe of *The Sydney Morning Herald* whose quest for the truth never relented) he thrust the plight of the foreign currency borrowers onto the breakfast tables of hundreds of thousands of Australians. McLennan was later to learn that the banks believed he had a 'sophisticated media network' and had used substantial funds to promote the cause. In reality he was a one man band. But every morning when his efforts produced a major newspaper story, he believed he could hear the toilets flushing in the head offices of the major banks.

Trevor King, the property developer, had pressing problems. His companies had substantial assets and the bank from which he had foreign currency borrowings was pressing ahead with a plan to sell all King's assets to recover outstanding monies. King had borrowed from Wespac's Brisbane branch. McLennan introduced King to John Garrett and he agreed to take on King's case. The bank appointed a receiver and had arranged to put King's properties up for auction. This was at a time when King had a substantial counter claim against the bank. If he lost all his assets and income through an auction process he would lose all his means to fight. There was no time to lose. Within thirty minutes of the auction's scheduled start, Garrett secured a Federal Court injunction against Westpac restraining it from proceeding. The court had said, in effect, that the bank could not sell King up while its customer was in dispute with it.

The decision, Eltran Pty Ltd v Westpac, was to stop the banks in their tracks. Before this the banks had sold up borrowers which denied them the means of fighting in the courts. The banks had an advantage. They had intimate details of a borrower's financial position and they usually controlled all their assets. In effect, they had a mortgage over the legal system and they ruthlessly exploited it. This called into question the entire justice system in many borrowers' minds.

McLennan recalls that all the banks involved in foreign currency loans treated the association and its members with contempt from the moment of the Eltran/Westpac judgment.

In the discovery process, as with the Sonters, thousands of documents had to be handed over. The legal expenses for the case were mounting up to millions of dollars. Trevor King had the foresight to squirrel funds away to back this legal fight to the death with his bank. Unlike other association members King never appeared to be ground down by difficulties and the seeming hopelessness of his circumstances taking on so powerful a corporate entity as the largest bank in Australia. He had known the risks of taking out loans in foreign currency. He did not plead ignorance in what he had committed himself to in the foreign currency arrangements. His case was based on his belief that the bank had not carried out his instructions in the placement of 'hedge' contracts. And he would set out to prove that the bank had been negligent in handling his instructions. He would claim that he had instructed the bank's foreign currency agents to implement 'stop loss' control. The bank had failed to carry out these instructions and he was furious with what had happened. The bank's tactic was to move as swiftly as possible to grab control of the defaulting or now greatly indebted customer, to effectively seize business cash flows, to disempower the customer by the removal of any resources with which to mount a counter attack. In Trevor King's case the bank had come within thirty minutes of achieving that objective.

McLennan recalled: 'I worked with Trevor King over many years, often spending weeks poring through endless documents and providing advice on complex audit trails. When I first started work on his case the bank had produced virtually no worthwhile discovery. Within two years, and after endless court battles, the discovery was massive. The relevant section of every document was extracted on to a computer data base. Every event, name, place and person could be tracked through thousands of documents. This was the first case where we employed technology to unravel the gobbledegook of documents provided by the bank. The result was devastating for the bank.

Trevor King eventually won an out-of-court settlement, Mc-Lennan providing tactical advice during the discovery process through his own knowledge of the way the banks conducted themselves, the documents they kept, their internal instructions to the branch networks on the marketing of foreign currency loans to customers and the duties that were imposed on the banks to protect clients. By the end of this harrowing process John McLennan and Trevor King were close friends with a common goal. It was a friendship forged through the adversity of the times and the high-stakes game with a corporation they viewed as ruthless with almost limitless financial capacity.

Legal Tactics

BORROWERS were starting to win inside and outside court. The first case won was Spice v Westpac. The borrowers' association thought this would provide a 'precedent' for all other cases but the bank successfully argued that each case was different. This lack of a 'precedent' was to cost borrowers millions of dollars in legal expenses.

Another win was Charabaglio v Westpac. Westpac appealed … and lost. The case Potts v Westpac was initially won by the borrower and then lost to appeal. The biggest loss by the borrowers was David Securities Pty Ltd v The Commonwealth Bank. The precedent set here was devastating for borrowers. By this time the banks were throwing millions of dollars into the legal battle and the borrowers could not cope with the massive cost of case preparation. It was clear to McLennan and the borrowers that the legal system was open to manipulation by the banks through endless interlocutory hearings and so-called notices of motion.

Hundreds of cases were started and failed when borrowers ran out of money and were quietly led to the slaughterhouse. The banks' tactics were simple. They settled any cases they thought would be won by the borrowers. So those that did get their day in court gave a distorted picture of the wider range of cases.

One borrower, Tom Quade, a farmer from western New South Wales, reported to McLennan that he had lost his case in court. McLennan was incredulous as the circumstances followed others already won by the Foreign Currency Borrowers. 'How could you possibly have lost?' McLennan said, sharing Quade's distress. Under evidentiary rules of the court, documents relevant in one case were not necessarily admissible in another.

To 'use' documents from one case in another was prima facie contempt of court. The banks exploited this to ensure each borrower never knew the extent of damaging documents which were available. The Westpac letters would later confirm this tactic. But the banks could not stop McLennan from using his knowledge of the existence of documents.

'In other words I could not show a borrower general policy documents produced in one case relating to the development and marketing of foreign currency loans even if the bank was in contempt of court for not having produced them in another. Might was right. What I could do, however, was to provide evidence to the court that I had knowledge of the existence of the relevant documents, their general description and class.

'This infuriated the banks and they tried on many occasions to entrap me into a contempt situation. To me it was a stupid and absurd situation that a bank could be in contempt by withholding documents and yet was protected by the court by holding anyone who caught them out "in contempt".'

Each case required separate and full discovery of all relevant documents with the banks contesting each document on the question of admissibility and relevance. Quade had run smack up against the legal system. McLennan took a huge risk. A solicitor, John Griffin of Ferrier and Associates, was one of the few lawyers McLennan had met who had a profound sense of justice and outrage over what was happening in the cases before the courts. It became apparent that the bank involved in Quade's case, the Commonwealth Bank, had withheld a huge amount of documentation in the discovery process. Equipped with McLennan's advice, Quade's lawyers appealed to the Full Bench of the Federal Court claiming that the bank had so withheld documents during discovery.

McLennan said: 'I was aware that if the Commonwealth Bank decided to become bloody minded they could try to nail me for contempt. Against this I had to weigh the fact that great injustice had been done and the Commonwealth Bank had obtained its justice by withholding substantial discovery. The documents were known as the G documents and comprised all the bank's policy documents showing the development, marketing and administration of foreign currency loans. Again, this decision was taken in the face of fear. I could not allow the lives of the Quades to be ruined by an injustice such as this. The risks were enormous but I knew that if the truth was put before the appeal court, I would be vindicated'. McLennan used knowledge of documents from another case to demonstrate the existence of similar documents in the Quade case. As it turned out Justice Marcus Einfeld accepted the evidence as did the High Court on appeal.

'We thrashed them', McLennan recalled. The Full Bench of the Federal Court declared that the Commonwealth Bank had won the judgement against Quade by 'misconduct'. The Commonwealth Bank appealed this decision to the High Court. Appeal dismissed. There was now a powerful precedent against the bank's tactics of 'non-discovery'. From then on the banks were terrified to withhold any documents. As well, with the banking industry awash with stories of the Foreign Currency Borrowers' success at court, the banks themselves started 'leaking like sieves'.

McLennan found that he was being personally blackguarded throughout the banking industry. He heard he was being denigrated 'as a nut case' by bank executives and lawyers dealing with foreign currency cases. 'These personal attacks made me realise that I was being very effective against them. One attack came from a prominent lawyer. I knew I was getting under his skin. You know when you are effective by the strength of the dirty tricks used against you. The irony is that all of the cases this particular lawyer ran, he lost. Who is the nut case?'

What was most devastating for the aggrieved bank customers and disappointing to observers of the process was the failure of the Australian commercial justice system to stop vexatious, delaying and other adversarial tactics. In fact the system thrived on this game—however costly it was to both the banks and their shareholders and the mental health and remaining financial resources of their once loyal customers. The Foreign Currency Borrowers Association believed that only one judge was prepared to call the injustice which so obviously existed—Justice Marcus Einfeld. Whether the documents so vital to establishing the truth had been obtained through 'discovery' or through leaking, Einfeld seemed to be unconcerned. It was not until 1994 that Einfeld 'stopped the rot', when in Greenwood v ANZ the judge remarked that the courts were sick of arguments over discovery and that the banks knew very well what documents should be discovered. He added that relevance was not an issue. The court would decide if they were relevant in the hearing. At one point in the proceedings to the amazement of McLennan and the consternation of the banks, Einfeld wished McLennan 'Merry Christmas' and told him to get the documents any way he could, short of stealing them. His final remark was that he did not care if they 'fell off the back of a truck'. As a result the bank was forced to produce a considerable additional discovery which was instrumental in forcing a substantial settlement for Ms Greenwood on the steps of the court.

The evidence through the leaked internal documents was building a picture that the banks had embroiled themselves in other questionable practices, including the taking of secret commissions without the knowledge or agreement of the customer or applying excessive margins in foreign currency exchange rates. One dealer declared that the foreign currency customers were 'like lambs to the slaughter'. So many customers never knew they were being ripped off.

Through all this the banks maintained an aggressive approach to the Foreign Currency Borrowers Association. The delaying tactics continued in litigation in progress. It was a document by document struggle, debilitating to desperate people who faced financial ruin.

Retaliatory Clauses

So great was one bank's fear of the Foreign Currency Borrowers Association that it adopted a new tactic to include clauses in settlement agreements which had the effect of banning the borrower from any contact with FCBA members or 'any other consumer organisation'. Any breach of this clause would result in a 'liquidated damages' fine of $1000 for each contact. They also demanded, as part of the deal, that borrowers 'dob in' the FCBA by giving the bank all copies of newsletters and correspondence. And this from one bank which would later demand its right to confidentiality. McLennan became aware that some borrowers were required to surrender copies of his own advice to their solicitors in the obvious hope of finding something on which McLennan could be dragged into court. To McLennan's enduring distress and regret some borrowers actually 'sold out' and agreed to the banks' demands in order to secure a settlement. 'They know who they are. They will have to live with their consciences,' he said.

The clauses in the settlement agreements read:

Return of discovered documents.

The Borrower shall return all copy documents provided to his legal advisers and experts during the action by (the bank) in the process of discovery or otherwise and all material obtained from or through the Foreign Currency Borrowers Association or any similar organisation within fourteen (14) days of the date hereof.

The borrower shall immediately sever any association or relationship (either personal or business) with the Foreign Currency Borrowers Association or any similar organisation. If the borrower breaches this provision he agrees to pay (the bank) ONE THOUSAND DOLLARS ($1000) by way of agreed liquidated damages for each and every occasion of any breach.

The existence of these retaliatory clauses in out-of-court settlement agreements has never before been made public. At the very least it was a denial of the civil liberties of the bank's customers and intimidatory and exploitative of their desperate financial circumstances. John McLennan was later to give a copy of one such agreement to the House of Representatives Standing Committee on Finance and Public Administration covering banking practices. Nothing was done to reprimand the banks.

A big breakthrough came in January 1991, but it was a breakthrough which almost destroyed John McLennan. He was to become the prime target for retaliation through the legal system.

Westpac Letters

OUT of the blue he received what became known as 'the Westpac letters'—two letters from Westpac's legal firm Allen Allen and

Hemsley to Westpac's chief general manager Corporate and International. McLennan first saw copies of the letters faxed to him from *The Sydney Morning Herald* journalist Anne Lampe. Copies addressed to himself arrived in the mail a day or two later. When he got the seventeen pages McLennan could not believe what he was reading. He was visiting a firm of solicitors in Sydney at the time when Lampe faxed the letters through to the fax number. She in turn had received the letters by fax from Belgium and wanted McLennan to confirm their authenticity. McLennan went into the toilet to contemplate the contents. The letters were a confirmation of all the Foreign Currency Borrowers Association had feared about Westpac's legal tactics. The letters had come to various addressees in Australia from Belgium. It was later to be alleged by Westpac that the letters had been stolen from the bank and were being used as leverage in litigation the bank had brought against Westpac's former foreign exchange dealer Naji Halabi and members of his family. This was unknown to John McLennan at the time. McLennan swears he did not know the identity of the source of the letters at the time he received them.

The letters were written by Allen's then senior partner Paddy Jones.

In the first, dated 26 November 1987, Jones reports under the qualification 'Absolutely Private and Confidential' on a searching review of 50 000 documents involving Westpac and its finance subsidiary Partnership Pacific Pty Ltd, which was the bank's vehicle for marketing the overseas currency loans. The letter summarised the history of PPL's internal management problems and the consequences:

In short, managed forex loans was a bad idea, introduced at the worst possible time, and badly managed.

Then came some staggering admissions:

1   According to PPL's own documents, PPL
    • told clients that it would adopt a conservative, 'when in doubt, hedge' approach to risk management.
2   PPL's own documents acknowledged that
    • PPL did neither of these things; and

- this failure caused loss which would not otherwise have been incurred.

3   Trading conditions during the relevant period were such that all a prudent manager could have done is to have hedged and stayed hedged for the duration. This
- was objectively what PPL should have done;
- would have been consistent with PPL's representations as to the policy it would adopt.

4   As a result of 1−3, a number of clients did significantly worse than the fully-hedged position.

5   PPL undoubtedly took points which, at best, exeeeded its entitlement and to which, in my view, PPL had no entitlement at all. PPL probably switched transactions between its own accounts and its managed borrowers accounts.

6   The exemption clause in the Power of Attorney signed by managed borrowers will not operate to defeat actions which are available to those borrowers based on
- point taking and deal switching;
- failure to follow the conservative management policy which PPL represented to clients that it would follow.

7   As a result of 1−6, it is likely that managed borrowers would succeed against PPL.

8   The measure of damages will be:
- the amount lost via the taking of points;
- the profit lost via the switching of transactions;
- the difference between the fully hedged position (plus, say 20 per cent to approximate the point at which clients should have been fully hedged) and the position actually achieved.

9   Clients will be slow to commence action because of:
- the breadth of the exclusion clause in the Power of Attorney will deter clients (who don't know of the deal switching and point taking and the damaging PPL documents) from commencing action;
- their lack of knowledge of how damaging PPL's documents are;
- the lack of success of OCL actions to date;
- the high costs involved.

10 Given 9 and given full-time hands-on management by a
    suitable executive having total responsibility, suitably sup-
    ported by state managers, it should be possible to keep
    liability at a manageable level.

Referring to the acknowledgements made in Westpac and PPL's
own documents the letter declared: 'Many more documents have
been examined and a number of them are very damaging ... All
those reading this letter should read these documents—they are
devastating'.

Allen Allen and Hemsley estimated the then liability at $12.5
million in assessing potential claims over the amounts borrowed
which could be proved to have not been fully hedged. Westpac's
legal advisers had endorsed a strategy to minimise the liability,
exploiting the ignorance of the bank's customers and the high costs
involved. 'Many borrowers (particularly in these troubled times) are
not flush with cash and they would doubtless perceive PPL would
defend proceedings grimly.' The letter emphasised that secrecy was
the key to a successful strategy of minimising liability.

John McLennan could not believe his eyes. Nor could Anne
Lampe at *The Sydney Morning Herald*. The newspaper highlighted
the leaked letters in its financial pages. The following day McLennan
and the Foreign Currency Borrowers Association went public. The
Hawke Government had earlier launched a federal parliamentary
inquiry into the banking industry after the Treasurer, Paul Keating,
had asserted that Australia's banks were not passing on falls in
official interest rates as a deliberate plan to recover bad debts
amounting to about $10 billion. The inquiry was to be headed by
Labor backbencher, Stephen Martin. McLennan tried to crank up
the pressure.

From *The Sydney Morning Herald*: Wednesday, 30 January 1991:

BORROWERS SEEK NEW INQUIRY INTO FOREX
By Anne Lampe

A borrowers' action group has called for a royal commission into
banks and for banks to reimburse clients for 'negligence and
incompetence' in the wake of allegations of mismanagement of

foreign currency risks by a Westpac arm, Partnership Pacific.

Westpac received a detailed report on what had happened at PPL and was warned by its lawyer, Allen Allen and Hemsley, it should 'take all practical steps to avoid PPL's weaknesses being known outside PPL/Westpac boards and senior management'.

The Borrowers Association represents more than 200 borrowers who took out what was promoted by Australia's major banks as low-interest foreign currency loans. A meeting has been called for this Saturday at the Royal Motor Yacht Club at Point Piper to discuss the association's response to the leaking of the highly confidential memo from Allen Allen and Hemsley written in November 1987 on 'what went wrong' inside PPL.

The memo outlined how Allens conducted a detailed investigation of allegedly incompetent management of forex risk transactions at PPL during 1985 and 1986, which resulted in some clients incurring large losses. It also focused on the charging of allegedly excessive commissions on transactions incurred on behalf of borrowers and the parking of transactions overnight to circumvent Reserve Bank guidelines.

A spokesman for the borrowers' association, Mr John McLennan, said the association had already made a lengthy submission to the Parliamentary inquiry into banking practices. But after yesterday's revelations in the *Herald* it would be adding to the submissions and would also be asking for a royal commission into the activities of Australian banks.

'The banks must reimburse their clients for their negligence and incompetence,' Mr McLennan said yesterday.

Allens' letter two years ago to Westpac chief general manager corporate and international, Mr Warwick Kent, estimated PPL foreign currency clients incurred capital losses of $33 million and were millions of dollars worse off by going to PPL than if they had remained totally unhedged or had been fully hedged.

The letter also said while PPL was exposed to legal action from former PPL clients, PPL had the advantage of the clients not knowing how damaging its documents were as well as often not having the legal means to mount an action.

PPL risk management services have been referred to in

several damages actions mounted by Westpac loan borrowers who were referred to PPL's forex services when their loans blew out. One litigant has estimated that excessive margins on transactions cost him more than $600,000. Another estimated commissions on his $1.5 million loan were more than $300,00. Mr McLennan gave advice on discovery of sensitive documents in cases that resulted in out of court settlement on behalf of borrowers.

'For two years I have fought (alongside) borrowers through the courts for better and further discovery and for two years the banks have dragged the borrowers through the courts maintaining that documents which we knew existed did not. It was not until certain top level documents starting with the Riley report (this was a report commissioned by Westpac in 1985 to examine the offshore loan debacle, noting the bank's exposure which was later estimated to be approximately $3 billion) were selectively leaked from Westpac did we begin to obtain better discovery.'

He submitted that in several cases Westpac claimed deal position slips and/or deal slips did not exist. It is these documents that enabled a borrower to establish how much the bank had taken in 'points' or commissions each time it undertook transactions on behalf of a client.

Mr McLennan said 'people have now been left financially destitute and many marriages have been destroyed. How can any bank justify using its privileged position to manipulate currency deals to make profits for itself knowing that such action would only add to heavy losses sustained by the fall of the Australian dollar and particularly when the bank also knew it was responsible for enticing borrowers to borrow offshore in the first place?'

John McLennan also made an appearance on that evening's edition of the New South Wales *7.30 Report* (interviewed by the author) in which he described the impact of the Westpac letters for struggling foreign currency borrowers.

The publicity quickly developed into a public relations disaster for Australian banks and Westpac in particular.

On 14 February, McLennan was advised by David Elder, the secretary of the parliamentary banking inquiry, that his submission to the inquiry was to be released for publication and he was to be a major witness. On 15 February 1991, the day the McLennan submission was released for publication, Westpac appeared before Justice Powell of the New South Wales Supreme Court in a closed 'ex parte' hearing and obtained orders against McLennan requiring him to appear before the court on 20 February 1991 to face 'examination' on where he had obtained the documents and to restrain him from making further use of them. The orders threatened McLennan with jail or confiscation of his property if he did not comply.

Unaware of this, McLennan had returned to Port Macquarie after the special meeting with the borrowers. With his growing obsession for the plight of the foreign currency borrowers, John and Chris McLennan had their own marital problems. John had moved out of the family home. On the Sunday night he was working on a supplementary submission to the parliamentary banking inquiry covering the issue of the 'Westpac letters'. He accepted a telephoned invitation to dinner with friends at their remote property thirty kilometres west of Port Macquarie. At 8 pm that night he was walking up the driveway to his friends' house. Dogs were barking. McLennan was confronted by a man 'who sprang from the bushes', and thrust a wad of documents about an inch thick into his hand. He was a process server who apparently had driven all the way from Sydney to 'serve' McLennan. To this day McLennan does not know how the process server knew exactly where to find him. His friends did not betray him.

McLennan was both fearful and furious at this latest tactic. He believed it was designed by Westpac to stop him giving evidence before the parliamentary banking inquiry where he was scheduled to speak and answer questions on behalf of the borrowers' association.

Westpac's tactics were now front page news throughout Australia and John McLennan was immediately elevated from a spokesman often quoted in the small print of the financial pages to the face behind the fight between Australia's banks and their own customers. In the process the public's anger about the banks, already apparent from the excesses of the 1980s, was exacerbated. Westpac's legal action to stop any publication of the Allen Allen and Hemsley letters also encompassed the media including the Fairfax publishing outlets and the Australian Broadcasting Corporation.

'Fight Them'

ON the Sunday night the orders were served, McLennan was still awake at 2 am writing a submission for the court and the parliamentary banking inquiry. He rang his friend Trevor King. King laughed when he heard what had happened. King simply said: 'They have shot themselves in the foot. You are a major witness before the Parliament ... fight them'. McLennan's supplementary submission to the parliamentary inquiry complained of intimidation by Westpac. How could a bank show such contempt for the parliament, freedom of speech and the Australian public?

He now believed he had to put his personal fear aside. Westpac was targeting him personally. He had to contest this, whatever the cost to his personal savings and assets. McLennan and his legal advisers decided on a counter punch. He sued Westpac and its managing director Stuart Fowler for defamation and abuse of process.

McLennan had been galvanised by his experience and the plight of the borrowers. 'One evening I sat on the river bank and watched a sunset. It was then I decided that even if the bank succeeded I would never give up. I would fight them with every ounce of energy in my body. I realised that if I allowed my fear of what might happen to consume me it would eventually destroy me.'

On 2 February 1991 Westpac had taken a large advertisement in the Murdoch press (the Fairfax press had refused to run the advertisement on the grounds that it was defamatory and sought to argue the bank's case while the press was restrained by injunctions).

NOTICE FROM WESTPAC

The Bank is aware that copies of two confidential letters from its solicitors, Allen Allen and Hemsley, have been disseminated under cover of:
• undated
• unsigned

- menacing letters;
- mailed from an unknown address in Belgium.

These actions are extraordinary. The letters in question are dated 26 November 1987 and 11 December 1987, are clearly CONFIDENTIAL and marked 'Absolutely Private and Confidential'. They are communications between the Bank and its solicitors and as such are privileged.

The two letters were obtained illegitimately. The Bank believes that those responsible for this unlawful conduct have done so to assist in legal proceedings commenced against them by Westpac. This behaviour is reprehensible and the Bank will pursue all remedies available to it. Furthermore, the Bank has taken court action and obtained Court Orders in the United Kingdom, New Zealand and in Australia in connection with this misconduct.

The Bank has been contacted by members of the community who have received this material and who have returned their copy to the Bank. Anyone who has received this material and not yet returned it or who may receive this unsolicited and threatening communication is asked to contact the Legal Division of the Bank (phone number) so that arrangements can be made for its return.

On 12 February the NSW Court of Appeal upheld Justice Powell's injunction restraining the media. In spite of its stated reasons for its litigation, most commentators condemned Westpac's action against McLennan as oppressive. There was a rush to get the letters tabled in Parliament where they would be covered by parliamentary privilege and not so-called legal professional privilege.

Media reaction to Westpac's 'gagging' of the letters through its court orders was damning to the bank. Fairfax and the ABC applied to the court to have the orders against publication lifted. McLennan claimed publicly that Westpac was trying to stop him giving evidence to the parliamentary inquiry. His written submission was already on the way to the secretary of the parliamentary committee of inquiry. The Westpac letters were now vital to that submission, he contended. Westpac also applied pressure to the Federal Parliament, approaching the president of the Senate to prevent the letters being tabled by Democrat Senator Paul McLean who had announced his intention so to do.

Senate Ruling

ON 12 February 1991 the president of the Senate, Senator Kerry Sibraa, ruled that the Westpac letters could not be tabled because they were sub judice—they were the subject of legal action then before the courts.

It emerged that Sibraa had made this ruling against the formal advice of the Clerk of the Senate who stated that under the sub judice principle, which was not a matter of law in the parliamentary context, the Senate President had the discretion to stop disclosure but advised that disclosure in this case would prejudice only Westpac's current efforts to suppress the documents in court. Against this was to be weighed the public interest in having the public informed of the contents of the letters. 'My advice is that you should not restrain Senator McLean from disclosing the documents in proceedings in the Senate on the basis of the sub judice principle, and that you make a statement to the Senate indicating your decision.'

Westpac's apparent tactics to gag both the parliament and the media made the uninvolved elements of both institutions more determined than ever to publish. The South Australian parliamentarian Ian Gilfillan tabled the Westpac letters in the Upper House in the last week in February, and media in South Australia, the Australian Capital Territory and Queensland ran some or all of the contents of the letters. Media in New South Wales and Victoria remained gagged. Justice Powell in the New South Wales Supreme Court declined to lift the orders restraining the media from publishing the letters. In his ruling Justice Powell said attempts had been made to portray the Westpac case as a power struggle between the legislature and the judiciary. While the judge did not believe it was his role to instruct any legislative chamber, he hoped that no parliamentary chamber would instruct him how to perform his judicial duties. The judge said it was his firmly held view that a clear case of contempt had been made against *The Canberra Times* newspaper, which reported on the contents of the Westpac letters read to the South Australian Parliament. And, he said, it could well be held that *The Sydney Morning Herald* and the ABC had been guilty of 'criminal contempt' by various reports intended or calculated to traduce and vilify Westpac to force it to abandon the further prosecution of proceedings involving John McLennan. The judge had accepted Westpac's argument that these media elements were conducting a campaign likely to deter Westpac proceeding in the ordinary way through the courts to protect its right.

On 20 February the Communist Party newspaper *Tribune*, with a circulation of 4000, published both of the Westpac letters before a court injunction was issued against it and as many copies as could be obtained were seized. It was the *Tribune*'s last act of defiance before its closure and the disbandment of the political party.

John McLennan continued to press his belief that Westpac was trying to stop his appearance before the parliamentary banking inquiry. He wrote to the parliamentary inquiry asserting that Westpac's legal action against him personally made him feel intimidated by the bank. He had to make an appearance in court to answer the court orders on 7 March. Tension was mounting. Media interest was intense. McLennan's appearance at court led the television news bulletins. And in an unprecedented move the Speaker of the House of Representatives briefed counsel Gary Downes QC to make a submission to a hearing before Justice Powell's consideration of the Westpac gag orders on McLennan. Westpac's lawyers immediately assured Downes that the bank was not trying to prevent McLennan giving evidence to the parliamentary inquiry.

The debate raged until 7 March when Westpac 'with the greatest reluctance' agreed to a request from the parliamentary banking inquiry that the confidential letters be tabled. But Westpac's action against McLennan continued. He faced massive legal costs to defend himself.

McLennan contends the bank knew it was going to release the Westpac letters to the parliamentary banking inquiry. But it did not tell McLennan. Even as he was being cross-examined by Tom Hughes QC, Stuart Fowler, the managing director of Westpac, was tabling the documents in Canberra.

On 13 March 1991 an article appeared in *Australian Business* magazine which set out the so called 'Halabi connection'. McLennan recalled: 'Until this time I did not know Halabi was trying to blackmail the bank into dropping fraud charges against him and had threatened to release the Westpac letters. I was furious that all this time the bank had known who released the documents but had attempted to blame me. My conviction, that the action against me was primarily aimed at stopping me from giving evidence to the inquiry, hardened'.

All the major banks had been at war with their foreign currency borrowers—Westpac, the Commonwealth Bank, the ANZ Bank and the National Australia Bank; the ultimate power of the Parliament of Australia to protect and defend the rights of the citizens of Australia had been set aside on this occasion. The honourable senators did not demur.

The judiciary, represented in this case by Justice Powell, had accepted the principle of 'banker-customer confidentiality' and 'legal professional privilege'.

Scales of Justice

BRUCE Donald, then head of the ABC Legal and Copyright Department, in an unpublished internal memorandum on Powell's judgment argued that the phrase 'legal professional privilege' was a red herring in the Westpac case.

The phrase seemed to divert the courts and the parliament from allowing the normal discussion of material which had, whatever the source, reached the public domain.

Donald argued it was a red herring because there was no special category of confidentiality surrounding legal advice. Of course legal advice was confidential just as most commercial communications were intended to be. But legal advice enjoyed no greater protection against breach of confidence than anything else.

He said: 'Once it [legal advice] has reached the public domain— for example by being published in *The Sydney Morning Herald* and being used by people far and wide to wrap up their fish and chips— it has ceased to be confidential'. Donald argued that Justice Powell had developed the principle himself when he sat in judgment in the so-called Spycatcher case. Powell had ruled that when MI-5's secrets were out—they were out. Powell's ruling in Spycatcher had been confirmed right up to the High Court. That should have been the end of the matter, except if the *Herald* could be shown to have breached a confidence and to be liable for damages, if any. Other people republishing the *Herald* report breached no confidence.

Donald argued that publication did not destroy legal professional privilege. The documents containing the legal advice, even if they had been made public, could not be used in the court cases to which they may relate. They may be of use in the public debate about the matter, but a court of law could not look at them in deciding any case. They remained privileged and inadmissible as evidence.

Like any leaked document (Cabinet, departmental, corporate) once it was out in the public domain, it was out.

Justice Powell's birching of the media following submissions from Westpac's lawyers illustrated a failing of lawyers and the law which seemed to regard a legal resolution of disputes as the optimal solution in an orderly society. The fact that the law was slow, expensive, technical and often out of touch with the public perception of 'justice' often escaped lawyers.

Westpac turned to the Distillers Case as a precedent in its attacks on media coverage of the plight of John McLennan, the anguished whistleblower. The Distillers case established a principle designed to inhibit public pressure being brought to bear on people where that pressure was such that they might refrain from relying on their legal rights.

Thalidomide was a pre-natal drug to control nausea. But the drug produced dreadful deformities in babies. When the victims sued its maker, Distillers, those victims had the immensely difficult task, under the restrictions of the law of tort, of proving the maker negligent. *The Times* of London ran a series of forthright articles critical of Distillers for having forced the victims through the courts instead of paying up regardless of the legalities. The English judges said it was contempt of court to bring such intemperate pressure to bear on a defendant that it would be discouraged from pursuing its rights at law.

Justice Powell relied on this principle when criticising the ABC and Fairfax for their Westpac coverage. The judge accepted Westpac's argument that these media elements were conducting a campaign likely to deter Westpac proceeding in the ordinary way through the courts to protect its rights.

In the Westpac case, the letters revealed the great difficulty of any injured party being able to defeat Westpac's reliance on its legal rights, namely to have the injured parties themselves prove the detailed and difficult case which Westpac's own lawyers were advising existed against it, the evidence of which had, to a great extent, been kept confidential.

Any ordinary person might well query any principle of law making it contempt of court to reveal these facts to the public, given that the very scales of justice were tipped so heavily in favour of Westpac.

The realisation by those following the events and legal tactics was that, if the media were gagged by the law, the Parliament could not be relied upon to then expose the facts to the public. But on 6 March Stephen Martin's parliamentary inquiry into the banking system redeemed the people's house, the House of Representatives, if not the Senate. It formally asked Westpac to publicly table the Westpac letters.

On 7 March Westpac's managing director Stuart Fowler appeared before the parliamentary inquiry and complained bitterly of the media campaign against the bank:

Despite the repeated court rulings in upholding the confidentiality of these letters, it is clear that there has been a deliberate and orchestrated campaign to:
- Publish the confidential letters and to destroy the bank's rights to pursue court actions by injunctions to retain that confidentiality;
- Vilify the bank as a litigant in the New South Wales court actions;
- Report court proceedings in New South Wales, where Westpac is a litigant, in a manner which in our opinion is both biased and unfair to Westpac;
- Engage in conduct in contempt of the Supreme Court of New South Wales;
- Pressure the bank into abandoning its rights to protect its property in the courts.

This campaign, timed to correspond with the commencement of this inquiry, has been conducted by certain journalists, interest groups and others prepared to traffic in stolen documents.

Stuart Fowler also attacked Democrat Senator Paul McLean for having made public statements outside Parliament at rallies and to the press and supplied copies of the confidential letters in circumstances which might amount to contempt of court and the spirit of Senator Sibraa's ruling on the sub judice convention:

The bank is also conscious of the impact of these wholly unjustified attacks on the credibility of Westpac and its 45 000 employees in Australia and in twenty-eight countries throughout the world, and their effect on its many customers and proprietors. This campaign has placed unprecedented pressure on the bank, the parliamentary inquiry, the legal system and the judiciary in New South Wales. These issues now have to be balanced against the principles and rights which Westpac has sought to protect as I outlined earlier. As a result, the bank has been forced into a position where, with the greatest reluctance, Westpac is prepared to accede to the request of the members of this committee that the confidential letters be tabled before you.

In doing so, I wish to make it perfectly clear that:
- Westpac believes it has behaved with the utmost propriety in taking the steps it has in the courts to protect its rights;
- the protection of banker-customer confidentiality remains of paramount importance to all Australian financial institutions and their customers. The bank has had that principle very much in mind in taking the steps it has in Australia and elsewhere. We recognise that the maintenance of banker-customer confidentiality is a matter of importance to this committee.
- Westpac like any other Australian citizen is entitled to the maintenance of the principles of legal professional privilege, described by the High Court of Australia as 'fundamental to the due administration of justice.' In acceding to the request from the committee, Westpac has not (and has never) waived the bank's claim to legal professional privilege in those documents.

Later in his submission Stuart Fowler accused John McLennan, and Democrat Senator Paul McLean, of making 'outrageous claims' that the Australian banks had destroyed the businesses and the lives of thousands of Australians:

No doubt Senator McLean and Mr McLennan will take advantage of their opportunity before this inquiry to repeat and elaborate on their allegations. As the commitee is aware, there are a number of pending court actions instituted by borrowers against banks, including Westpac, arising out of these foreign currency loans. The appropriate place for those claims to be tested was in the courts.

However, your committee and the public should know that, in relation to Westpac's approximately 850 loans offshore at October 1985, there have been no bankruptcy notices issued; only ten matters where action has been taken in respect of security— only three of which have resulted in the sale of security properties.

These facts, said the managing director of Westpac, spoke for themselves. The Westpac letters and the legal battle over their leaking had become the biggest crisis of confidence for customers in the post-war period and Australians have remained sceptical about banking practices to this day.

The bank had invoked the 'principle' of bank-customer confidentiality—confidentiality for practices which resulted in severe disadvantage for its customers. Stuart Fowler's statement may yet emerge as the greatest piece of hypocrisy in the history of Australian banking.

Pat the Tiger

WHILE this was unfolding John McLennan was facing the biggest test of his life. The pressures he had placed on himself through his personal involvement with the foreign currency borrowers was having a destructive effect.

With his counter claim against Westpac of abuse of process and defamation McLennan was to spend the next twelve months on a constant procession to and from Port Macquarie to Sydney. No sooner had he returned home than Westpac put on another notice of motion. McLennan had to spend days, then weeks, preparing complex and detailed affidavits refuting Westpac's claims. In all he spent $140,000 in legal costs. By the end of the process his finances were exhausted and he was in grave jeopardy of losing everything.

John McLennan's marriage to Chris had ended and she had received a generous property settlement. 'I knew she and the children would be safe from Westpac who would have showed them no mercy. This was little consolation for Chris who suffered greatly because of the marriage break-up. For this I will always be sorry.'

McLennan said: 'By this time I was very angry that the legal system would allow a vexatious litigant to continue to pursue its claims, knowing that they had been clearly refuted. I was angry that the Parliament refused to further intervene. It was clear to me that despite the so-called protection for witnesses provided by Parliament, when it came to the crunch, the Parliament was content to let me battle alone. I laid formal charges of harassment and intimidation of a witness against Westpac. They were dismissed. The Parliament did not even exercise its powers and seek documents or examine those who initiated the legal action against me.

'My fear grew. It pervaded my whole being and I spent many sleepless nights. I knew that if I gave in to my fear the bank would win. Fear is like a cancer. It grows if you feed it. I soon learnt that the only way to treat the "tiger" was to pat it on the nose and get on with life. I resolved that I must either crash through or crash. Each time the bank knocked me down I was determined to get up. Eventually I knew the truth would come out and when it did the public would respond. Westpac was starting to bleed. Accounts were being closed. The media turned on them. Not because they had made mistakes, but because they tried to cover it up. In the end I knew that the only person who could beat the bank was me. Nobody was going to rescue me. I had to do it on my own.'

John McLennan appeared before the banking inquiry on 20 March 1991. Unfortunately because of the bank's action against him he was unable to properly prepare much of the documentary evidence he would have liked to have provided. He had no research support but gave a chronological account of his involvement with the formation of the Foreign Currency Borrowers Association.

The House of Representatives Standing Committee on Finance and Public Administration headed by Labor Party backbencher Steven Martin came to Coffs Harbour for the hearing. McLennan, feeling the intense pressure of the legal action against him, had dined at the Anuka Resort, Coffs Harbour, before the hearing with committee members and Anne Lampe of *The Sydney Morning Herald*. Chairman Martin assured him that he would be 'protected' against the bank. McLennan felt far from protected. He woke on the morning of the hearing with a blinding headache and was violently sick. When he arrived at the hearing room, he watched in amazement as senior officials of Westpac and a phalanx of lawyers from Allen Allen and Hemsley filed in to the vacant seats. His words at the committee hearing were covered by what is called parliamentary privilege, meaning that he could not be sued for anything he said there or legally pursued in any way. McLennan anguished as he saw the legal representatives take copious notes as he started his oral evidence. He was conscious that anything he did say could be taken down and used against him in the actions Westpac were pursuing him in the courts. His words to the committee may not be used. But the intelligence they gathered from his admissions and comments in this forum could be turned against him before the courts. McLennan felt far from protected by 'parliamentary privilege'. He felt intimidated.

Many of the foreign currency borrowers had already refused to give evidence because of what had happened to McLennan in the action launched against him by Westpac. And, regrettably, McLennan also knew many employees of the banks who may have been available to stand up and be counted in this affair had changed their minds when they saw what was happening to John McLennan. Who could blame them?

McLennan did not feel he was the nemesis of the banks as some media reports were now painting him. With what remained of his life savings after the end of his marriage to Chris and his own personal bankruptcy at stake, not to mention his mental health as his personal relationships suffered under the strain, he said he felt how a woman in a domestic violence case must feel: trapped and totally intimidated.

Nevertheless, he confronted his fear and began his evidence to the committee. He traced the sequence of events in some detail, particularly the legal tactics of the banks in the individual cases in which he had been a consultant.

While the banks had threatened to have the borrowers cited for 'contempt of court' if they tried to use documents discovered in one case admitted in another, McLennan made the telling point:

> So far I have not seen any action against a bank for contempt of court for failing to produce adequate discovery. I would ask this committee to look at that aspect in great detail. We can supply you with many instances of what we believe to be contempt of court.
>
> One bank, the Commonwealth Bank, as I understand it, has supboenaed the high school records of borrowers, and all banks subpoenaed the minutes and attendance records and files of the Foreign Currency Borrowers Association. They have also invaded the privacy of our meetings to serve threatening and menacing letters. I wonder how the banks' boards would treat similar intrusions by the Borrowers Association.
>
> One process server tried to serve documents, a letter, on the 12-year-old son of a woman who was a friend of mine. And you wonder why I think I have been harassed. In all this time, not once did the bank seek to phone me or to discuss the matter in a reasonable way.

Concerning the PPL documents, or the Westpac letters as they were known, McLennan said:

> Much has already been said about these documents but it appears to me that no one is willing to say what they really mean. The bank and/or its employees stole, yes, stole money from its clients. Whichever way you look at it, the taking of a secret commission incorporated in exchange rate is stealing; deal switching is stealing. The bank used its trusted and privileged position to take secret profits and to make the borrowers' already tenuous position worse. I can think of no other worse example of corporate immorality.
>
> Senior persons in the bank and its solicitors set out to deliberately cover up the theft and deliberately frustrate the legitimate claims of aggrieved borrowers by manipulating the legal system. If there has ever been a scheme to pervert the course of justice, this had to be it. The bank has attempted to muddy the waters in claiming, in an aggrieved manner, that the documents were stolen from it. In other words, someone stole the evidence about them stealing the money. I do not condone people stealing documents

and I had nothing to do with it but I think you have to get the whole thing in perspective.

And later in his evidence:

I draw your attention to an article in *Australian Business* which states that Westpac knew who leaked the PPL letters. This article was on the newstands at the very time the bank had me in court trying to find out who leaked the documents. So why did they obtain orders against me to present myself for cross examination as to the source of the documents, under threat of confiscation of property and/or imprisonment? I reiterate my previous advices that the bank deliberately set out to intimidate me and ask that the matter be again considered by the Speaker.

McLennan took the committee through a range of revealing internal banking documents indicating mismanagement of foreign currency loans and a dangerously flawed international lending policy by the major Australian banks.

On Westpac's aggressive marketing of foreign currency loans from the late 1970s McLennan said:

To even a casual observer (internal documents) show a clear picture of a product which evolved without any clear direction and was seized upon by the corporate and international division because of its fee and interest-earning capacity. The corporate and international division was in conflict with the domestic bankers who were wearing the flak from disgruntled borrowers. The documents reveal that the bank well knew that the average unsophisticated borrower could not manage the offshore exposure, and borderline proposals were approved to achieve market share. Even when the Australian dollar drastically depreciated, it was not until mid-1986 that an appropriate management structure was established to manage the situation. Then it seemed more intent on covering up than trying to assist borrowers. The bank's legal advisers were paranoid about litigation, hence the directive that no advice was to be given.

The fear of litigation appears to have paralysed the bank's

decision-making process and left the borrowers with no advice after further falls in the Australian dollar. It would appear that the Chief Manager, Retail Lending, Mr Frank Cass, General Manager, Retail Banking, Mr McInnes, and General Manager, Credit Policy and Control, Mr Frank Ward, tried desperately to halt this type of lending. But the corporate and international division persisted until the potential losses and concern from Chief Manager, Europe, eventually forced a halt. By that time the bank's exposure was considerable—$2.6 billion or 6.6 per cent of total assets.

Throughout his oral evidence John McLennan did not personally attack Stuart Fowler, the managing director of Westpac. He let his submission and the analysis of facts and documents do the talking.

But on Fowler's own assertions of the bank's due regard for borrowers, McLennan submitted:

> I note Mr Fowler's claims that the bank did not bankrupt people. However, I am sure that those people who were left with no assets after being coerced into signing indemnities would have a different interpretation of this strictly legal interpretation of bankruptcy. When we talk about bankruptcy we talk in generic terms—if you have nothing left you are still bankrupt. However, given the opportunity and the right environment, I know all the disputes within the banks could be resolved and the trust in the fine traditions restored. It may take some time and a lot of pain, but in the end it will be worth it.

Weak Report

WHEN the Martin committee's final report was tabled, John McLennan and the Borrowers Association were bitterly disappointed. Given the evidence of all the documents submitted to the committee about Australian banking practices the final report, they felt, was weak. It was noted that the banks had a constant procession to Canberra to lobby. The Australian Bankers' Association, the industry body funded by all the banks, had even installed a representative 'to advise' the Martin committee. The ABA representative was privy to all 'in camera' evidence taken by the committee. While the propriety of the particular representative was not in question, to the borrowers it did not seem right. The Martin committee refused to allow a consumer representative similar access to it.

While the Martin committee condemned the foreign exchange loan product it failed to provide any formal mechanism to ensure outstanding disputes were settled. Nor did it address the issues of the many cases which had run on, at great cost to the litigants, on inadequate discovery. The issue of the manipulation of the justice system was ignored.

The banks had announced that they would mediate outstanding disputes. But in reality the borrowers believed they did little to settle disputes and many were still running before the courts in 1996.

With the media battle over the Westpac letters resolved, coverage subsided. While John McLennan had the satisfaction of a public hearing of his own attack on Westpac and the banks through the inquiry, his life and death struggle with Westpac in the courts continued. He faced weeks in court as the lawyers' meters ticked rapidly over.

On 16 June 1992 John McLennan and Westpac reached an out of court and 'undisclosed' settlement of their actions against each other. Anne Lampe in the *Herald* reported that McLennan had counter-sued Westpac and its then managing director Stuart Fowler citing alleged defamation and abuse of process as causes of action.

The claims and cross-claims have dragged on since then, with Mr McLennan's legal bills reportedly reaching close to $150,000. One day last year a short court appearance cost him $15,000. Mr McLennan could not discuss figures yesterday, but grinning broadly, said he was 'very happy' with the negotiated outcome.

As part of the settlement, McLennan had to hand to Westpac any documents relating to the bank which were provided in court proceedings which had been settled or determined, as well as any unsolicited material he had received. In reality he had none. He had to hand over to Westpac thirty or more documents relating to a lengthy investigation of the bank by the Australian Tax Office (which had hired McLennan as a consultant) and which had been obtained from him by the ATO exercising its powers of acquisition. These documents were to be shredded in the bank's offices in McLennan's presence.

McLennan told Lampe: 'All I fought for were the foreign currency loans cases and I got caught in the cross-fire'.

Given all this personal ordeal and trauma, would McLennan do it again? His answer: Yes.

I would do it again. I have always been a fighter. I have always stood up for my beliefs. I would, however, do it differently. I should have represented myself and I should not have settled when I did. Had I known the devastation I was causing to Westpac I would have driven on until the truth finally came out. I guess I just could no longer bear the pain on my own. My personal life has suffered. Instead of drawing away from my family I should have drawn them to me for support. I now agonise over the trauma my family suffered, particularly my children who watched helplessly as I withdrew into a world of legal battles and loneliness.

I suppose what tormented me most was that although I was a target for the bank—and they knew the pain I would suffer—nobody in the bank suffered. 'The Bank's after all just an entity with no body, no conscience, no soul. The bankers involved did not have to put their assets on the line. They got paid regardless and I was just a bloody nuisance to them. For me it was a life and death struggle and that is why I won.

I have had two disastrous relationships since my marriage break up and, to my great regret, transferred my distress to my partners who deserved better. I am sorry for the pain I caused them. Unfortunately, my intensity and passion make me a difficult person to live with. Perhaps now ... the future ... is the time for me, for my happiness.

Legal System has Failed

MCLENNAN believes the legal system has failed miserably. From his bitter experience he believes the judiciary must take a more interventionist role and stop powerful litigants from abusing the legal process. Recourse through the courts was simply beyond borrowers whose banks controlled all their finances. 'Discovery is easier today. The banks know that I know where the goodies are buried. But they still play the game and resist production until the last minute. What a waste of legal resources.'

After the final settlement of his personal fight with Westpac John McLennan collapsed with exhaustion. 'I slept for many days. I felt I had been betrayed by the legal system, the Parliament and, to some extent, the Foreign Currency Borrowers. Where were they when I needed them? I was fighting their battle. Many had achieved quite substantial settlements while I waged war with the banks. Worse still some of my "strategy advices" were copied and circulated to other litigants who then used them to obtain settlements from banks. A few came forward to thank me. Many did not. This has left a nasty taste in my mouth. Finally I realised that what I did, I did for myself. If I sought recognition from others I would have failed. I won for myself. If others benefited then, so be it.

'I wish I could reveal the terms of my settlement. I want to be able to show what it cost the bank but yet I cannot bring myself to be plunged into more litigation. I know I won. That is the most important thing of all.'

Since settling, and in fact right through the entire saga, John McLennan has continued to act as a consultant to bank customers in trouble. In 1992 he formed the Foreign Currency Borrowers Association in New Zealand and has provided advice to borrowers in New Zealand ever since. In 1997, the Jim Bolger/Winston Peters coalition government responded to consistent representations of McLennan and the foreign currency borrowers and announced a judicial inquiry into foreign currency lending and the Bank of New Zealand.

By 1996 McLennan had consulted in more that 250 matters involving banks, with settlements or court judgments of several hundred million dollars being achieved.

'I wish I had a percentage of all those settlements. In reality I have earned a modest living from consultancy fees. In many cases borrowers even haggled over payment of fees after I had facilitated settlements for them. There is good and bad on both sides.'

In 1995, after a substantial victory in a matter involving the

ANZ Bank, McLennan was retained by the National Farmers' Federation to advise them on the most effective way to settle about thirty outstanding foreign currency loan disputes between Australian farmers and the banks. As part of that strategy he has completed a major submission to the Australian Competition and Consumer Commission.

The process of mediation established by the banks to 'appease' the Parliamentary committee of inquiry was unsatisfactory to the borrowers. The mediator had no power to impose a settlement and the banks simply went through the motions. When the dust had settled they again quietly put the borrowers to the sword of the legal system.

John McLennan believes there must be a system of dispute resolution in commercial banking similar to the Ombudsman scheme if consumers are to be given any effective and inexpensive redress over banking malpractice or mismanagement.

By 1996 it was believed there were still fifty cases of litigation between banks and their customers before the courts of Australia. In the five years to 1996 legal costs in all the cases were estimated to have exceeded $100 million.

The media focus on the Westpac bank eventually produced further revelations about the bank's balance sheet and the stated value of its assets. Westpac had to purge its board and underwent the biggest write-down of assets in Australian banking history. Managing director Stuart Fowler retired to be replaced by an American banker, Bob Joss.

McLennan still believes that much of the problem for the bank stemmed from the Westpac letters and the public storm which erupted. 'Had the bank owned up to its mistake and settled disputes with honour—as the National Australia Bank did—they would not have been diverted from the more pressing problems of managing their potential bad loan exposure.

'I have watched with horror as bankers have sold their souls for the "company line". Even the judiciary have commented that bankers often tell what they think their employers would want them to say rather than the truth. The irony is that many of the dedicated bankers who so cold-bloodedly put so many borrowers into financial ruin have since been retrenched.

'When I was a child I was relentlessly beaten by a group of bullies when I attended Rozelle school following the transfer of my father from Queensland to Sydney. Each day the beatings were worse and I feared for my life. Prior to that I was a happy child, free of fear, at peace with the world and myself. I soon learnt the hard way that if I did not stand up for myself no one else would. I struggled with my fear and then decided to fight back. One day I defeated the ring leader of the bullies in a bloody and vicious fight. From that day on I bore the scars. To this day I mourn the loss of my peaceful childhood.

'It seems to me that any society which suppresses individuality and healthy conflict runs the risk that it will develop a culture where "yes men" flourish, as corporate morality is corrupted by employees who have abdicated all responsibility for their own personal integrity.'

John McLennan believes the crisis in Australian banking in the late 1980s and early 1990s had the potential to collapse the banking industry. He estimates that the banks lent $3 billion offshore which blew out to $6 billion. In the end no banker had been impeached by a court. In spite of being disbelieved by the courts not one banker was charged with perjury. In spite of the recommendations of the Martin committee that the Westpac letters be referred to the National Crime Authority and various State fraud squads, in spite of the admissions of theft and fraud contained in the documents, no investigation ever appeared to take place.

In retrospect, a Royal Commission headed by a determined investigative leader, and using the full range of coercive powers, was what was needed.

McLennan has made representations of the House of Representatives Standing Committee on finance and public administration to recommend the establishment of a specific Finance and Banking Consumers Association. This body would have the statutory powers of an ombudsman but would cover private sector commercial and business transactions. 'We have consumer organisations that will provide support and advice involving everything from a toaster that doesn't work to a motor vehicle but none will become involved in disputes with banks.' A code of conduct for banks still has not been implemented.

CRADLE TO GRAVE

'We didn't have to use propaganda—the facts spoke for themselves.'

'Cradle to grave
Cradle to grave
Lead harms our children in the cradle
Puts lead workers in the grave'
Song by Elizabeth O'Brien, Co-ordinator of the LEAD (Lead Education and Abatement Design) Group.

'Elizabeth O'Brien's child has a high lead level. I'm sorry about that, but she is trying to solve her kid's problem at an enormous social cost.' Spokesman for the Australian Institute of Petroleum.

THE HOUSE was just what they wanted. It had four bedrooms, a big backyard and a reasonable (for Sydney in 1990, that is) price tag: $230,000.

When Elizabeth O'Brien, then heavily pregnant with her third child, inspected the federation-style house in Moonbie Street, Summer Hill, in Sydney's inner west, she believed she was on to a good thing.

Husband Greg thought so too. The Moonbie Street house was just over the road from the local school. If they could get the house, one of the major problems facing their growing family would be solved—transportation to and from school. The O'Brien family obviously needed bigger premises. With another baby on the way their renovated terrace in Summer Hill, which they had bought six years earlier, would no longer comfortably meet their needs. Elizabeth, 34, and Greg, 35, with their two boys, Alex, 5, and Eric, nearly 3, walked through each room imagining what life would be like living in that space. They looked longingly at the backyard big enough for the boys to ride their bikes around the trees and garden beds.

In the front yard Elizabeth O'Brien paused for a moment. She had noticed something.

Directly opposite the house was what looked like a factory. There was a chimney of sorts. Not a very large one. Perhaps five metres high. Elizabeth asked the real estate agent what sort of factory it was. The agent did not know. Later Greg strolled across the road and knocked on the factory door to inquire: What do you do here? 'Lead foundry,' he was told. The Thomas Thoms Pty Ltd foundry manufactured lead and aluminium roof flashings and damp courses for the building industry. The mention of the word 'lead' caused Elizabeth O'Brien concern.

Years before when she had been teaching in the Sydney suburb of Rosebery to the south of the city, Elizabeth recalled, there had been a problem involving lead. It was around 1979. One of the teachers told her about a study of children's blood at their school. Blood samples had been taken from a large number of children in a university research project. Apparently they all had high concentrations of lead in their blood. 'That's why they're all so stupid and so difficult to teach,' the teacher in the staff room had said during a break. Stupid? Difficult to teach? Elizabeth O'Brien had remembered this description.

Now she was confronted with a dilemma. They wanted the Moonbie Street house. There was no argument about that. But the chimney stack across the road was a worry. What to do? If in doubt, as mother would say ... ask.

Elizabeth O'Brien had learnt to be inquisitive. As a student she had scored above average in Art, Maths and Biology in an education interrupted by constant moves from country Queensland, to Melbourne, to suburban Sydney. Her mother, Noela, had packed up Elizabeth, her two elder sisters and an elder brother in 1964 and left husband and home in Kingaroy after a long period of marital difficulties. For a time the young Elizabeth was boarded at a Catholic convent in Murgon, near Kingaroy. It was an experience, Elizabeth recalled, which put her off religion for life. She was the youngest boarder in what was an oppressive regime where she suffered beatings, ridicule and disapproval over her parental separation. In 1964 separation after irreconcilable differences was considered a sin against the holy institution of marriage.

Fortunately, Elizabeth and her sisters were soon reunited with their mother and brother who had moved to Melbourne. A year later a former teacher, who was embarking on a new career, came to live with the family. Life under the new regime was not easy.

It was an era of parenting in which 'children should be seen and not heard' and Elizabeth recalls having to put her hand up at home if she wanted to ask a question. The television had been tuned to current affairs. She reacted by switching her mind away from current affairs, the media and politics.

But she did have an innate talent for research. Her mother was a secretary, researcher and writer.

At 17 Elizabeth left the family nest and had to fend for herself. She shared flats and houses and with the help of a scholarship she studied to become a teacher. She paid the rent and funded her later studies at Sydney University by odd jobs and ended her formal education with a degree in science, majoring in botany, and a Diploma in Education. She also studied for and achieved a Graduate Diploma in Health Education and developed an interest in women's fertility and personal development issues.

Her social life was busy. She had a variety of student boyfriends and joined a rock and roll band as lead singer. It was called Hot Spurs, or sometimes, Behind Enemy Lines. They played around the pubs and rock venues of inner-city Sydney in Newtown, Glebe and Redfern and regularly went on tour to the north coast of New South Wales. After three years in the classroom, Elizabeth took a break for a year and travelled to Europe, Asia and Africa with a young man, Greg, who was an industrial chemist. They started a family and settled back home in the Blue Mountains. Alex was born in 1985 and Eric came along in 1988 after they had moved to the terrace house at Summer Hill.

Jars and Spoons

NOW in 1990, with another baby expected soon, what were they going to do about the house in Moonbie Street? Elizabeth decided to telephone the State Pollution Control Commission, listed in the telephone book as a division of the NSW Environment Department.

She kept notes in a pad by the telephone. She wanted to know about the possibility of contamination at the Moonbie Street house. She wanted to know if the house was safe for habitation as it was so close to a lead foundry. No one could give her a specific answer to the question. The local council kept no records on contamination. The Pollution Control people kept no specific records of affected streets or houses next to lead fallout facilities. Elizabeth found out the names of laboratory researchers who might know something. One said she should ask if long term residents in the area had had their blood checked to see if they had been affected by lead from the Thomas Thoms foundry.

With Alex and Eric she knocked on the door of the house in Moonbie Street and explained to the owners that she was interested in buying their house. They had been living in the area for thirty years. She asked them directly if they would be prepared to have a blood test to see if the house was safe to live in. Not surprisingly the owners declined.

On the advice of one of the researchers she had spoken to on the telephone, Elizabeth then went back to the Moonbie Street house. She carried three empty glass jam jars and three tablespoons. She took a tablespoon of soil from the front garden and placed it in one jar and took two samples of soil from the backyard, one from the garden closest to the Thomas Thoms chimney stack. On a piece of paper in her pocket, Elizabeth had the address of the Australian Government Analytical Laboratory in Pymble in the far north of Sydney.

She recalls that the trip with the jam jars and Eric and Alex was an ordeal with Eric being particularly out of sorts. She had to break the car journey three or four times and at one stage stopped at a park to allow the children to play. The trip took several hours as a consequence. Eventually, a heavily pregnant woman, with two young children complaining alongside, fronted the counter at the Pymble laboratory and presented the three glass jars. Requests from ordinary citizens for soil analysis were a rare event. The laboratory's clients were usually government agencies and large corporations. Elizabeth asked the laboratory staff to fax the results through to Greg's fax number at work. Greg was working for an Australian paint manufacturer.

When the fax arrived several days later they did not know what to make of the soil analysis results. There was no written interpretation. Sample one, from the front garden, showed the presence of lead by 3200 parts per million; sample two from the backyard showed 3700 lead parts per million while sample three, the one closest to the stack, measured 5700 parts per million.

What did that mean? Why was the backyard higher than the front yard?

Elizabeth rang the SPCC (State Pollution Control Commission, later to become the NSW Environment Protection Authority) for an explanation. One of the staff looked up the available reference on lead in soil and read over the telephone the advice that lead in soil of more than 300 parts per million would indicate that 'further investigation' was recommended. Further investigation? What further investigation? She was told that the SPCC literature did not advise what was a safe level of lead in soil or, if high concentrations were found, what should be done about it.

Three hundred parts per million. Five thousand, seven hundred parts per million. The soil must be highly poisonous.

Lead is what is called a neuro-toxin. For decades its poisonous effects have been known with lead poisoning affecting painters with what was known as painter's colic. Elizabeth had discovered through her telephone conversations that the University of New South Wales Department of Analytical Chemistry had done the most research in Australia on the prevalence of urban childhood lead poisoning, including the study at Rosebery, the school where she had worked eleven years before. In fact that study had been the most comprehensive undertaken in Australia with blood (a finger-prick-blood sample) taken (with parental permission) from 407 children. She learnt that the Rosebery study had been a major factor in Australian authorities moving for the introduction of unleaded petrol in 1985. One of the effects of serious lead poisoning in children was that it could affect intellectual development. Children exposed to lead could also suffer hyperactivity, temper tantrums, fatigue, frequent infection and increased allergic reactions. The Concise Medical Dictionary defined lead as 'a soft bluish-grey metallic element that forms several poisonous compounds. Acute lead poisoning, which may follow inhalation of lead fumes or dust, causes abdominal pains, vomiting and diarrhoea with paralysis and convulsions and sometimes encephalitis. In chronic poisoning a characteristic bluish marking of the gums ('lead line') is seen and the peripheral nerves are affected: there is also anaemia'.

When Elizabeth and Greg looked at the lead levels from the Moonbie Street house they had a decision to make. They decided not to buy. The alarm bells were ringing. They could not afford to risk the health of their sons and the new baby. With her awareness of lead now raised, Elizabeth O'Brien became an activist. She and Greg eventually bought a house in Dulwich Hill about a kilometre away from Moonbie Street. She wrote a formal complaint to the SPCC about Moonbie Street, wanting to know why this house and similar houses near the Thomas Thoms foundry had not been declared lead contaminated. If it had taken her this much effort to get answers it was obvious that other affected residents were living in blissful ignorance.

Thank heavens, they thought, they had found out about the soil contamination at the house. They could take evasive action. The new house was still close enough to their chosen school. At least they could now relax. But they remained worried about Moonbie Street. They asked the real estate agent what prospective buyers would be told. To his credit the agent said buyers would be told the truth: there was a lead problem at the house.

Pollution Control

ELIZABETH O'Brien felt a responsibility to let other families around the Thomas Thoms foundry know of her discovery of soil contamination. Young children ingesting lead particles on their hands outside and inside their houses were at serious risk of poisoning. Elizabeth attended a meeting of the local Nursing Mothers Association and discovered that one of the women attending there had actually bought the Moonbie Street house (for substantially less than the O'Briens had been prepared to pay) and the new owners were about to move in. Elizabeth assessed what her personal obligations were under these circumstances. Surely the responsibility to warn residents, particularly those with young children, rested with the SPCC, particularly as this body now knew of the lead-contaminated soil. The new family had two young children. They were going to be placed at risk immediately. If she was a mother in those circumstances she would want to know. The original owner had changed estate agents. The new buyers of the house were unaware of the lead problem.

Elizabeth prepared a hand-written note explaining the results of the soil analysis and the interpretation that lead levels in the yard were way above safety levels. She delivered the letter to the woman's address late at night on the day before they moved to the new home. At the time she thought, 'Well—I've done my best'. She heard nothing. Then two weeks later the telephone rang at home. It was the woman. She wanted a meeting to discuss the problem. They were contracturally committed to buying the Moonbie Street house. The woman and her husband were incensed that nothing had been done officially to warn them. Pollution 'control'? What a sick joke.

In June 1991 the couple took possession of their contaminated house. There was no formal advice available from any health or pollution agency on what to do to inhibit lead particle ingestion by the family. Here was a family at serious risk. By October 1991 the husband had prepared a thirty-page report on lead contamination in Summer Hill in a deliberate effort to embarrass the authorities into taking some responsibility and fully researching the problem.

One of the scientific officers of the State Pollution Control Commission, Bill Balding, had been prepared to help. He advised the residents' group on the toxicological effects of lead and of the various restraints on the SPCC. By this time the O'Briens and the other family had been joined by another Summer Hill parent, Kerrie O'Donnell.

The group negotiated with Thomas Thoms foundry management and some more soil analysis was conducted at the company's expense in nearby residences. The results, when presented to the concerned parents, showed a maximum soil lead level fifty times the 300-parts-per-million benchmark at which the Pollution Control guidelines recommended 'further investigation'.

The deficiencies in the legislation and the failure of the authorities to have a remediation plan were now glaring. There was no statutory lead limit at which decontamination or remedial action was mandatory. The pollution control authorities operated on 'guidelines' which were still in place in 1996. These 'guidelines' were set by the ANZECC—the Australian and New Zealand Environment and Conservation Council—a body comprising Ministers of the Crown. These 'guidelines' did not comprise any action plan for the decontamination of soil procedure to follow.

Elizabeth and her increasingly anxious group got by on the helpful advice of Bill Balding. As a scientist Balding was objective and unemotional. He read all the international scientific literature on lead contamination and passed this on to the group.

Around this time another University of New South Wales study project was underway, headed by Jason Bawden-Smith, who announced in the local press around Glebe, Balmain and the inner city that UNSW was taking blood samples from children to test lead contamination. Sixty-five extra children were offered by concerned parents who allowed their children to give what is called a 'venous' sample where blood is drawn with a syringe from a vein in the child's arm. The study became known as the Mort Bay survey, based as it was on fifty children from Mort Bay in Balmain.

The results were staggering. Fifty per cent of the children in Mort Bay and other suburbs near the central business district of Australia's largest city had blood lead levels above a new American 'level of concern', established by the United States in 1991 at 10 micrograms of lead per decilitre of blood. In the American definitions now being distributed, any blood lead reading above 10 micrograms per decilitre was called 'lead poisoned' by the US Centers for Disease Control. Research in the United States and elsewhere since the early 1970s had indicated an imperative to keep lowering the 'level of concern' because of adverse symptoms apparent in all long-term studies into lead poisoning.

Elizabeth O'Brien's group read about the Mort Bay survey in the local newspaper. Balmain was then both a heavy industry and residential peninsula right on Sydney Harbour. There were many petrol storage tanks around the harbourside and there were specific sources of lead contamination. But the findings indicated a broader problem.

Reading the Mort Bay survey material Bill Balding advised the group that, given the widespread nature of lead poisoning, there was only one thing for it. Bill said: 'The SPCC can do nothing about soil lead results. Go get your kids tested'. Bill Balding soon after compiled the NSW Lead Issues Paper. The group would always be grateful for his honest appraisal of the known research and his practical advice.

Elizabeth O'Brien considered Bill's words. She and Greg had taken evasive action when they decided not to buy the Moonbie Street house and she thought: 'I don't have to get my kids tested'. She sat on Bill's advice for two months. Then one day she arrived home to find baby Harrison 'helping' Daddy with the gardening. He had a dirty chin. Elizabeth was furious. Their soil had never been tested for lead so the baby would have to be tested.

Harrison had been born on 22 September 1990. By October 1991 he was just twelve months old. Elizabeth believed that half the children in the Mort Bay area had been in areas of lead concentration—or what was known as 'point source' contamination near a fuel depot, plumbing workshop, power station and ship-breaking yard.

The metropolitan media all but ignored the issue at this time. How was public ignorance to be confronted if the media did not inform it of the health impacts of ongoing exposure to lead contamination?

Blood Tests

ELIZABETH and Greg decided to have their three children's blood tested for lead contamination. There were no publicly available guidelines or advice on how this was to be done. So they organised for samples to be taken through Jason Bawden-Smith and took baby Harrison, Alex and Eric to the inner-city Rozelle Hospital where there was a nurse, who was a paediatric venipuncturist (a specialist in taking blood from children). To secure the blood test they first had to have a referral from a general practitioner. Each test would cost $30—or just $4 after the Medicare rebate of $26 was received. Alex and Eric went bravely forward to give their blood samples. Baby Harrison was a different matter. He was most distressed at the intrusion and pain from the needle jab and screamed with full force into the nurse's ear.

The O'Briens had to wait two weeks for the results of the blood analysis. Elizabeth returned to the GP and was told that Harrison's sample was 'slightly above normal'. What did that mean? The GP was applying the then Australian standard or 'level of concern' of 25 micrograms of lead per decilitre of blood and calling this 'normal'.

To her alarm Elizabeth found that even by this measure her baby son had an elevated blood lead level of 31 micrograms per decilitre. On the US interpretation of 'level of concern' Harrison O'Brien was being poisoned by lead. The GP's interpretation of the analyst's report was amiss and so was the advice given on what to do about it ... 'Perhaps you should slap him if he puts his fingers in his mouth'. Elizabeth left the GP's surgery, never to return. Such was the nature of the ignorance infecting suburban medicine.

Eric's blood analysis showed a blood lead level of 13 micrograms per decilitre while Alex's showed a reading of 14.

Through her now considerable knowledge of experts in the field of blood lead interpretation, Elizabeth had located Dr Garth Alperstein, a South African who had run a lead program in New York City. Alperstein worked for the Central Sydney Area Health Service. Harrison was just twelve months old. All the research indicated that unless his blood lead levels could be reduced to 10—the US 'level of concern'—or below before the age of two years, the risk of permanent damage to the child's intellectual development was high.

With Harrison there was no time to lose. Alperstein came to address a meeting at Kerrie O'Donnell's house in Summer Hill and later visited the O'Brien home. He spent well over an hour inspecting for possible lead sources—checking the roof space and the back yard where what was once a lawn had been reduced to a dusty bike track by the children's play. Alperstein noted with satisfaction the bark chip covering of the soil in the front garden but inside the house he looked with concern at the carpets throughout the living and bedrooms. They had to go, he advised.

To achieve a child's blood lead level below 10 when contamination was all around you, was a parental nightmare akin to paranoid vigilence. A child could lovingly pat a family pet which had come in from the garden and innocently transfer lead particles when he inevitably put his fingers in his mouth. The GP's method of slapping was certainly not advised—removal of the invisible source was the answer. Toys which lay around the house and yard had to be regularly washed. Carpets had to be vacuumed but not when the child was in the vicinity because of ambient lead dust stirred up by the process. Wall, door and kitchen surfaces had to be wiped incessantly and hard surface floors thoroughly wet mopped every day. A new awareness of hygiene was imperative. It would drive any parent mad—but Harrison's long term development now depended on this.

The Australian National Health and Medical Research Council had set the 'level of concern' for blood lead at 25 micrograms per decilitre in 1987. Less than a decade before, in 1979, there had been no recommended 'level of concern'. As a rule of thumb a benchmark of 40 micrograms had been set. Harrison's blood lead level of 31 was at that time one of the highest levels yet exposed by Jason Bawden-Smith. At last there was some local media attention as a result of which fifty extra children (from the Summer Hill area) were tested by Bawden-Smith and his Public Health Unit team. When these results came in Harrison's reading was the second highest.

This news only added more pressure to safeguard Harrison's long term future. The discipline required to maintain the hygiene put added stress on the family. Alperstein recommended a dietary iron supplement for Harrison—Liquid Fergon. Iron inhibits the uptake of lead by red blood cells, that is, iron acts as a protective factor against further lead poisoning. The household was re-organised to fight lead.

Alperstein reported that a South Australian study in Port Pirie had found that up to 7 IQ (intelligence quotient) points could be lost for each 10 micrograms of lead per decilitre found in a child's blood. Professor Anthony McMichael of Adelaide University had looked at the blood lead levels of 700 children over the first four years of life. The South Australian study confirmed longitudinal epidemiological surveys around the western world. The effect on intellectual development could be averted if blood lead levels were reduced in the shortest possible period of time to limit long term exposure to lead contamination.

Because of the publicity generated by Elizabeth O'Brien, a medical consultant employed by Associated Octel, the world's leading manufacturer of lead additive for petrol, offered to help with Harrison's monitoring. Elizabeth and Greg rejected the offer although the consultant insisted he was motivated out of genuine concern.

The O'Briens stuck doggedly to their hygiene regimen for six months. At times it seemed all too much, with the children crying out for attention and play while both parents worked to ensure that cleaning, wiping, mopping, washing tasks were completed first.

After six months Harrison's blood was tested again. The analysis showed some success for all the effort. Harrison's blood lead level had dropped from 31 to 17 micrograms of lead per decilitre. This, however, was disheartening. It indicated that long-term exposure seemed unavoidable as the explanation for the slow fall in the blood lead level. Elizabeth still suffers a 'hefty dose of Catholic guilt' for having put off the blood lead test for two months. She would never know whether Harrison's blood lead level was much higher, the same, or lower at ten months of age.

Alperstein reported that a World Health Organisation analysis of all recent long-term studies had declared that two to three IQ points would be lost for every 10 micrograms of lead per decilitre of blood. And a New York study had found that if you reduced blood lead levels in babies to below 10, the 'level of concern', within the first two years of life, impact on long-term intellectual development would be negligible.

Harrison by this stage was eighteen months old. The race was still on. The carpets had to go. But it was no use polishing the old floorboards in the house. Cracks between the floorboards were obvious collection points for lead particles. Elizabeth borrowed $10,000 from her mother Noela and had the O'Brien floors covered in completely flat cork tiles. The carpets, impregnated with lead from household paint removal and atmospheric fallout, should have been drenched with water before they were pulled up. But no one was around to tell Elizabeth this and Harrison's blood lead level rose slightly following the carpet removal before again continuing the downward trend.

Elizabeth learnt that you could detect the presence of lead particles. You could see the black heavy dust on shop window sills along busy streets with cars and trucks rushing by. If you rubbed this dust between your fingers you would soon see greasy marks on your fingertips. That was lead, heavy, immovable, highly toxic lead. And the horrible realisation was that lead was everywhere in a big city. The city was poisoning our children. The modern convenience of the automobile was a toxic trap with an invisible, insidious fallout.

In 1991 in Australia, with all the domestic and international research then available, absolutely nothing was being done to alert the public. The oil companies which put the lead additive in petrol, ostensibly to aid the vehicle's performance, took no pro-active or pre-emptive responsibility for the damaging health effects of petrol fallout.

Time had almost run out for Harrison O'Brien. While determined household hygiene further reduced his blood lead levels it held at around 15 micrograms per decilitre of blood from the time he turned two to his third birthday. Given the possible high level of lead exposure in his first twelve months of life, Harrison's condition could have been worse, but the distress for the family at not being able to reduce blood lead levels to below the US 'level of concern' was heart-wrenching.

Elizabeth O'Brien's silent outrage at her GP's ignorance and misinterpretation of the data from the children's blood tests was a turning point. From the moment Harrison's blood lead level had come in at 31, an urban activist had been created. But some still believed there was nothing to worry about with a 31 microgram reading. Symptoms of sickness only occurred, it was said, from a blood lead level of 45 and upwards. Readings of more than 70 micrograms were said to produce severe stomach pains or sleep and eating disorders, diarrhoea or constipation in adults, while a child with a blood lead level of 70 or more could be expected to behave 'aggressively'.

But lead was largely a hidden poison which made its way via the bloodstream to all organs of the body, into the skeletal bone itself and into the brain tissue. Lead poisoning was really a silent epidemic. But this epidemic still was not notifiable under health laws and regulations. An infectious disease was notifiable, and rightly so, to protect people. But not lead poisoning.

The Lead Group

BY the end of 1991 Elizabeth O'Brien stood at the centre of a self-constructed network of Australians with a vital concern about lead poisoning in children. They met in the O'Briens' front cork-tiled, wet-mopped room and formed the LEAD Group Inc—short for Lead Education and Abatement Design. They purloined the O'Briens' word processor and set to work, disseminating their material through the local community and local press. With the synchronicity that came to the aid of the campaign on many occasions, Elizabeth asked the Canon Corporation to donate a photocopier just after one of their young staff members had died of kidney failure brought about by lead poisoning she had suffered as a child. Canon donated the copier and a free service agreement which they still supply.

They called a public meeting and about twenty people turned up at the O'Briens' living room. They asked their scientific experts to form the Technical Advisory Board of the LEAD Group and to address their growing membership.

Elizabeth and her colleagues worked without pay or reward to alert the parents of Sydney and interstate callers with practical advice about how they could abate the effects of lead; how to get a blood test; how to interpret the result when Sydney's pathology labs at that time would give no written interpretation. The LEAD Group soon produced a seven-point plan for Australian parents on how to protect their children and started research into the practices of oil companies and the growth of freeways and cars in Australia.

They discovered that leaded paint had been phased out of the Australian market in 1970. But there remained an immense problem with the leaded paint which had been used on houses for decades. Renovators had to be warned about the effects of lead contamination when they came to strip down their walls for repainting. Leaded paint was a 'point source' of contamination in homes. The LEAD Group issued advice on how to decontaminate a lead painted house. Dry sanding was out. Only wet methods which did not disperse dust or flakes were recommended.

Each day the sum of their knowledge increased dramatically through the network of amateurs and scientists. Some days the telephone rang with fascinating and disturbing information. The most disturbing aspect was that Australia seemed to be well behind other developed countries in the public health policy response to lead.

They discovered that in 1985 the Japanese Government had ordered a complete ban on the sale of leaded petrol and that by 1992 the Americans had phased down the amount of lead in petrol to 0.026 grams of lead per litre.

In Sydney lead added to the petrol amounted to 0.4 grams per litre—16 times the US level. Some other parts of Australia allowed 32 times the US level. By the start of 1992 the LEAD Group discovered that in spite of the introduction of unleaded petrol in Australia in 1985, 60 per cent of the market was still leaded petrol, compared with only 1 per cent in the United States.

Ignorance was the enemy which had to defeated. By this time Elizabeth O'Brien was a full time campaigner operating from the front room of their Dulwich Hill house. Before long the shelves she assembled on the walls of the room were groaning with a library of scientific papers and books on toxicology and lead contamination. The telephone started to ring with queries from nearby residents; from elsewhere in the city of Sydney, from the country, from interstate and eventually, from abroad.

At one stage the group toyed with the idea of calling their campaign project PARABLE—short for Parents And Renovators Against Blood Level Excesses. In a world of competitive commercial markets, competitive charities and competitive worthy causes, this was deemed to be too obscure and too biblical.

People needed education. Of that there was no doubt. But government also needed education. Activism produced through the Thomas Thoms affair had exposed the fact that guidelines and regulations were deficient and institutions with the stated objectives of protecting the public from environmental pollution lacked both knowledge and will.

The Campaign

THE LEAD Group and its members decided to embark on a strategy of grass roots campaigning while providing a service to the public. At the same time they would attempt to engage the politicians directly in the consciousness-raising effort. They put out media releases but there was little interest.

The counselling service provided by The LEAD Group became vital to the decisions of many people confronted with lead contamination in their homes. The LEAD Group would interpret the blood lead level analysis, and advise on the strict hygiene regimen which must be used to defeat the poisoning process, and refer people to anyone who might help them.

On 19 May 1992 The LEAD Group started their political lobby through a letter to the top—in Australia's case the then Commonwealth Minister for the Environment, Ros Kelly. The letter asked the Minister to order the Commonwealth Environment Protection Agency to carry out a cost benefit analysis of lead risk reduction in domestic environments and to develop a strategy for the elimination of childhood lead poisoning. It asked that the National Health and Medical Research Council lower the recommended blood lead level of concern to the 10 micrograms per decilitre already set in the United States.

The letter asked that the EPA lay down the infrastructure to deal with thousands of individual cases which would be exposed by targeted screening of at-risk children. The LEAD Group sought the Minister's assurance that legislation and public education programs would be devised to accelerate the phase-out of leaded petrol and that money set aside for urban renewal be channelled into de-leading contaminated domestic sites.

The LEAD Group quoted the latest research that lead poisoning was one of the most common and preventable paediatric health problems of the time.

The concern about adverse effects on central nervous system functioning at blood lead levels as low as 10 ug/dL is based on a large number of rigorous epidemiologic and experimental studies— Centers for Disease Control, October 1991.

Dr Geoffrey Duggin, Head of Toxicology, Royal Prince Alfred Hospital, Sydney, predicts that 40 per cent of twelve to 48-month-old children living in older urban areas in Australia have a blood lead level above 10 ug/dL.—ABC *7.30 Report*, 23.3.92.

The letter to Ros Kelly eventually got The LEAD Group through the door of the Federal Government and in spite of her many perceived faults in the partial distribution of sporting grants, Minister Kelly's intervention on childhood lead poisoning was to be a historic contribution to the health of Australia's children. But it took Elizabeth O'Brien's LEAD group five months to get through that door. Meanwhile The LEAD Group networked with other environmental groups, most notably Greenpeace, the popularly supported international environment organisation.

Ros Kelly met a deputation of people vitally interested in lead contamination from The LEAD Group, including Lynette Thorstensen from Greenpeace and Theresa Gordon, an environmental campaigner from NO-LEAD, a Newcastle group which represented Australian communities affected by point sources of lead such as mines and smelters. Ros Kelly's adviser on the subject, Paul Bainton from the Environment Protection Agency, was a key influence on what was to follow. With his Minister a strategy was drawn up with the objective of switching as much of the Australian domestic car fleet to unleaded petrol as soon as possible. It was then estimated that 30 per cent of cars (pre-1986) were technically able to run on unleaded petrol and thereby to substantially lower the air lead level around the country.

The meeting with Ros Kelly also produced planning for what became known as the Lead Round Table conference of 1993. The process of raising the consciousness of the Federal Government and the agencies charged with protecting public health was aggravating and slow. Agencies were quick to make excuses but painfully slow to move to implement any strategy.

On 10 June 1993, more than a year after The LEAD Group's letter to the Minister, the Federal Government lowered the blood lead 'level of concern' from 25 and set 10 micrograms per decilitre of blood as the national goal below which all Australians should be, especially nought to four year olds.

The week before the lead round-table conference there was something of a media breakthrough. Journalist Kate Legge, writing in *The Weekend Australian* reported:

Elizabeth O'Brien is no Karen Silkwood.

She has not been run off the road before an appointment to brief journalists on the health risks of the nuclear industry. But her single-minded campaign to rid the environment of lead has put powerful commercial interests offside.

Lead is not as sexy as plutonium. There are no stories of two-headed goats grazing on contaminated sites. No stories of birth defects, or terminal cancers troubling the communities living nearby. In massive doses, lead can be fatal, but this is the exception. At the lower levels more commonly recorded there is evidence the damage may be invisible and insidious. It does not maim the body. It impairs the central nervous system. Discounts the IQ.

The horrors of starving Ethiopians and the devastation of war in Bosnia make it hard to get worked up about the threat of stunted intellectual growth. But in a competitive global economy where brains count more than brawn estimates that up to half of Australia's children may exceed the internationally accepted level for concern signals a significant national handicap.

Legge's article had come at just the right time for the round-table conference. It canvassed the latest scientific research in Australia and, most significantly, exposed the lead industry's motivation behind its resistance to the immediate phase-out of leaded petrol which was on the agenda at the conference.

Legge quoted Associated Octel chief spokesman Bill Perreau in a 'disarmingly frank' explanation of the company's motives.

Business is business and 70 per cent of Octel's approximately $700 million annual turnover is related to leaded petrol. The company is diversifying belatedly, as Perreau put it: 'We need a bit of time to fund these acquisitions, otherwise we go out the door at a great rate of knots'.

There in *The Weekend Australian* was the problem. Legge

contended that the debate about lead in petrol had turned positively vicious.

Legge reported:

Pam de Silva, a scientist with the Victorian occupational health research firm AMCOSH, is sceptical of the claims that higher blood lead levels cause lower IQ.

'There is another side to the whole story,' she said. 'The reason you get a relationship between lead in blood and IQ is not because of the lead in blood but because lower IQ causes blood lead. Children with a lower IQ are slower to grow out of the habit of putting things in their mouth.'

There were reported to be major deficiencies in Australian research databases on lead because of different methodologies. But, Legge wrote, such objections had not changed the international consensus that even relatively low levels of lead may be harming the health of children.

The article also quoted Rod Corinaldi, spokesman for the Australian Institute of Petroleum. He was reported to be adamant that lead exposure did not warrant all this attention. In a personal reference to Elizabeth O'Brien, Corinaldi was quoted by Legge as saying:

'The issue is driven by people who don't deal with the broader public health agenda,' he said.

Corinaldi is convinced his opponents have lost the plot. 'Hard science is being denied credence by politically motivated groups with genuine concerns. Elizabeth O'Brien's child has a high lead level. I'm sorry about that, but she is trying to solve her kid's problem at an enormous social cost.'

Kate Legge gave the last word to the activist:

O'Brien won't buy that one. She says whatever happens now will be too late to correct any adverse effects from her own son's blood lead level. 'I'm fighting for the next generation,' she said.

The Round Table

ON 29 July 1993 in Parliament House, Canberra, 160 invited representatives, advisers and observers from state and federal government, the oil industry, regulatory agencies and consumer groups gathered. No one could say they were not consulted.

Ros Kelly opened the Round Table Conference on Lead in Petrol with a prepared speech. But far from engaging in a discussion, the Minister took as read that there existed an adverse health impact of lead fallout from petrol.

Minister Kelly said:

> The purpose of our meeting today is to talk about how we, as a nation, can reduce the amount of lead in petrol and increase the use of unleaded petrol. In this way, we can begin to solve the very serious problem we have of a large number of children in Australia being adversely affected by lead. In discussing this problem, the number one priority must be the health of young Australians.
> ... You are all here because of your knowledge and your important responsibilities in relation to the lead problem. Many of you have been heavily involved in developing and implementing programs for lead reduction at the State and local level.

Minister Kelly then asked for a national response from those assembled:

> The issue of lead in petrol is not a new one. Eight years ago Australia decided to phase out the use of lead in petrol altogether. All new cars imported or produced in Australia since 1986 have been required to run on unleaded fuel.

The health imperative required the accelerated phasing out of lead in petrol. The Minister put up five propositions to the meeting to avoid any further lengthy debate and to take immediate action.

But the Statements of Consensus produced at the end of the day, while being a great step forward, were disappointing to Elizabeth O'Brien. Instead of firm deadlines to achieve a complete phase-out there was no legislated compulsion on the oil industry, which had moved towards phase-down only after it was pushed.

STATEMENTS OF CONSENSUS

- It was agreed that there are compelling health reasons to reduce lead in petrol. To do so should be a principal element in a national lead abatement strategy.
- There was broad support for a national approach with recognition of regional/state circumstances. There was universal agreement that the problem was serious and warranted urgent action by all concerned.
- There was agreement that petrol sourced from Victoria and NSW move to 0.2 g/L by the end of 1994 and that other States move to 0.3 g/L by 1994 and aim to get to 0.2 g/L by 1995 provided that octane demand can be significantly reduced. It is encouraging to see that oil companies have given a commitment to move towards 0.2 g/L by the end of 1995. A total phaseout should be achieved as soon as practicable.
- There was significant support for reduction in octane rating of leaded petrol to 96 in 1994 (or even lower) to accelerate lead phasedown on the understanding that the impact of such a reduction is further assessed between now and then.
- There was support for urgent study of the possibilities and implications of the use of additives such as MTBE (methyl tertiary butyl ether) as a substitute for lead.
- There was unanimous agreement on a national education campaign targeted at consumers and petrol station operators to be undertaken as a partnership initiative between governments, industry, unions and community and trade organisations with a particular focus on the health benefits and information at the pump. There was also support for the suggestion that the name of Super be changed to Leaded petrol.
- Without delaying action, there was support for selective studies in partnership with industry and other relevant bodies such as NHMRC of the incidence and distribution of blood lead levels to monitor the effectiveness of the interventions.

- The importance of a price differential was emphasised by many participants. The economic and equity implications were noted. The importance of an incentive element in a total package and the fact that the cost of manufacture of leaded fuel was now greater than that of unleaded was recognised. Price differentials of between 2c and 5c per litre were canvassed. While the community groups, Victoria and some industry groups strongly urged the case for price differentials, some State and Territory governments emphasised their reservations.
- The need to monitor the effects of measures adopted and to reassess strategies in 12 months time was emphasised. At that point vehicle modification and possible vehicle replacement strategies may have to be considered.
- The public transport option was also pointed to as deserving closer consideration.
- It was agreed it would be useful to investigate the way that premium ULP might contribute to reducing lead use in the longer term.
- Finally it was agreed that all governments would work towards the development of a National Lead Abatement Strategy including appropriate strategies for remediation of areas with site-specific lead problems.

At last Australia was going to move out of its Third World exploitative attitude to childhood lead poisoning—or so it seemed.

At the round table forty-six people were allowed to speak including Elizabeth O'Brien who argued that the tax from the price differential be used to fund the national lead abatement strategy. Representatives from the South Australian Health Commission tabled the results of sixteen surveys of lead contamination around smelters and mines.

Every major petrol company was represented at a senior level: Ampol, BP, Shell, Caltex and Mobil. Ministers or their senior bureaucrats from every state and territory signed off on the communique. Elizabeth O'Brien had a seat at the table as a delegate of the national peak organisation Consumers Health Forum (CHF). Theresa Gordon represented Greenpeace.

It had taken a letter to a Minister and a wait of five months to get a meeting and another year before all interest groups in Australia could be assembled to confront the problem. But what was most disappointing was the resistance at the round table to put a deadline date on the phasing out of leaded petrol in Australia. Significantly the communique commited the parties only to: 'a total phase-out should be achieved as soon as practical'. Elizabeth O'Brien remains angry that when confronted with over-whelming scientific evidence of the effects of lead poisoning on children the regulatory agencies, governments and petrol com-panies did not strive for the quickest most cost-effective solution possible to lead contamination.

The Federal Government was not prepared to legislate without industry agreement. The education and advertising campaigns were welcome. The price differential between leaded and unleaded petrol was a good tactic. By mid-1996 it had raised more than $350 million, precious little of which had been spent on lead abatement. But only through legislation could more children be saved from lead poisoning.

And this lack of willingness to set a limit on contamination was in a country with a car fleet estimated to be one of the oldest in the western world. Australians kept their old cars on the road and they all used leaded petrol. At the round table the petrol companies had lobbied hard for a no deadline statement. They had won that one but at least the issue was up and running.

Elizabeth O'Brien and her supporters had moved for the phase-out deadline for the sale of leaded petrol in Australia to be 1995. The move was overruled after intense lobbying from petrol company representatives in the luncheon recess. Lobbyists were seen to be overjoyed and rather smug when no deadline was set in the final communique.

Other countries had no trouble setting deadlines: the United States had set 1995 as its final phase out of leaded petrol; Canada 1993; Austria 1991 and New Zealand 1996.

As the advertising campaign to persuade car owners of des-ignated makes to switch to unleaded petrol got underway, there was much more work for the LEAD Group to do back in the front room office at Elizabeth O'Brien's house at Dulwich Hill.

There were newsletters to get out, blood-lead analyses to be interpreted, referrals to be issued to worried parents, house inspections and lead decontamination advice to be given. The group had been operating on a voluntary basis for many months. The telephone would ring constantly. The subscriber list for the newsletter was growing.

In 1994 the Federal Government gave The LEAD Group $10,000 to help defray administrative costs, and $150,000 in 1995. This was enough to employ three people. Minister Ros Kelly secured the money through the National Lead Abatement Strategy after it was approved by the Federal Cabinet.

Elizabeth O'Brien's network of allies had grown substantially from the round table meeting. They now included Dr Diane Horvath from the National Health and Medical Research Council who had spoken passionately about the health effects of elevated blood-lead levels.

Other ideas to attack the problem had been floated including a car exchange program or 'cash for clunkers' buyout schemes to give poor Australians, or those from what is known by economists as lower socio-economic backgrounds, an incentive to upgrade their vehicles.

The emphasis also swung onto the Federal Government's Better Cities program which to many seemed to be an aesthetic debate about urban design and freeway construction rather than making cities healthier places in which to live.

In spite of the compelling evidence that cars poisoned our children, governments were just not prepared to think of lateral solutions to this major urban problem. Some large cities had tried innovative solutions. Toronto in Canada had redesigned its public transport system to address consumer concerns about security and convenience. Public transport there had been made more secure and more frequent and integrated at bus/train/tram/taxi interchanges to give a better service.

There was so much more to do to educate the public. Ros Kelly had carried the day in the Federal Cabinet and the abatement strategy was put into place with $4 million to $5 million to be spent on the education campaign for the unleaded petrol changeover. The television ads starred the Australian actor Gary Sweet urging motorists to take the right step and switch to unleaded petrol so no harm would come to our children. There were 150 models of pre-1986 cars on the list which could take unleaded petrol immediately without modification. That was about a third of the estimated Australian car fleet of eight to nine million vehicles. From February 1994 the price of leaded petrol went up by 1 cent a litre with another 1 cent being applied in August 1994. There had been criticism that the price differential would hurt the poor who could not afford to upgrade their cars. But it was pointed out in the limited debate then apparent about the issue that the children of the poor were the ones who would benefit the most from the incentive to switch to unleaded petrol.

The LEAD Group was hoping that the money raised from the 2 cents a litre price differential would go to the priority list they had drawn up for lead abatement. But such was the nature of government that the many millions it raised went in to consolidated revenue.

In a cynical way it appeared that the government's revenue raisers had seized on the health concerns voiced by The LEAD Group and health agencies merely to raise revenue.

In an article in *The Australian Financial Review* on 11 August 1993 reporter Tom Burton had written: 'The new petrol tax will affect more than 3.3 million cars and raise about $160 million a year'. Whatever the real politik, the pricing structure was having the desired effect. Unleaded petrol sales indicated a massive switch-over in the Australian car fleet.

The LEAD Group also started to lobby to persuade the petrol companies to replace the lead additive in petrol with the non-toxic MTBE used in the United States. This was an immediate practical solution but was met with strong resistance by the petrol companies. The great shame was that it would have cost just 2 cents a litre to replace all the lead in petrol with imported MTBE thus effecting an immediate lead phase-out. Instead the 2 cents a litre was taken as tax and disappeared into the ether.

The Fall-Out Continues

FIGURES would show that the peak of leaded petrol use in Australia was reached in 1986 before unleaded petrol was introduced for sale to motorists. But while that was a welcome trend, lead fallout continued to mount in ceiling dust in homes through the country. The lead had been accumulating in homes for fifty years from leaded petrol and for decades prior to that from wood and coal burning.

The ignorance about its toxic effects was overwhelming to the small group of activists operating on three telephones and a fax machine. With The LEAD Group's help whole houses could be decontaminated. It would cost householders $500 to have their attics and other areas vacuumed by specialists.

Elizabeth O'Brien reflected:

It was a cradle to grave struggle. I even wrote a song ...
    Cradle to grave
    cradle to grave
    lead harms our children in the cradle
    puts lead workers in the grave ...
We have struggled without mainstream media support for years, with some exceptions. And we have never felt the need to exaggerate the facts or circumstances ... let alone lie. The facts about this speak for themselves.

The O'Brien family's rigorous hygiene efforts eventually reduced young Harrison's blood lead level to 10 by age three and to seven by the age of four. The experience made the family more determined to ensure that other children were not similarly poisoned. 'Lead additive for petrol is a dangerous compound processed by only a couple of plants in the world. It has to be handled by men in space suits,' Elizabeth said.

On 29 March 1996 *The Sydney Morning Herald* reported that Australia's most extensive survey of lead levels had found 75 000 children aged one to four suffer from such serious lead poisoning their intelligence was likely to have been damaged.

However the study found that fewer Australian children had the higher lead levels that previous research suggested. A 1993 study estimated that up to 53 per cent of children had levels over 10 micrograms of lead per decilitre of blood (microg/dL), a level research shows will damage a child's intelligence by between one and three IQ points by the age of four.

The article also reported a blood lead survey of 700 Sydney pre-schoolers by Dr Mira et al which found that 25 per cent of the children within 10 kilometres of the CBD were above the national goal. This put paid to the notion that the NHMRC's target had been achieved in Australia's largest city and raised the question: Had the national study used rural blood lead levels to dilute and draw attention away from significant urban lead hotspots across the nation?

For the $1.1 million national study, commissioned from the Australian Institute of Health and Welfare by the Commonwealth Environment Protection Agency, researchers visited 2215 homes and took blood samples from 1575 children.

Overall, 7.25 per cent had lead levels above 10 microg/dL of blood. Nationally this represented about 75 000 children. Of these the survey suggests 17 000 children have lead levels about 15 microg/dL, a level causing further damage to normal brain function.

The national goal is to have 90 per cent of children under four with lead levels below 10 microg/dL by 1998. This appears to have been achieved.

How the NHMRC ever decided that nearly 100 000 pre-schoolers was an acceptable number to be poisoned was beyond the belief of The LEAD Group and its supporters.

Elizabeth O'Brien, still working to eliminate lead poisoning, was quoted in the article as saying it was 'unacceptable' that 75 000 children should suffer when the sources were well known.

By mid-1996, pathology laboratories had only just started issuing written interpretation of blood lead analysis. There remained no statutory level of lead contamination in soil, dust or paint at which decontamination must occur.

The abatement strategy was expected to be abandoned by the newly elected Howard Government. Federal funding for The LEAD Group ceased and only the New South Wales Government was prepared to pay for The LEAD Group's vital advisory and referral service for New South Wales residents only.

There remained no deadline for the complete phase-out of leaded petrol in Australia. Thirty-eight per cent of cars were still running on leaded petrol in spite of the successful phase-out in other developed countries by the mid-1990s. Lead continues to accumulate in house dust throughout Australia.

By 1996 the Thomas Thoms foundry, however, was a model of responsibility. The company's principal, Paul Thoms, announced to the group of concerned residents that after 113 years in Summer Hill the company was moving to an industrial estate in Brisbane. They would leave behind a housing development—after decontamination of the soil which the company would conduct at its own expense. The company required no urging or threat of legal sanctions (not that any were forthcoming) from the health or environment authorities to clean up its site. Paul Thoms had declared that a toxic industry simply should not be in a residential area.

The world environment summit in Rio de Janiero produced many 'motherhood' statements on abatement strategies but, predictably, progress was slow. Lead is the only toxin to be mentioned individually in consensus statements from the United Nations Commission on Sustainable Development and the Habitat 2 Conference of 1996.

Lead contamination was an international problem affecting the development of the world's children. It was a preventable problem which did not require the shut down of industry or place individual countries at an economic disadvantage in world trade and productive output. Health workers, objective scientists and environmentalists all knew the case against lead was compelling. But such is the compromise of politics that the final solution to lead contamination in Australia, in particular, has not been embraced by the national government. Until this occurs Elizabeth O'Brien will keep up the pressure for better management of the world's most researched toxin.

For NSW residents, information on lead poisoning prevention is available from:

NSW Community Lead Advisory Service
c/- The LEAD Group Inc.
P.O. Box 161
Summer Hill
NSW. 2130
Telephone: 02 9716 0014 or 1800 626 086
Fax: 02 716 9005

(The NSW Community Lead Advisory Service is funded by a $300,000 thirteen-month grant from the NSW Environment Protection Authority. Residents of other states or territories should write to their state, territory or federal environment ministers.)

AFFORDABLE SAFETY?

'There can be no doubt that the assertions made by Dr James have been inimical to the interests of her employer.'—report on Helen James' 'disloyalty' to the Civil Aviation Authority.

H ELEN JAMES is a woman with a strong sense of what is right and wrong. She can also follow her passions single-mindedly. She is a 'staunch Presbyterian' with a streak of moral righteousness, leavened by a sense of humour and the ridiculous. Her life in Australia, her family background, her shyness and commitment to academic study shaped a woman unafraid but mindful of the perversity and corruption of power and authority.

In 1995, James became a 'whistleblower' who was to be exposed to national publicity through her conflict with her employer, the Board and senior management of the safety regulator, the Civil Aviation Authority. James was forty-eight and a veteran senior public administrator and policy analyst. She had not led a cloistered life in the corridors of bureaucratic power. She had confronted conflict within her own family, had broken with convention, achieved brilliantly in academic study, and been a witness to a bloody movement for democracy in South-East Asia.

When the time came to make a stand, Helen James, with sole financial responsibility for her six children, had to put everything on the line. To her there was no other choice.

James was born in Brisbane on 13 March 1947. Her father, Walter Phillip Dudley James, was a World War II Lancaster bomber pilot who served in Europe in what was known as Australia's 'colonial squadron'—No. 15 based at Mildenhall. Helen still has a cherished photograph of her father and his crew. Her mother, Alice, like her father, was born in Queensland. Helen was the eldest of five children—three boys and two girls. On his return to civilian life, her father resumed his pre-wartime occupation of school principal.

Following her father's promotions the family moved from Raglan, west of Rockhampton, to Bribie Island, Townsville, Mackay, Mt Isa and Brisbane, then to her father's last post as principal of Broadbeach School on the Gold Coast.

Helen's capacity for learning was prodigious. In her teenage years she regularly studied to four o'clock in the morning, a habit continued throughout the years of her university studies.

In the 1950s and 1960s many young women left school at fourteen to take up secretarial positions doing typing and office work until they married. Helen was determined to avoid that fate. She worked hard to earn her father's approval and was determined to go to university.

As she grew up, this bright young girl developed an interest in South-East Asia. She remembers at the age of seven standing in the kitchen of her family's house on Bribie Island and listening to the ABC radio news report on the defeat of the French army at Dien Bien Phu in Vietnam. She thought: What were they doing there in the first place? It was the beginning of a lifelong commitment to Asia, its peoples and cultures.

At high school first in Townsville, then at Mackay where her father moved during her Senior year, she managed to extricate herself from the soul-destroying 'commercial' subjects forced on her by her family and chose straight academic subjects for matriculation. She scored eight As in the Queensland Junior examination and five As and a B (in mathematics) in the Senior Matriculation examination. She was just sixteen at the time and found that she had won five educational and teaching scholarships including an Oriental Studies Scholarship to the Australian National University in Canberra. This was her first choice and she went to live at Bruce Hall at the ANU, again studying into the early hours of the morning, almost living at the university's Menzies Library. She was painfully shy, under-socialised and very withdrawn. She took her meals (a bag of sandwiches) to the library so that she could keep studying.

There were Asian students attending the university who also spent time in the library. One student from Thailand befriended her, often waiting outside until late at night to talk to her. Her friend was very persistent and eventually became her boyfriend. His name was Vinit Phinit-Akson, a Colombo Plan student then studying economics. He was twenty-three, she was eighteen. They went out together for six months at the end of which time they became engaged to be married. The announcement in the Canberra newspaper was shown to her prospective father-in-law, then in Djakarta as Thai Ambassador and Dean of the Diplomatic Corps, by an Australian diplomat before Vinit's letter advising of the engagement reached his parents.

While Vinit's family was extremely kind and welcoming, Helen's parents were shocked and outraged. She remembers that she and Vinit were invited to a garden party at Government House, Yarralumla, during Lord Casey's term, after the engagement was announced. But for fifteen months until their marriage on 21 March 1967, the young couple experienced her parents' opposition. At one point, her father threatened court action to stop the marriage.

By the end of 1966 Helen had passed all her examinations and was due to move to a further year's study to achieve an honours degree in Oriental Studies. She had majored in Indonesian language and Literature and South-East Asian history. Instead, in the face of mounting pressure from her family, she decided to leave Australia with her future husband and to marry him in Thailand.

On 6 January 1967 they flew to Djakarta and stayed with Vinit's parents at the Thai Embassy. A short while later they went to Bangkok where together with Vinit's mother, sister and other family members, they were married in the family home on Soi 49 Sukhumvit Road, Bangkok.

Both Helen and Vinit took up academic positions at Thammasat University, Bangkok. Helen was appointed coordinator of the Department of Linguistics, responsible for a staff of thirty-five American teachers, before she was twenty-one years old. As part of their work, Helen and Vinit worked with the late Professor Alan Markman on the Rockefeller English-language project at Thammasat University. In mid-1969 Vinit won a Rockefeller Scholarship to undertake graduate studies in the United States at the University of Pittsburgh, Pennsylvania, and Helen won a teaching fellowship to the same university.

They both completed MA and PhD degrees in three years and four months. Vinit's postgraduate degrees were taken in linguistics and Helen's in English and American literature. One of her four specialisations was Early American literature. For her dissertation she studied the works of the American writer James Fenimore Cooper, who between 1820 and 1850 produced some forty volumes of fiction and sixty volumes of non-fiction. This body of work covered every genre of American literature. Helen's dissertation *James Fenimore Cooper: A Critical Study of His Religious Vision* remains a perceptive analysis of the nature of Cooper's moral world. Cooper was one of the early American dissenters who, in his writings, regularly lacerated the politicians of his day for their moral cowardice and scrutinised the nature of moral action. It was this element which attracted Helen to Cooper's works.

During their years at the University of Pittsburgh, from 1969 to 1972, American society was wracked by the country's involvement in the Vietnam war. There were demonstrations and sit-ins at their university while at the Kent State University (in neighbouring Ohio) the massacre of student demonstrators by the American National Guard occurred. Helen did not participate in any of the demonstrations. She had been in Bangkok during the North Vietnamese Tet offensive of 1968 and from her knowledge of communist subversion of democratic movements in South-East Asia did not think that sit-ins were warranted in the situation.

By the time Helen was twenty-five years old, she and Vinit had three degrees each and two children, both born in the USA. At the completion of their studies, in early 1973, they decided to return to Thailand and live where they had already built their home next to Vinit's family home in Soi 49 Sukhumvit Road, Bangkok. Both returned to their posts at Thammasat University, Vinit in the Department of Linguistics and Helen in the Department of English Language and Literature, Faculty of Liberal Arts.

In 1973, Thailand was technically a constitutional monarchy whose government was in the hands of a corrupt military dictatorship led by Field Marshall Thanom Kittikachorn and his deputy, General Prapass Charusatiara. In 1971, Prime Minister Thanom had abrogated the constitution and resumed martial law. Throughout 1972, various civil and student groups were agitating for restoration of a constitution. By mid-1973 opposition to the military government was beginning to concentrate in certain student power groups centered at Thammasat University. Thirteen students who became known as the Democracy 13, challenged the government, demanding a constitution. One of them was a student of Helen's in the fourth year Shakespeare Seminar she taught for honours students. The subsequent arrest and imprisonment of these thirteen students led to the people's revolution of 14 October 1973 when parts of the Thai population rose up and overthrew the US-backed military dictatorship. October 14 is known in Thai history as Martyrs' Day in honour of the many students and citizens who gave their lives when, against overwhelming odds, they marched from Thammasat University down Rajdamnern Avenue against the tanks and helicopter gunships of the Thai military.

Surviving student leaders later met with His Majesty King Bhumibol Adulyadej and members of the Thai Royal family in the grounds of Chitrlada Palace. To avoid further bloodshed, the King advised the dictators Thanom and Prapass, together with Thanom's son, Narong Kittikachorn, who had fired on students from the helicopter gunships, to leave the country. They did so that evening, 15 October 1973. It appeared that democracy had triumphed.

The year 1974 was euphoric in Thailand as a civilian government under the astute leadership of Professor Sanya Dhammasak, rector of Thammasat University, was charged by the King with the responsibility of drawing up a new constitution. But the euphoria did not last long: soon the conservative forces began rebuilding their power bases.

Democracy Struggle

BY 1975 North Vietnam had conquered the South, and North Vietnamese soldiers had swept through Indochina. At the same time the ruthless Khmer Rouge had unleashed genocide in Cambodia. The Thai student movement was split by factionalism and infiltrated by agents of both the extreme right and the extreme left. By 1975, the student leaders had become increasingly isolated from their popular bases of support and easily fell prey to reactionary forces, particularly the two extreme right-wing groups, the Krating Daeng and the Nawaphon (New Force).

On 6 October 1976 there was another bloody confrontation at Thammasat University, between supporters of these two right-wing groups and the student forces, followed by a coup d'etat and installation of an extreme right-wing government under a civilian judge, Thanin Kraivixien. He was a trusted friend of the Royal family and had the responsibility of ensuring that Thailand did not fall prey to communist elements.

Helen was deeply moved by the carnage, by the treatment of the young students, and by the violent destruction at Thammasat University. Thousands of students and citizens had either fled to the jungles to join the communist cadres or gone abroad to avoid the actions of the extreme rightist government. At this moment in Thai history, civil war seemed very close. In late 1978—by which time Helen and Vinit had six young children—Prime Minister Thanin was replaced and a more moderate military regime installed. By 1980, under the astute leadership of General Prem Tinsulandonda, a policy of national reconciliation was implemented and amnesty declared for those students who had fled to the jungles.

During the years 1973 to 1980, Helen had been teaching not only at Thammasat University but also in the graduate school at Chulalongkorn University. She had been appointed Head of Department at Thammasat University in 1977 and a Visiting Professor at Chulalongkorn University in 1974. As head of the department she had seen the actions of many groups, both left and right, and it had become clear that it would be wise for her and Vinit to take their family to a safer environment. It was with great regret that she left Thailand, but also with a sense of overwhelming relief when the family boarded the plane for Singapore, then to Melbourne. In moving around with her young family, Helen had to be very careful to keep accurate documentation and to have all her children on her Australian passport. This precaution stood her in good stead.

Having been away from Australia for almost fourteen years, Helen felt like a refugee when, on arrival at Melbourne in the early hours of the morning, a diligent Immigration Officer peered at the family and barked, 'Does anyone here speak English?' Helen thought to herself, nothing has changed in all the years away.

The family moved to Canberra where Helen and Vinit had many fond memories of their student days. Helen worked first at ANU teaching American Literature with the late Professor Bob Brissenden, then decided to pursue a full-time career with the Australian Public Service. From 1981 she worked as a senior public administrator, policy analyst and bureaucrat in Canberra in the Departments of Communication, Foreign Affairs and Prime Minister and Cabinet.

Her marriage to Vinit ended in 1984 although he stayed on in Australia until 1989 when he returned to Thailand to take up a position as Head of the Department of International Relations at a private university in Bangkok.

In those years Helen raised her young family by herself, worked hard, and continued to watch closely the developments in Thailand and elsewhere in South-East Asia. Only in recent years, with political stability restored, has Helen returned to Thailand, a country and people she dearly loves. She continues to have a very close relationship with Vinit's family with whom she stays on her frequent visits to Bangkok.

In 1988, seeking a change of direction and hands-on management experience, she accepted a position as Director of Personnel at the newly formed Civil Aviation Authority or CAA as it became known. She was to be responsible for a staff of sixty-five.

Joining the CAA

HELEN James found an organisation struggling to find its feet. In the prevailing political climate of privatisation and economic rationalism, the new CAA had been split from the old Department of Civil Aviation (DCA) to operate as a statutory body. It had its own Board and chief executive officer. Its statutory objective was to regulate commercial flying operations efficiently and cost effectively. The new CAA retained many of the old DCA staff and the political baggage which inevitably came with established work practices and attitudes. Slowly, over the next two years under Colin Freeland and Alan Rainbird, the CAA melded itself into what James believed to be an energised and relatively cohesive force. She enjoyed her work and she was appointed manager of the Corporate Secretariat and worked directly with the CAA Board.

In 1990 the CAA was shaken by a 'tornado'. Dick Smith, the Australian aviator, adventurer, entrepreneur and former Australian of the Year, was appointed chairman of the board following the death in January that year of Alan Woods AO. The Smith Board appointed a new CEO, Frank Baldwin, with a brief to pare the CAA's operations right back to make it more efficient and account-able. 'Affordable safety' became Dick Smith's mantra. In pursuit of this goal, management and staff jobs were abolished; some 2000 staff left the CAA on redundancy packages and the composition of the Board turned over rapidly. Many experienced safety regulatory staff lost their jobs. Helen James watched as morale within the organisation plummeted. Amidst stringent cost-cutting measures which often seemed to her more like settling of old scores, executive management numbers increased and salaries skyrocketed.

At the same time, the Australian aviation industry was made self-regulating with many delegations formerly exercised by CAA/DCA being transferred to the industry for implementation. The philosophy was that only a safe airline stays in business so it is in the interest of each airline to maintain high safety standards. All this was at the time when increased external costs were being imposed on the industry as well. These activities sparked vigorous debate both inside and outside the organisation with many critics saying that self-regulation was akin to putting the fox in charge of the chicken coop.

At the end of his two-year-term in February 1992, Dick Smith retired as chairman and was replaced by Ted Butcher, already a member of the Board and a former head of the National Rail Authority.

The engineers' union, the ALAEA (Australian Licensed Aircraft Engineers Association), was concerned that many skilled staff had been removed in the rush to save money and that safety standards had been dangerously compromised. Union officials held a series of meetings with management to try to address the concerns. In March 1992 Ted Butcher established a Board Safety Committee, chaired by former Qantas pilot and CAA Board member, Captain Alan Terrell. Helen James was made secretary to that committee. While safety issues were back on the agenda, the problems were not solved and were in fact increasing. The CAA was heading for more trouble.

In January 1993, CEO Frank Baldwin left the Authority after an inquiry by Ian McPhee (former Fraser Government minister then working as a Melbourne-based consultant) into Australia's new air traffic control system. The Australian Advanced Air Traffic Systems (TAAATS) found that Baldwin and his general manager had mishandled the tender process. Another CAA general manager, Doug Roser, was temporarily appointed to replace Baldwin as CEO.

In February 1993 the CAA Board appointed Alan Terrell to investigate the CAA Safety Regulation Division. Helen James, as secretary to the Board Safety Committee, was asked by Terrell to be co-ordinator of the investigative group assembled to do this work. The group included Laurie Foley, a freelance aviation consultant and former CAA senior manager in the Safety Regulation division, George Grunbaum, a senior CAA manager, and Bill Edwards, delegate of Ron Cooper, the CAA's chief safety officer. Cooper had refused to be personally involved in the investigation.

Doug Roser was keen to become the CAA's permanent CEO and wanted the CAA to be seen as an efficient organisation. He gave the investigation group three weeks to gather all available information about safety regulatory operations and one week to write a 'consensus report'. The implication was that, if all parties did not sign, the report would not be accepted. The members of the group knew that their report could be significant for the safety and well being of the flying public. The mood, according to James, was one of feeling immense pressure to have the report both accepted and acted upon.

For three weeks in February the investigators toured the country, talking at length to CAA staff, industry and unions. Their investigations covered all major capital cities. The level of paranoia in the organisation was high. So much so that in some places many of the interviews were conducted 'in camera'. Many of the people approached said they would not talk in front of some CAA officials for fear of repercussions. Some of the evidence was quite alarming. Helen James, as secretary, kept a complete record of all the interviews they conducted. When the committee returned to headquarters at 25 Coronation Avenue, Glebe Park, in Canberra, they got down to the task of writing their report. They worked into the night to reach Roser's deadline. Occasionally informants would ring in with additional information they wanted included in the final report.

On the day before the report was due, the investigative group received a call from an engineer who told them that he had just assessed a World War II Polish-built MIG 15 plane and decided that it was not airworthy. The engineer told them his decision had been over-ridden by CAA officials. The very next day the plane crashed in an airshow, killing the pilot and his passenger and putting hundreds of on-lookers at risk. The plane had passed within twenty metres of a stadium full of school children. James and the rest of the committee were shaken by the news. They were now more determined than ever that safety procedures regulated by the CAA should be upgraded to proper levels.

Re-writing

BECAUSE of the constraints involved in preparing a consensus report the investigative group had to choose their words carefully. They did not want to include anything which might give the Board grounds to dismiss it. They decided to make no official recommendations, instead identifying a series of key problem areas for action by the Board and management. However, the chairman of the investigative group, Alan Terrell, together with James and Grunbaum, wrote a paper for the CAA Board which included their more serious concerns, in particular their fears about falling safety standards. As was the custom, papers prepared for the CAA Board first went to the CEO for endorsement. When it was returned to Helen James she found that two crucial paragraphs relating to the safety problems had been removed and the rest of the paper had been re-written.

The Terrell group had written in summary of their findings:

Effects on Safety. There was considerable but mixed comment in regard to any reduction in existing safety levels. In fact there was a suggestion that it may be improving, although this was related to economic necessity rather than regulatory effect. There were views that when economic pressures were brought to bear on an operator, safety margins were likely to be affected.

There was concern that unless the matters identified above were urgently addressed a significant safety concern would become evident.

This passage had been re-written and now read:

Effects on Safety. It is notable that the report does not address safety issues. Mixed comments suggest that in many respects safety levels have been improved, but over all there is no conclusion that safety has been impaired or deteriorated.

While the original report proposed a detailed course of urgent action and oversight, the re-written report proposed that the CAA Board merely note the report's contents and refer it to management 'for review and prioritising the concerns raised with a requirement to report back to the Board Safety Committee with details of proposed rectification action'.

The thrust of the original report had been radically changed.

Helen James was horrified and immediately protested to Roser. But in the ensuing discussion Roser refused to make any changes and dismissed James from his office.

Alan Terrell then wrote a second report to the CAA chairman, Ted Butcher, in which he expressed his regret that only part of his report had been presented to the Board and reiterating his concerns about safety standards:

It is in my opinion . . . a fact that safety standards/levels have been reduced so that they are closer to the regulated margins. It would be most surprising if this were not so, as in essence what has occurred is that the industry has been deregulated, the Authority has been commercialised, policy has insisted on devolution wherever possible and delegation where this can be controlled, and the country is experiencing a major economic downturn, all at the same time. Summing all that up, standards are certainly lower, the essence of the argument would be: are they too low? A major accident would determine this but it is the Authority's—and the Board's—

responsibility to ensure this does not happen. The position in General Aviation may already be below an acceptable level if the insurance statistic showing a 40 per cent increase in GA claims between the early 90s and late 80s can be translated into operational events.

It emerged later that this report was neither tabled nor shown to other board members at that time. So the CAA Board, the body charged with air safety in Australia, was not then fully aware of the gravity of the safety problems uncovered by the Terrell committee. In the meantime Alan Terrell's term came to an end and he was not re-appointed to the position, nor was he asked to brief the Board on his findings.

Rumours began to circulate within the CAA that some of the informants, people who had spoken to the Terrell inquiry, were being unexpectedly removed from their positions and some people feared that their telephones had been tapped. As a result, a network began to grow around the country, made up of CAA employees who were genuinely concerned about falling safety standards and the negligent attitude of CAA management. They tried to draw attention to what they saw as a disaster waiting to happen.

And happen it did.

On 11 June 1993, only a few months after the debacle over the Terrell report, Helen James's worst fears were realised. On that day a Monarch Airlines Piper Chieftain plane crashed when it tried to land at Young, west of Canberra, in bad weather. Seven people were killed in the tragedy. The Civil Aviation Authority went into defensive mode. The accident was investigated by the Bureau of Air Safety Investigation. It soon emerged that the Bureau was highly critical of CAA actions. Nothing effective changed in the CAA's approach to safety. There was change at the top, however, with the departure of Ted Butcher as chairman and his replacement with General Peter Gration, former head of the Defence forces.

Dr Helen James worked quite closely with the new chairman and developed a sincere admiration for him. On several occasions she spoke to him about the safety problems she had observed. Gration appeared to be shocked.

In the meantime, in early 1994, Doug Roser was appointed Chief Executive Officer of the CAA. Laurie Foley, the aviation consultant, talked to both Gration and Roser, briefing them on the current problems, particularly the situation relating to Seaview, a small airline which was causing much concern to the safety regulatory staff.

By this time Helen James was aware that she was unpopular with the organisation's management. Although she was aware she had done nothing wrong, her feelings about safety issues and the problems within CAA were known and she began to feel the consequences of her independent attitude. Her immediate supervisor removed staff from her control and took away some of her functions. James felt she was in an increasingly untenable position. She began to suffer badly from the stress of the situation and developed pneumonia.

But for a time she continued, coping with the difficult atmosphere at work. She still tried to make sure that senior people in authority in the Civil Aviation Authority were aware of what was happening. But the stress took its toll and she became ill once again. As is the way in bureaucracies, certain tactics can be adopted to deal with a person deemed inappropriately employed. Helen James's job was upgraded, requiring that it be advertised. As she now expected, the job was given to someone more junior than herself. On 5 August 1994 Helen James took stress leave. But before she left the Canberra offices of the CAA she had a last talk to Gration and left convinced that he would take some action.

In 1994 the Civil Aviation Authority was an organisation under siege. The Bureau of Air Safety Investigation report on the Monarch accident was scathing. In May the Opposition spokesman on transport, John Sharp, made a speech in Federal Parliament in which he claimed the CAA was not regulating small airlines and was out of control.

In July the Minister for Aviation, Laurie Brereton, appointed Peter Morris, a former Minister for Transport now returned to the backbench, to head a parliamentary inquiry into aviation safety standards. This seemed to be a sign that things might change. While she was still on stress leave, Helen James and Laurie Foley each prepared submissions to the inquiry.

James now knew that her career with the CAA was effectively over and she began to search for a new job. In the meantime the

CAA itself suggested that she might like to take redundancy. After thinking about it for a while, it seemed to be a good idea and she agreed. The redundancy departure was to be effective from the end of November. With the redundancy payment (after fourteen years of public service) she decided to buy a place in the country for her children. Together they found an ideal property and negotiated to purchase it when the redundancy payment was made.

But on 2 October 1994 the unthinkable happened. An Aerocommander aircraft, belonging to Seaview Air, crashed en route to Lord Howe Island from Newcastle. The pilot and all eight passengers were killed.

This latest accident had a dramatic effect on Helen James. She felt that something had to be done to try to ensure that safety was improved. The public outcry which followed the crash intensified as media reports were broadcast questioning the regulatory checks on Seaview Air by the CAA. It was widely reported that Seaview Air had been allowed to continue flying even after CAA inspectors had reported major problems with the crashed aircraft's maintenance. The Minister called in the Federal Police to investigate allegations of links between CAA staff and Seaview Air.

Going Public

IN early November Helen James was talking with her colleague Laurie Foley in his office. They were both concerned about what had happened. Foley had decided that it was time to talk about the issue publicly. He was going to meet with Peter Cassuben, a reporter from ABC TV's *7.30 Report*, in his office. James sat in on the meeting and a discussion about all the circumstances took place, off the record, as the journalists would say. Later, over coffee, Cassuben heard about James's concern at the watering down of the investigation committee's report to the CAA Board. 'That's the real story,' the reporter declared. He then asked Helen James if she would be prepared to tell her story with the television camera rolling. James thought about it for a while, then after weighing all the factors, including the consequences, both personal and professional, she decided that she would give a television interview. If the public and politicians are made aware then something may be done to improve safety standards, she thought.

Cassuben had a credible witness in Helen James. In the interview she told the story of the doctored addenda to the Terrell report and said that the CAA was 'riddled with deceit'. As the camera rolled she produced her 'blue book' in which she had recorded the concerns of CAA employees around Australia and told how their testimony and courage in speaking out had been ignored by CAA management.

When the James interview went to air there was uproar. The day after the broadcast Minister Laurie Brereton ordered two CAA Board members to investigate James's allegations. Doug Roser stood aside while the inquiry was held. Meanwhile James braced herself. Within a few days she received a letter from the CAA threatening her with legal action and demanding the return of the documents she had shown on the *7.30 Report*. She was also notified that her redundancy payout had been deferred pending further investigation. She had worked at CAA for long enough to understand the culture and was under no illusions about what she could expect in personal reprisal even though she was only days away from officially exiting the organisation.

In the weeks that were to follow she had to draw on all her reserves of strength. She suspected that her telephone was tapped and for a while even thought she might end up in jail. But she had a lot of support from family and friends. Letters of support, stimulated by the publicity, arrived from all over Australia, many from strangers who believed in what she was doing.

Laurie Foley and other colleagues who had been trying to draw attention to the problems within the CAA applauded her actions. Even her bank offered her extra funds to pay for any extra legal requirements and the owner of the land she had planned on buying offered to wait until her redundancy was paid out.

On 3 December the CAA Board was presented with a report which exonerated Doug Roser from any wrong doing although it asserted that the Terrell Report had been altered by another CAA Board member, Ron Yates. Under pressure from Brereton, Roser resigned his position and left with a large redundancy payment.

In what appeared to Helen James to be revenge, the Board

immediately appointed Australian National University Professor of Law, Dennis Pearce, to investigate Helen James's own conduct in the affair. Pearce initiated a full scale inquiry and wrote to James, ordering her to appear before him at the National Convention Centre. Her lawyer, Hugh Selby, advised her against going and attended himself to tell Pearce that his client would not be there. Selby arrived at the convention Centre to find Pearce sitting in solitary splendour on a podium surrounded by recording devices to take down the evidence.

Helen James had been confronted with five allegations: that she had removed CAA documents when unauthorised to do so; that she had retained documents; that she had allowed the ABC access to confidential documents and information; that she had made statements to the ABC inconsistent with her duty as a CAA employee; that her behaviour constituted misconduct.

In January 1995, Helen James took her family for a short holiday, trying to escape from some of the stress that had built up. On their return and before she had set foot in her house, a letter from the CAA Board was hand-delivered to her young daughter. It informed James she had been found guilty of misconduct and would, subject to any final representation from her, be dismissed forthwith: 'Professor Pearce has completed his investigation and presented his report, a copy of which is enclosed for your information'.

The letter and report were in her opinion ludicrous. In his report Professor Pearce had criticised her for having spoken to the media about her concerns instead of following 'normal channels'. Yet she had spent the two and a half years since the submission of the Terrell Report trying to do exactly that. In that time there had been two major aircraft crashes.

Professor Pearce found that the allegations were made out. James was under a duty not to disclose. 'Broadly speaking, an employee owes a responsibility to an employer to do nothing that is inimical to the interests of the employer.' There were exceptions, Pearce noted, but James was not asserting criminality.

There can be no doubt that the assertions made by Dr James have been inimical to the interests of her employer. The CAA has been subjected to intense criticism in the Parliament and the press as a result of her statements. The former Chief Executive Officer became the subject of an inquiry to determine the truth of the allegations made against him by Dr James (and was exonerated). Dr James has disclosed confidential information to the public via a television program knowing that the information was confidential and that she was under a duty not to disclose it.

Professor Pearce also dealt with the issue of 'whistleblowing' as a possible defence for James's behaviour. He stressed that there was no Commonwealth legislation then present which exempted a person from liability for the consequences of their actions on the basis that they were acting as a 'whistleblower'.

In press reports Dr James is quoted as saying that the Seaview crash was the final motivation for her making her concerns public. On the other hand it is to be observed that Dr James' main concerns appeared to relate to an event that had occurred some twenty months previously. This is the only specific matter to which she refers. All other comments are of a general nature. She had not pursued this specific issue internally. Further she had applied to work for the person against whom she levelled the criticism of altering the relevant document. It was only after she failed to gain appointment to that position and appeared to have secured an early retirement package that she aired her concerns in public. These were matters that I wished to pursue with Dr James but was unable to do so by her choosing not to talk to me. In the absence of this opportunity I am unable to reach a conclusion on what motivated Dr James to have acted as she did.

Professor Pearce ruled on the question of penalty for Helen James's misconduct:

From the Authority's viewpoint, it does not seem to me that it is possible to do other than terminate Dr James' employment. She occupied a key position in the Authority that required the highest level of trust and discretion. Her access to what I understand are regarded as the most important documents held by the Authority demanded of her the utmost good faith. She took some of these documents and made them publicly available to a very wide audience. She also made most damaging statements that have cost the Authority dearly in terms of public standing and confidence and were, I gather, instrumental in inducing the then CEO to resign. It is impossible to think that the employment relationship could continue in the light of Dr James' conduct.

With support from the Opposition spokesman on transport, John Sharp, Helen James appealed to Minister Laurie Brereton for justice. At the end of January, just before the CAA Board was to meet to implement her dismissal, Minister Brereton issued a directive, ordering the Board to desist all action against her and immediately settle her redundancy payment. The media publicity had generated substantial public support for her stand and she had apparently become too hot to handle:

> I, LAURENCE JOHN BRERETON, Minister for Transport, acting pursuant to subsection 12(1) of the Civil Aviation Act 1988, DIRECT the Civil Aviation Authority to do the following:
> 1. Take no action to terminate the employment of Dr Helen James on any ground relating to the matters that are the subject of the report of 9 January 1995 by Professor Dennis Pearce to the Civil Aviation Authority.

After privately seeking legal advice about the legitimacy of the Minister's directive, and finding that it could not ignore the Minister's orders, the CAA Board was forced to allow Helen James to leave the organisation with all her employee entitlements. However, two Board members resigned over the issue and one member requested that she return the personal reference he had given her when she went on leave.

Victory

HELEN James first learnt of her victory when a CAA delivery car arrived at her house and a letter was thrown down at her door. It contained a copy of the Minister's directive. 'It was fabulous to get that letter and to know that I had been vindicated at last,' she said.

More than a year later Helen James can recall some of the ridiculous incidents in the saga with her usual sense of humour.

It helped that she was fully aware of the capacity of the organisation for reprisal and that she felt one step ahead of the tactics used against her. She also knew that, deep down, her detractors could not touch her, even if she went to jail for having spoken out.

'If you don't become emotional and you can see the funny side of things, it will get you through,' she advises. Although she was denied the title or status of 'whistleblower' by the Pearce inquiry because she went 'public' with her concerns, her treatment followed the by now normal practice of corporations towards those who do blow the whistle—shoot the messenger.

The support Helen James received from her family and friends was very important to her emotional survival. One morning, when things were looking fairly grim, she had a telephone call from someone she was about to start working with. The caller simply offered his support. It meant a great deal to know that people were feeling for her.

The Whistleblowers' Association also contacted her to offer support. In the end she supported others in the same predicament, talking to people who were being vilified for doing their duty.

On 6 June 1996 Coroner Peter Gould's investigation into the Monarch crash of June 1993 was released. Gould condemned 'slipshod' management, concealment and deceit. He declared that the Civil Aviation Authority—the body charged with ensuring the safety of the public—could have averted the Monarch disaster if it had not turned a blind eye to Monarch's shoddy operations.

Gould found that CAA had gone out of its way to protect charter operators from regulations. Both the CAA and the Air Transport Council had ample warning that Monarch was a 'disaster waiting to happen'.

The CAA and the ATC had received many complaints about Monarch in the months before the crash. 'The CAA management refused in the face of persistent and overwhelming evidence of blatant breaches of the regulations to revoke the airline's air operating certificate which it was required by law to do. It placed the commercial interests of its "customers" above the safety of the public.'

James believes that what toughened her more than anything else was a sense of personal perspective. In South-East Asia and Thailand in particular, she had seen human beings struggling for democratic principles often at the cost of their lives, taken in sometimes brutal political reprisals. In spite of her personal circumstances and her responsibilities to her children she placed her wellbeing at great risk to seize an opportunity to warn the public about what was going on within the CAA. She had not set out to be disloyal. Had she been motivated by self interest alone she could have kept her mouth shut and collected her redundancy payout without any additional aggravation. But when an opportunity to break the silence over the CAA's corporate response to safety presented itself she spoke out, willing and ready to suffer the consequences. Fortunately, public consciousness about the value of genuine whistleblowers had been raised sufficiently for that extra political pressure to ensure the consequences were not prolonged. Australia is blessed with a relatively stable political system and a sometimes appropriately inquisitive media. Other countries in our region are not so blessed.

James stood against an arrogant, careerist and uncaring mentality within the Civil Aviation Authority. What the authority, its Board, management and staff did after the exposure of laxity or negligence within it, was now very much open to full public scrutiny.

The travelling public had been made aware that there were some within the body charged with regulating safety who were prepared to put the physical welfare of passengers before their own careers. Helen James would never be officially thanked for her own courage. But, more significantly, she had the support and thanks from those who knew what she had gone through.

Helen James now teaches Thai language and cultural history at university, a job which she loves. She has been able to put the past behind her, as part of an experience that in many ways she can feel proud of.

INCOMPATIBLE WITH COMPANY OBJECTIVES

'There was red-coloured dirty liquid bubbling up out of the ground. The men were ankle deep in it and it smelt very strongly of diesel.'—Eyewitness to Groote Eylandt fuel spill, 4 April 1996.

'Hey Rob they've found your leak!'—A former crew-member's phone call to Dr Robert Savory, March 1995.

'Whether you're a greenie or a BHP shareholder, this is bad news.'—Dr Robert Savory, March 1995.

'Incompatible with company objectives.'—Former employer's statement on Dr Robert Savory's Social Security Employment Separation Certificate, 15 February 1994.

THE BHP job advertisement was enticing. GEMCO, BHP's manganese mine subsidiary on Groote Eylandt in the Gulf of Carpentaria, wanted to appoint an 'environmental co-ordinator' to maintain 'the highest possible level of environmental excellence' on the island.

Manganese had been mined on Groote Eylandt for twenty-five years. The island is 2300 square kilometres of near pristine Darwin woolly butt forest with lush tropical rivers and rocky escarpments rich with Aboriginal paintings. There is a small mining community of about 1000 at Alyangula on the north western side of the island. Living alongside the miners are the Aborigines—the traditional owners—some 1200 in number, who administer the island through the Anandilyakwa Land Council.

Dr Robert Savory was living in Toowoomba, west of Brisbane, with his wife, Jennifer, and three children when he spotted the advertisement. Excitedly he prepared his application and attached his curriculum vitae. He had appropriate qualifications for mine rehabilitation work.

Savory, 52-years-old in 1990, was looking for a fresh challenge. Born in Kenya in 1938 to dairy farmer parents of British extraction, he was an only child whose friends and playmates were the children of the black workers employed on the farm. Young Robert's parents were devout Christians who shared their love of their God with the blacks. The family spoke Swahili as a second language.

Savory's father, Dick, had worked in Australia as a jackaroo before settling in Kenya. The father taught the boy to crack a stockwhip and recite Banjo Patterson poetry. His father's stories of life in Australia became part of Robert's early conscious memories.

Young Robert had a rugged boarding school secondary education at the Prince of Wales School in Nairobi and at Clifton College, Bristol, in England. He was admitted to the University of London's Wye Agricultural College and then went to Rhodesia (later Zimbabwe) to complete a Masters degree in soil science. There Savory married an English girl, Clare, and applied for and accepted a teaching position at Gatton Agricultural College in Queensland around 1961. Within a year he had taken out Australian citizenship. Three children, Helen, Richard and Philip, were born in south-east Queensland. But his new wife pined for home and Savory went back to Africa where he worked on pasture research at the University of Malawi. He prepared his PhD thesis over the next eight years concentrating on pasture improvement and fodder crops for small-holder farmers. He was employed by the United Nations Food and Agriculture Organisation to help the farmers of Malawi and Botswana.

Savory's writings appeared in the publications of the National Academy of Sciences in Washington DC. They included self-help guides to soil conservation and pasture improvement, the development of legumes in agricultural systems and seed farm growing— 'never plough a steep hill ... never cultivate near a creek ... build contour bunds to stop soil erosion ...'

Work for the FAO was challenging. Results had to be produced in the shortest possible time. Corners were cut. But the Savorys had a great lifestyle with personally satisfying rewards. He had been a conservationist from his early days on his parents' farm and he shared his mother's love of birds.

Savory says now he had never been an argumentative type in his relations with others but he had always held firm views. He remembered once, aged about thirty, clashing with an academic superior, an American-born professor with an abrasive style. The tough American had lost most of his fingers during bomb demolition work in World War II. The stand-up difference of opinion, Savory found, did not destroy their relationship—it cemented it. Savory determinedly had stated the facts. Facts were facts. The American did not readily concede. But the often abrasive put-down of such conflicts was this time replaced with a tone of respect. When Savory left this job, his family was touched to see tears in the American's eyes as they said their farewells.

By 1980 his marriage to Clare had ended and Savory returned to Australia where he took up a variety of jobs not related to his usual field. He felt he had become a rolling stone around southern Queensland. In the mid 1980s he met and married an Australian woman, Jennifer. Jennifer had children of her own and with a new family eventually comprising three, Jamie, Cristy and Anna, Savory needed a good job to help meet the children's needs.

BHP Manganese or GEMCO (Groote Eylandt Mining Company) were happy to employ him. Savory found GEMCO managers Bob Wunder and Murray Fox to be unusually enlightened for miners in an industry often associated with redneckery. Savory's duty statement, for what was to be a new position, had to ensure that the 'traditional owners' wishes were complied with'. The successful applicant had to maintain the 'highest possible environmental standards' and be in charge of a team to help clean up the mining leases on Groote Eylandt and rehabilitate more than 200 hectares of mined land. Wunder and Fox had interviewed Savory for the job. He was flown to Groote Eylandt for the interview and was offered the position soon after. Murray Fox told him it was his view that if GEMCO did not get on top of the environmental and rehabilitation problem caused by the very grimy manganese mining operation, '*it will come back and bite us on the bum*'.

The Challenge

SAVORY went ahead of his family to start work. A GEMCO house on the island came with the job. Jennifer and the children joined him within a few months. His challenge was to turn BHP's rhetoric and professed environmental commitment into reality. Jennifer was thrilled for him. 'He thought he'd died and gone to heaven,' she said.

Savory's work was to be part of BHP's routine management performance appraisal. This was the first time Savory had worked in the mining industry and he approached his new job with gusto. Fox and Wunder, practical mining men, knew about bad public relations through previous industry impact on the environment. Savory started the task of compiling an environmental audit of BHP's mining leases.

His reports and action plans drew high praise from head office. His rehabilitation work involved the slow process of tree and plant regrowth at the mine site. The environmental coordinator's duty statement also required Savory to monitor all aspects of environmental impacts from mining operations and facilities. Just near the Alyangula jetty where the tankers loaded the manganese was a 16 million litre tank farm—seven huge storage tanks filled with diesel fuel, the biggest 15 metres high.

Savory, a soil and tree specialist, had no technical knowledge of bulk fuel storage and management procedures. However, reports of a 10-tonne fuel spill into the ocean at nearby Gove in 1990 alerted him to the potential for a similar disaster at the GEMCO tank farm. The Gove spill had been caused by the chance combination of relatively minor mechanical faults and human errors. Savory's first inspection of the GEMCO tank farm in May 1991 revealed that such a disaster was just waiting to happen. All the stormwater drain valves in the impermeable bunds (3-metre high walls) that protected the massive fuel tanks, were found in the 'open' position. Any fuel leak would have immediately discharged through the 20 centimetre pipes into the ocean 20 metres away.

By nightfall on the day of the inspection a total of seventy-four faults had been identified and the more obvious ones, such as 'open' valves, had been secured and padlocked. Savory sent a memo to the Finance and Administration manager detailing all the more obvious engineering problems and faults that he, a tree specialist, had identified at the tank farm. It was this experience with the slackness of environmental protection at the tank farm which first made him feel insecure about GEMCO's fuel storage facilities.

By the end of 1990 Savory had produced a comprehensive summary of GEMCO's environmental status on Groote Eylandt. Mr N.T. Allen, BHP's Manager of Environmental Services, had memoed Wunder on 27 December 1990: 'Please pass on my compliments to Rob Savory and others involved'.

While the work continued Savory had to come to terms with the prejudices of some of the local whites, most disturbingly among GEMCO's management. At an induction meeting soon after his arrival he heard one man say of Aborigines in general: 'The reason why Aborigines can't hold their liquor is because they are genetically defective'. Savory overheard the same man call the Aborigines 'those black pricks at Angurugu' on a number of occasions.

As part of his duties Savory often took BHP executives, including directors from Melbourne, on tours in four-wheel drive vehicles to show his rehabilitation work at the mine site.

On one occasion another GEMCO manager said: 'Well Rob, you're doing a good job but personally I couldn't give a shit about the environment'. Savory held his tongue.

And on another occasion when he requested a small welding job from a workshop boss, he was told: 'If it has nothing to do with getting rocks out of the ground, down the Rowell highway (the 20 kilometre road from the manganese mine to the jetty) and on to a ship, your fucking job goes to the bottom of the fucking list'.

Awareness of environmental damage and its effect on the public standing of the company were apparently high at least at some senior levels. On 29 July 1991 a memo from Jerry Ellis, the CEO of BHP Minerals in Melbourne, was distributed to GEMCO management.

US Environmental Survey. The attached press cutting has been sent to me reporting the results of a survey which found 84 per cent of Americans believe that damage to the environment is the most serious crime a company can commit. It does not matter if the figure is 80 per cent or 50 per cent. The message is clear and I suspect many people elsewhere in the world, including Australia, hold similar views. The newspaper article serves as a timely reminder that we all must take appropriate care in the management of environmental issues over which we have control or where we have responsibility. A mistake could place our good reputation in jeopardy and I would like you to reinforce my views on the management of environmental isues with your management and staff.

In this enlightened atmosphere Savory felt under appropriate pressure to drive through to the objectives he had taken on. On 23 July 1991 Carl I.K. Berglin, Director of Mines for the Northern Territory Government in whose jurisdiction GEMCO operated, wrote to Savory praising his submitted environmental management plan:

> Initial departmental reaction to the plan has been favourable. In fact, the Acting Secretary of the Department (of Mines and Energy) expressed the opinion that it could serve as a model which other mining companies might do well to follow ...

In early 1992 Savory started his first detailed environmental audit of GEMCO's fuel and oil facilities and operations. He would now report to a new general manager as Bob Wunder had moved up the BHP career ladder.

Discrepancies

IN the process of the audit, fuel records for the previous two years had been checked. The audit covered the amount of diesel pumped from BP tankers which visited the island every three months to refill the storage tanks. When matched with the records of how much diesel was being pumped to the electricity generating powerhouse and through to the nearby bowser to keep the mine trucks and vehicles running, there were found to be significant discrepancies.

Long serving GEMCO employees told Savory that the company had earlier drilled for and found underground diesel leaks in the vicinity of the powerhouse. Savory obtained confirmation of this from GEMCO's engineer at the time, Ken Farrell, who was now in a more senior BHP position in Western Australia. Farrell directed Savory to where the drill holes had been located—two of them were still visible, but blocked with gravel.

By 3 June 1992 Savory had located the remaining drill holes and was investigating the cost of hiring a drill from the Northern Territory Government to attempt to clean them out.

On 18 June 1992 there was a meeting of senior BHP executives with GEMCO management on Groote Eylandt. Savory produced a handwritten assessment of environmental risk problems covering oil and fuel spills, manganese discharge, biological issues, soil erosion, greenhouse effect and visual impact. He listed the 'risk' on a scale of zero to five. For example, oil and fuel spills:

RISK ASSESSMENT

Fuel Loss from underground pipes/tanks   (Scale 0–5)

Environment impact	1–2
Cost of prevention	2
Cost of remediation	5
Adverse publicity	5

Savory had assessed the environmental impact as low, the cost of prevention as reasonable but the cost of remediation and adverse publicity likely to affect BHP's public image as high.

GEMCO management did not act on his memo.

The cause of any leak was not physically apparent. Years earlier, Savory was told by old timers on the island, there had once been a sheen of oil across Milner Bay but locals put it down to one of the trawler operators spilling diesel during refuelling. The sheen disappeared with the next choppy sea. There was no sign of seepage around the tanks or the pipes which had been laid underground to link the huge storage tanks to the bowser and the powerhouse. There was a 'negative variance' of around 5000 litres of diesel each week between the master fuel meter and all outlets.

Savory was told during discussions with BP and GEMCO management there could be numerous reasons for the variance. The meters might be faulty. There could be mathematical errors by those monitoring the flow of fuel. There could be evaporation of the fuel in the tropical heat of Groote Eylandt.

Nothing happened. Savory went on with his duties. He continued to raise the tank farm problem in reports and memos. On 31 July

1992 in a memo prepared for a management report to Gerry Ellis he wrote: 'You may wish to mention lost diesel under powerhouse'.

On 2 September 1992 there was a meeting of GEMCO and BP officials, including Savory, to organise a survey of the tank farm following Savory's efforts to have the problem acknowledged. But the minutes of the meeting were recorded without Savory's remarks about the possibility of a substantial leak yet to be identified from the tank farm or pipes to the outlets. Savory asserts he asked a BP engineer: 'How do you account for the discrepancies in the fuel records over a two year period?'

According to Savory a GEMCO management representative replied: 'I don't want to talk about that now. There could be all sorts of reasons'.

The BP fuel engineer had been invited to attend the meeting as a consultant to GEMCO following Savory's 1991 audit of the tank farm which had revealed many minor problems. Savory recommended a more specialised study and he cannot explain why the question he raised was not recorded in the minutes of the meeting. The study never happened.

'The Enviros'

SAVORY learnt that on Groote Eylandt he was in a different world. He started to adopt the rough language of the miners and became more aggressive to win their respect if he could not win their trust. He mixed with the workers assigned to his environment section and soon found himself counselling some of them through a variety of personal problems. He worked at building a team which became known on the island as 'the enviros'. Whether the term was used affectionately or contemptuously depended on the individual who used it.

Soon after raising his concerns about the fuel discrepancies Savory faxed to BHP senior management a note detailing further concerns about meeting GEMCO's environmental commitments. He was working very long hours trying to keep on top of his range of duties, particularly the rehabilitation of mined land.

His wife, Jennifer, tried to integrate with the society of wives at

Alyangula. She accepted responsibility for running the Brownie Guide group and mixed with both the 'staffie' wives and the 'wages' wives as GEMCO employees were colloquially ranked. But when Robert started to encounter difficulties with GEMCO management over environmental problems, Jennifer realised she was being ostracised by the 'staffie' wives.

The atmosphere eventually became intolerable and Jennifer and Anna, who was with them at the time, left Groote Eylandt in early 1993 and went to live in Darwin.

Non-communication

BY 1993 Savory's 'Environment Department' within GEMCO had been formally established with a workforce of ten operators—employees considered to be surplus to the manganese mining operation. Savory converted these 'rednecks' into a productive, happy and proud crew and reported later that the year 1993 was the most successful rehabilitation season on company record. GEMCO's environmental efforts attracted praise from government departments of the Northern Territory, the CSIRO and BHP management in Melbourne.

But, in spite of this, Savory's advocacy of environmental awareness now started to really aggravate some of his colleagues within GEMCO.

On Sunday, 19 September 1993, Savory organised volunteers on Groote Eylandt to take part in the inaugural Clean Up The World Day. Jambana Lalara, chairman of the Anandilyakwa Land Council, gave his support. The volunteers borrowed a bulldozer and mobile crane from GEMCO. They had two clean-up objectives: to dig up and bury all exotic sisal plants brought in by the Church of England missionaries in 1921 to use for making rope and string—the sisal had spread into surrounding native bush and was a prominent and unwanted weed—and to collect, crush and bury about 200 rusty 44-gallon drums left around the abandoned World War II airstrip on the island.

Groote Eylandt's contribution to cleaning up the world was mentioned in despatches—a newsletter from the United Nations

Environment Program in November 1993. At the end of an exhausting day pulling up sisal and collecting drums there was the obligatory barbecue on the beach. Savory, openly passionate about the environment, enjoyed the exhausted company of his supporters. But there were enemies.

GEMCO's management had changed and now Savory was communicating with his employer by memo and report. What he was reporting did not find favour. In a draft report he submitted on the tank farm review a senior BHP environmental manager wrote in the margin, 'Don't overstate the significance of oil spills'.

Savory's agitation in getting his job done was grating on senior executives anxious to demonstrate their higher production priorities—that was what mining was all about—and his reports and requests for minor expenditure approvals were being left unanswered.

By November 1993 the 'enviro crew'—Savory's well-trained crew of rehabilitation workers—was disbanded by GEMCO management. Savory was furious. They were to be replaced by eight untrained Aborigines. While he welcomed the opportunity to train the Aborigines, Savory complained that the removal of all his trained operators just before the beginning of the wet season would have a catastrophic effect on GEMCO's rehabilitation programs. He pleaded that his crew did not want to move back to manganese production jobs and asked that they be allowed to remain for a time to 'train up' the Aborigines as plant operators. His request was refused.

The crew left and after a considerable delay five Aborigines were recruited but subsequent absenteeism dwindled the workforce to zero on some days. The rehabilitation program almost came to a halt with less than two hectares of old mined land being replanted with seedlings. Savory reported angrily that it was unlikely the target of twenty hectares would be met.

Nevertheless, his work for BHP and GEMCO was the subject of what he heard was a very favourable performance review, but for some reason it was withheld. He was never to receive it.

On 9 December 1993 Savory received an annual salary review letter from GEMCO human resources manager Mark Stone:

Dear Rob ... The company has completed the annual salary review and I am pleased to advise that your new salary is $70,675.00 effective from 1 December 1993. I would like to take this opportunity to thank you for your support during the year. We still have many challenges ahead in 1994 and I look forward to working with you to achieve our business objectives.

The Dismissal

ON 4 February 1994—eight weeks later—Savory was sacked. He was stunned. He had been called into Mark Stone's office and handed a letter and told to read it.

You have indicated during 1993 and confirmed in January this year that it is your intention to leave GEMCO, the timing of this being determined by the success of your search for alternative employment.

This leaves GEMCO in a difficult position in planning for the future. This, combined with our previous discussions about whether you and GEMCO management are heading in the same direction, requires me to take action.

Accordingly, you are hereby given three months' notice of termination of employment from close of business today. I do not require you to work out this period of notice.

Savory walked back to his company house with the letter in his hand. A GEMCO truck came by the house and dumped a container on the front lawn. He was instructed to pack up personal effects and leave Groote Eylandt on the next plane, in two days time. The container was to follow by barge later.

There was to be no formal company farewell dinner with traditional trappings of barramundi and speeches of appreciation. Instead his old 'enviro crew' operators helped him pack his belongings and then threw a party for him at the Alyangula Recreation Club. It was reported that the speeches were colourful, but honest . . . and heartwarming to Savory.

One of the Environment Coordinator's tasks had been to eradicate feral cats from the island. On Savory's last, hot summer night on Groote Eylandt some mischief-maker left a dead cat in Mark Stone's washing machine.

In Darwin Savory rejoined Jennifer who gave him moral and practical support. It took him some days to collect his thoughts about what had happened to him. He started writing letters to BHP senior management appealing for support. No support was offered.

In one letter Savory outlined his theory of the reason for the dismissal:

> This issue relates to the fact that I was not prepared to lie to the Anandilyakwa Land Council and the Department of Mines and Energy as to the total area of substandard land near Angurugu that could be upgraded on an annual basis ...
>
> After three and half years of total commitment to GEMCO I was devastated by having my employment terminated at six hours notice.
>
> I have worked consistently to fulfil my mandate with GEMCO, working sixty to eighty hours per week with no additional remunerative reward granted at the recent performance review.
>
> I acknowledge that there have been conflicts in the past with previous managers. These have been resolved and I have then been allowed to get on with my job to the best of my ability.
>
> My commitment has always been to the environment, to BHP's long term reputation, to BHP's shareholders, to the Aboriginal owners of Groote Eylandt and to my own workforce.

There was to be no acknowledgement from BHP or GEMCO of Savory's pleadings. He demanded settlement of claims for a list of expenses, including air fares, relocation and medical expenses. He was later to settle out of court for a small additional once-only sum of money in complete settlement of outstanding claims.

Savory considered his position. It was desperate. He had just been sacked by BHP, Australia's biggest company. His employability at the age of fifty-six was effectively destroyed. He agonised about what he could do. Eventually he decided to fight back.

Before he withdrew his family from Darwin to Brisbane, Savory contacted the Darwin office of the ABC's *7.30 Report*, a nightly current affairs program. He spoke to reporter Kelly Nestor and recorded an interview which, when it went to air, created a stir.

In the interview Savory's language was cautious. He questioned GEMCO's commitment to the environment. He told of the discrepancies on fuel tank readings: 'I went back over two years of information … 1990 to 1992 and found there appeared to be a discrepancy of more than 5000 litres a week. And again I went to management. I put it in writing. I was told 'No, we'll investigate it'. Nothing happened'.

In response to the *7.30 Report* item the Department of Mines and Energy in Darwin announced it would investigate Savory's claims. GEMCO said the claims were groundless but that the company would cooperate with the DME.

Savory and his family left Darwin for Brisbane. Their future was uncertain. He started searching for work, sending out job applications. The phone did not ring. Eventually he applied for unemployment benefits. To obtain the dole the applicant's previous employer is asked by the Department of Social Security to supply what is known as an Employment Separation Certificate. Beside the question, 'Give reason for unsatisfactory work performance', a GEMCO official had written in Savory's certificate:

"Incompatible with company objectives."

Meantime on March 10 1994—a month after his dismissal—GEMCO's public relations machine counter-attacked Savory's public bucketing of his former employer.

In the *Eylandt Echo*—the company newsletter distributed on the island with the slugline 'GEMCO—committed to safe production' under the masthead—there was an article in bold type on page three:

FUEL LEAK ALLEGATIONS PROVED INCORRECT
Independent Company Finds No Leaks in Fuel Pipes

Last week senior Department of Mines and Energy personnel visited GEMCO to complete an investigation into allegations that fuel was being lost from company storage tanks.

The allegations were made by an ex-GEMCO employee on the ABC TV programme *The 7.30 Report*.

As a result of the allegations, GEMCO employed an independent company to come on site and pressure test all pipes which carried fuel at the Tank Farm and at the Powerhouse.

No leaks were found in any of the pipes and all pipes were found to be sound.

At the time, GEMCO Manager Bill Scheel said: 'The allegations made on *The 7.30 Report* resulted in an intensive investigation by the Department of Mines and Energy.

To date, the Department has not found anything of concern, but they will continue the investigation during an on site visit in mid-March.

On Tuesday and Wednesday, 15th and 16th March GEMCO was visited by the Department of Mines and Energy's Secretary, Director of Mines, Environmental Project Officer and Chief Environmental Scientist.

The DME personnel spent two days touring our operations and holding discussions with GEMCO Management.

A full report about the visit will be prepared by the DME in due course. However, Senior Public Affairs Officer Warren Paull said: 'We were able to justify to the DME that there was no leak. We have had all pipes pressure tested by an independent authority and everything was found to be sound'.

Manager Bill Scheel said: 'Even though fuel loss is not a problem, there is room for improvement in the way that fuel is managed. The investigation has not been an enjoyable experience, but it will benefit GEMCO's operation in the longer term'.

Savory's public shot at GEMCO had missed. In the process he had been discredited by 'independent' company assessment. He was finished.

Jobless

JOBLESS in Brisbane, Savory had nowhere to turn. The months following his abrupt departure from Groote Eylandt carried the same despair experienced by many active but unemployed Australians. Self-esteem was gone, depression set in, good humour was rare. There was an underlying anger. The loss of a good job under these circumstances and his final discrediting at the hands of the company and its independent assessment were a crushing burden to carry.

Savory had invested his savings in real estate in the city of Toowoomba west of Brisbane on the Darling Downs. With his sudden dismissal and lack of subsequent employment, he was forced to sell. In the rapidly falling market of then drought-affected Toowoomba, he lost a lot of money.

As well, the Savorys' marriage, which had suffered on Groote Eylandt, deteriorated even further.

The Phone Rang

In late February 1995, a year after his dismissal, Savory was still unemployed. His position appeared hopeless. His attempts to secure work, any work, had failed. He had applied for numerous environmental positions in the mining industry but had achieved only one interview. When he had tried to explain the circumstances on Groote Eylandt and his previous employment he saw the interviewer's eyes glaze over and felt his prospects disappear.

One day the telephone rang at home. Savory heard the beep-beep-beep of a long-distance call. It was a friend, one of the old enviro crew from Groote Eylandt.

'Hey Rob!' he shouted down the phone. '. . . They've found your leak!'

Savory heard how GEMCO workers had been digging a trench to lay a new pipe to the bowsers when they found contaminated soil. A back-hoe had scooped up diesel-contaminated earth. GEMCO PR issued an immediate press release declaring the find to be only 2 or 3 metres around the pipe.

On 23 February 1995 the small independent newspaper on the island, *The Paradise Post*, run by journalist Kate Hale, reported: 'Fuel leak causes closure of bowsers—environmental disaster claims denied'.

Savory contacted *The 7.30 Report* in Sydney and the program moved on the story. Groote Eylandt residents were contacted by phone and amateur video footage was taken of diesel-contaminated water being pumped from bore holes.

The videotape, despatched by courier to the Sydney ABC, recorded eyewitnesses' accounts of what they had seen. From one: 'Every location they've been into around the tank farm and as far down as the beach area and foreshore they've been bringing up diesel. Everybody knows that diesel is bubbling out of the ground'. From another: 'Everyone seems to think it could be a disaster ... there was red-coloured dirty liquid bubbling up out of the ground. The men were ankle deep in it and it smelt very strong of diesel'.

In an interview recorded for the ABC story, Savory was challenged about his attitude towards the company: 'What we had was a potential for a very large contamination of the soil and rocks which would cost a lot of money to be remediated, and also which would attract very bad publicity to the company. And I was carrying this. I was telling management, I was saying, "Hey look!", very quiet and confidential ... didn't discuss with anyone outside the company, only with senior management ... and nobody listened to me! And sure I got aggressive. I got pissed off!'

The 7.30 Report put Savory's claims to BHP. Significantly, Jim Rothwell, BHP's manager Manganese, confirmed that there was a major fuel spill on the island.

In the item broadcast on 6 April 1995 Rothwell said: 'Of course, any spill is significant. We don't have an estimate as yet. We've done some drilling. We know it's in a confined area, we know there's been no movement of oil into the marine environment and we believe we'll be able to clean it up'. Rothwell declined to be drawn on Savory. The program reported: 'As for the man who blew the whistle BHP won't comment, compensate or vindicate'. Jim Rothwell: 'Dr Savory did some good work for us. I don't think it would be fair to comment on the reasons for his leaving'.

Savory was vindicated. But with his elation at so public a vindication there remained private bitterness at the circumstances.

The positive publicity, at last, opened some doors. Two days later he was contacted by the Queensland Department of Minerals and Energy and offered a job—a temporary special projects job rehabilitating abandoned mine sites. Savory was over the moon. He had offered to go back to Groote Eylandt to help in the clean up. That offer was rejected. He wrote to BHP to seek 'full exoneration for my dismissal' demanding financial compensation for the 'stress and hardship caused to me and my family by the abrupt nature of my dismissal and by the fact that I have been unemployed for over a year'. He told BHP that recent investigations by independent persons on his behalf had disclosed that his dismissal by GEMCO had seriously affected his future career. The company made no admissions. There would be no public exoneration.

BHP Manganese had engaged the environmental clean-up company Dames and Moore to assess the problem on Groote Eylandt. They began sinking bore holes in a pattern to try to assess the extent of the contamination. With each drill there was a 'gusher'. At first there were reports that the diesel was 'fresh', that it was a recent leak. But subsequent tests revealed that the diesel recovered by the pumps was 'old'.

The diesel, which was sitting on top of a water table, was now being recovered by the pumps and stored in drums for later use.

By 7 December 1995 the drilling had been going on all year. An item in *The Australian* newspaper that day broke the news that Savory's warning of a substantial leak, up to 10 million litres, was on the way to being correct.

The Northern Territory Government will consider laying negligence charges against BHP after estimates of a diesel oil spill at the GEMCO manganese mine on remote Groote Eylandt in the Gulf of Carpentaria were revised dramatically upwards.

BHP confirmed yesterday the spill could be as much as three million litres of diesel—ten times more than the worst-case scenario outlined by GEMCO management when the leak was discovered during routine excavation and repair work at the mine's fuel depot in February.

The discovery was 13 months after BHP had sacked GEMCO's environmental scientist, Dr Robert Savory, who had repeatedly told management that a major fuel leak had occurred.

The report said ninety-two bore holes had been drilled to

evaluate the extent of the spill. It reported that tests to that stage probably indicated that the sub-ground structure was such that the leaked oil had not seeped into the adjacent marine environment. 'Instead, it is held safely in a clay, kidney-shaped pool 250m by 150m sitting on top of the water table'.

The paper quoted the Territory Minister for Mines, Mike Reed, 'very specifically not ruling out charges at this stage because this remains a developing situation and I am leaving all my options open'.

Robert Savory had found work at last. He was hired by the Queensland Department of Mines in September as an Environmental Officer on a salary half that he had received from GEMCO. But it was work. And Savory felt relieved that his reputation had been restored.

He reflected that in the stress of the situation at Groote Eylandt he had acted on the available facts although even now the company would claim that Savory's original allegations were 'flawed'.

If he had his time over would he do it all again? He has these reflections on his experience as a whistleblower:

It's not easy to go around saying: 'I'm right ... BHP is wrong' when I've only been in the industry for two years and BHP is the fabled Big Australian! However my knowledge of the *facts*, no hunches here, gave me the strength to persevere. What amazed me then and now was how bloody stupid they were.

I guess I had the advantage of maturity and having knocked around the world a bit. Maybe if I had been a yuppie and a recent graduate with my foot on the first rung of the corporate ladder, my approach would have been different.

It is not easy to stand up to hard-nosed bullying Canadian and American mining managers who have little respect for the Australian environment or for environmental workers.

The experience has tempered me in fire. If I am sure of my facts I will never again hesitate in speaking out immediately and forcefully. And had I not submitted those written reports and kept copies when the fuel leak was discovered I would, for sure, have copped the blame.

Anyone who is in a position of responsibility and sees him/

herself being drawn into a vulnerable situation should:
- put all communications in writing—it's okay to send handwritten memos in order to maintain confidentiality;
- ensure memos are routed to your supervisor's supervisor;
- keep a photocopy for daily reference;
- send a photocopy to your solicitor for safe keeping;
- keep a diary.

You should stick to facts, absolute concrete facts, exact or verbatim records of conversations, without any embellishment. If you know you are telling the truth, then you can look anybody in the eye, be it the Chief Executive of BHP, the Board of Directors or a magistrate or judge, and never falter.

I did not start out to be a whistleblower. It was forced upon me by GEMCO management at the time. I am sure if I had gone to the blokes who'd hired me, Bob Wunder or Murray Fox, with my suspicions and fears about fuel leaks, they would have immediately ordered a full and open investigation. GEMCO would have turned a negative into a positive.

Originally from 1990, 1991 to early 1992 I had a very positive attitude towards BHP-GEMCO and was never a radical greenie type looking for trouble. If I were I wouldn't have been appointed.

Part of the problem is:
- the Northern Territory is very far behind the other states as far as environmental legislation is concerned. GEMCO operates under two or three 'special conditions' formulated 30 years ago when the manganese leases were first granted.
- Groote Eylandt is isolated—the GEMCO leases are effectively 'off limits' to the Australian public.
- the Aboriginal landowners are, in fact, treated with scorn, in spite of the corporate rhetoric.

There is a prevailing corporate culture that production is paramount to everything else.

Personally I have gained tremendous personal strength from this experience. I learnt who my real friends are. My 'staffie' colleagues deserted me in droves. Even one bloke I had really supported over three years stabbed me in the back. But the operators, not only the enviro crew, were loyal and supportive. I guess they are pleased to see the bosses with a black eye. On the debit side my marriage has suffered, my mental health has suffered and I am broke.

With 20/20 rear vision I now know I should never have gone to Groote Eylandt. Jennifer saw it back in 1990 after I arrived on Groote and while she was still back in Toowoomba before joining me. She said I should quit and return to the family in Toowoomba. So, on balance, I am very much the loser.

However, if I hadn't blown the whistle BHP would not today be called to account for its disregard of the environment over many years.

Savory's public stand produced calls from the Northern Territory Opposition and the Northern Territory Environment Centre for the parliamentary censure of BHP. There was evidence that the Northern Territory administration was at last seriously questioning the explanations and assurances it had always received from BHP. Public relations strategies and glib remarks via press releases would not work anymore.

The remediation of the contaminated land at Groote Eylandt was expected to go on indefinitely. If the job was to be done properly thousands of cubic metres of contaminated earth would have to be treated to remove the absorbed hydrocarbons. GEMCO told its staff in late 1996 that the underground plume of lost diesel was more extensive than first thought.

An item in the industry journal, *The Minerex Report*, said that the plume might also be closer to Milner Bay. More than 3 million litres of diesel were believed to have leaked. GEMCO was reported to be planning a $1 million membrane barrier along the foreshore of Milner Bay. 'This would impede the underground flow of fuel in or on the groundwater to prevent any unacceptable impact on the marine environment'.

GEMCO had spent $2 million managing the fuel loss and had recovered more than 600 000 litres, pumping 3000 litres of diesel from the ground every day. GEMCO had appointed an independent marine environment advisory group chaired by Dr Russell Reichelt, the director of the Australian Institute of Marine Sciences. The journal reported that the management program included a marine habitat survey in Milner Bay and a detailed risk assessment.

The total cost to the company? This remains unknown. Savory holds to his original estimate of $10 million. The Groote Eylandt spill is expected to be confirmed as one of the largest from fuel storage tanks in Australian history.

On Friday, 1 March 1996, GEMCO was fined $45,000 (the maximum allowable fine was $50,000) after it pleaded guilty to having breached Section 16 of the Northern Territory Water Act. Magistrate Mr I. Gray SM said in judgment:

> The obvious dramatic feature of this case is the sheer size of the discharge. It was an enormous discharge and one which is far in excess of the amount of pollutant discharged in any of the cases which have been referred to me.
>
> ... Fortunately, perhaps fortuitously because of the geological features of the area there has in fact been no measurable contamination of either the water supply to any residential community or of the open sea. It must be conceded though that by virtue of the size of the discharge there was at least theoretically the potential for very serious environmental impact and damage.
>
> ... The leak was discovered during routine upgrading of pipes. It's significant and it's conceded that it was not discovered during any form of routine testing or inspection of pipes. This suggests and again it's not seriously argued to the contrary that there was an inadequate set of procedures for the regular assessment of the condition of the underground pipes.

DERELICTION OF DUTY

'It's not a case of privatising ANL ... you couldn't give it away ...'—Federal Transport Minister Laurie Brereton, 22 August 1994.

'It is alleged by a number of parties present at the meeting that Laurie Brereton told the Maritime Union of Australia that ... he would ratfuck the board of ANL.'—Submission to the Senate Finance and Public Administration References Committee inquiry into the Australian National Line.

'The actions and statements of Laurie Brereton in respect of ANL are inconsistent with his responsibilities and duties as a Minister of the Crown.'—Captain William Bolitho, former chairman, Australian National Line.

ANL—THE AUSTRALIAN SHIPPING LINE, carrying the Australian flag and crewed by Australians, was established by the Commonwealth Government because of wartime necessity in 1939. A Shipping Control Board was set up to requisition, charter and build ships in the interests of the war effort. After the war, requisitioned ships were returned to their private owners but the re-named Australian Shipping Board continued to operate the wartime-built ships and vessels captured from the enemy. After a decade of indecision and talk of mergers with private shipping lines, the Menzies Government established the Australian National Line on 1 October 1956 under the Australian Shipping Commission Act to operate a fully government-owned shipping operation.

For most of its existence the patriotic dream of a viable national flag carrier was just that—a dream. ANL struggled to compete in one of the most ruthless international industries where rust buckets under 'flags-of-convenience' crewed by slave labor and corrupt foreign governments desperate for currency could undercut the more scrupulous shippers.

On many occasions during its history ANL was close to insolvency. As a government-owned enterprise, however, there was the political will to keep it afloat and the Australian flag flying in coastal and international waters.

In October 1982 the will to keep ANL going was still apparent. The secretary of the Federal Department of Transport, Ray Taylor, telephoned William Bolitho at his Buchan woolgrowing property in Victoria. The Minister, Ralph Hunt, wanted to appoint Bolitho, then 51, a commissioner of the Australian Shipping Commission, which traded as the Australian National Line.

'It'll be only two days a month,' Taylor had said at lunch, 'a day to read the board papers and a day at a meeting. It'll give you an opportunity to catch up with your old mates and you can keep an eye on the operation.' It was an attractive offer. Bolitho had gone back to the farm and his five rapidly growing children after spending many years away at sea and in tough management jobs on shore in the shipping industry. He had promised his wife, Bridget, that he would retire to the farm they had bought to spend as much time as possible with the children before they embarked on careers of their own. Bill Bolitho had met and married Bridget while working out of the United Kingdom in 1955.

A day or two a month in Melbourne and some stimulating challenges trying to play the shipping game from the corporate boardroom were just what he needed. But it emerged that Ralph Hunt and his permanent head Ray Taylor had laid an enticing trap that would take almost all of Bolitho's time for the next thirteen years and end with his dismissal in highly contentious circumstances. What was to unfold would test Bill Bolitho to the limit.

ANL Technically Bankrupt

ANL was technically bankrupt in 1983. Its annual financial statements showed a loss for the year of $26 million, and total accumulated losses of $41 million. It was massively overgeared with debt of more than $600 million and a fleet of ships which were old and fuel inefficient. The average age of the fleet was more than twenty years.

The fuel inefficiency of the fleet was a major concern particularly after the so called oil price shocks of the 1970s. ANL was run almost as a public service department, avoiding any commercial realities, and had massive overheads and overstaffing. Politicians, always willing to porkbarrel voters, had used their influence to keep unprofitable services going, particularly the passenger trade across Bass Strait and coastal trade routes to North Queensland and Darwin where marginal parliamentary seats were seen to be a concern. The then board also believed that a number of very expensive and commercially inappropriate vessels had been built in the State dockyard at Newcastle for similar political purposes.

What to do? Consideration was given to closing down ANL in 1982–83. But the Commonwealth Government would have to accept losses of $110 million in government loans to ANL and expose itself to between $100 million and $200 million in payouts to satisfy a long list of ANL creditors and financiers.

The choice then facing the government was stark: to close down a statutory authority, the Australian Shipping Commission, and watch the conflagration of taxpayers' money, or trade out.

To trade out, the Board would have to drive through a major restructuring of ANL and convert the $110 million government debt to equity. To ensure ANL could recover its losses over time the entire Australian shipping industry would have to be reformed. Bolitho had come to the Australian Shipping Commission at a crucial time.

A year after Taylor's phone call, Captain William Bolitho was appointed chairman of the Australian Shipping Commission and the restructure started in earnest. In that time there had been a change of government in Canberra and the new Transport Minister, Peter Morris, had assured Bolitho that he and the government would work with the Commission to reform not only ANL but also the Australian shipping industry. Bolitho had ordered a financial analysis of the enterprise immediately he was appointed chairman and reported to Morris that liabilities exceeded assets by $200 million. They agreed it would be no use reforming ANL if the industry framework did not enhance its prospects for long term viability.

The canny, laconic seaman, his hair now white with experience, enjoyed the early years of rebuilding. His influence in the industry was growing as ANL continued to redevelop its core businesses.

Bill Bolitho: Off to Sea

BOLITHO was born and educated in Victoria. He was the fourth of six children and had a stable and happy childhood attending the Chelsea and George Street State Schools at Fitzroy. He did reasonably well at maths and English and was an average footballer, cricketer and boxer.

In 1948 Bolitho got a job with the old Broken Hill Proprietary Company's ore and steel carriers and spent four years shovelling iron ore and painting ships. By 1952 he had decided on a maritime working life and sat for his second mate's foreign-going certificate, finding work with the British Indian Steam Navigation Company and rising to the rank of chief officer.

But when he was just twenty-four and working as third mate on overnight cargo work in the East Pakistan port of Chittagong (servicing the ports of Colombo in Ceylon and Karachi), Bill Bolitho faced a test of his character.

Because of the shortage of space on the dock the local agent had issued instructions that cargo be loaded in strict turn of arrival in order to prevent shippers bribing their cargo on board and queue-jumping. Bolitho stuck to these orders, which were written in the night order book. He refused to accept a particular cargo of betel nut. No room. He could not disadvantage other earlier arrived cargo. Bolitho also refused a substantial bribe offered by the Indian shipper and sent him on his way.

Later that night he was called to the cabin of the first mate who, apparently, had been awakened by the Indian shipper and pressed to take the cargo. The first mate instructed Bolitho, in front of the Indian shipper, to take the cargo.

Bolitho, the subordinate in this situation, was confronted with a dilemma. Thinking quickly he replied that in order to take the cargo he would have to make an entry in the ship's log and that he would require the first mate to make an appropriate entry in the ship's log and amend and sign the night order book. The mate backed down. The cargo was not shipped. Bolitho later wrote: 'I never forgot the sight of the unfortunate mate having to grovel before the Indian gentleman over a petty bribe he had obviously accepted and it drove home to me the lesson of Napoleon's dictum, The hand that gives is above the hand that takes'.

In 1956 he sat for his foreign-going master's certificate in London at the Sir John Cass Nautical Institute. Two years later he returned to Australia to do odd labouring jobs for the Victorian Main Roads Board and worked on fishing boats at Port Welshpool. He was back at sea as a deck officer for BHP soon after and quickly rose through the maritime ranks to be appointed master in 1964. He was Captain of the 6000 tonne *Iron Monarch*, an ore, coal and limestone dolimite carrier. By now he had been around the world several times and spent some time in various shore supervisory jobs as wharf manager, stevedoring, traffic control and charter work gaining an overall knowledge of all BHP's shipping operations.

In 1966 BHP promoted Bolitho to superintendent of its shipping operations, responsible for the operational efficiency of the fleet and all stevedoring and port activities. In 1968 he left BHP to return to sea as Master of the 50 000 ton bulk carrier, *Ore Regent*, supervising the conversion of this vessel in Italy to Australian standards, and started Clutha Development's shipping operation carrying bauxite between Weipa and Gladstone in Queensland.

In 1969 he joined the American Dillingham Corporation as Australian project manager developing its shipping subsidiary John Burke Pty Ltd. By 1972 he was general manager, Dillingham Marine Group and was directly responsible to the chief executive of the company for the net profitability of John Burke, Mason Shipping Pty Ltd (a landing barge and small coastal shipper operating in North Queensland, Papua New Guinea and Indonesia); a rail-sea service between Brisbane and Thursday Island; a Geraldton boat yard; a prawning company in Queensland, and a Western Australian boat building and repair company.

Dillingham had serious cash flow problems in its American parent company and Bolitho was given the task of disposing of its Australian marine assets. During this process he made a presentation to the big Australian transport company, Brambles Industries Limited.

They hired him. He became general manager of Brambles Marine Group, administering twenty separate commercial entities covering Sydney harbour ferry services, repairs and maintenance, offshore oil exploration, deep sea diving, shipping agencies, stevedoring and hydrographic survey.

By 1979 he was appointed a director of Brambles Holdings Limited, a subsidiary of the publicly-listed Brambles Industries Limited. By 1981 his knowledge of the transport and shipping industry was recognised when the Fraser Government appointed him a member of the shipowners panel of the 'Crawford inquiry'—Sir John Crawford's inquiry into the revitalisation of Australian shipping.

True to his promise to Bridget, Bolitho retired from Brambles in July 1982 and moved to the Buchan farm they had bought some years earlier.

Rebuilding ANL

As chairman of the Australian Shipping Commission, Bill Bolitho used his vast knowledge of the vagaries of international and coastal shipping, transport and stevedoring to monitor the rebuilding of the Australian National Line. In 1987 he was appointed the inaugural chairman of the Australian Shipowners' Association, the employers' lobby which previously had been dominated in another form (the Australian Chamber of Shipping) by foreign shippers with little interest in the development of Australian-owned shipping.

He also served four years, appointed by the Hawke Government, as a director of Qantas Airways, to 1991.

ANL struggled for ten years from 1983 to tackle its massive problems. The ANL Board (the Wran Board appointed in August 1994) for the financial year 1993/94 recorded in its annual report to its shareholder, the government and people of Australia, that ANL had a positive net worth of $26 million and a fleet of ships with an average age of eight years. The $26 million was posted after massive provisions had to be declared by the Board at the insistence of the Commonwealth Auditor General. When those technical provisions were removed, Bolitho contended, ANL had a net worth of more than $100 million.

Bolitho later said in a submission to the Australian Senate: 'Even on the lower figure of $26 million net worth in the audited accounts, however, the actions of the Board and ANL management over the decade from 1983/84 have resulted in a benefit to the taxpayer in excess of $200 million. Translated into 1994 dollars this is a massive taxpayer benefit in excess of $300 million.'

Sitting on the ANL Board with Bolitho in 1994 were Barry McGuiness, the managing director of ANL, and Morella Calder, a maritime law solicitor who had the rare distinction of being licensed to practice at both the New South Wales and New York bars. She held the appointment of deputy chairman. Also aboard were Donald Dyer, former general manager of the AIDC (Australian Industry Development Corporation), a board member of the Export Finance Insurance Company, former chairman of the Textile, Clothing and Footwear Development Authority, and chairman of the public Sports Fashion Group; John Hurlstone, former managing director of AMPOL; Robert Kidman, former Queensland manager, National Australia Bank; Graham Glenn, former secretary of the Industrial Relations and Administration departments, former commissioner of the Commonwealth Public Service Board and chairman of the Safety, Rehabilitation and Compensation Commission; Colin Freeland, former secretary of the Aviation and Housing Departments, former CEO and MD of the Civil Aviation Authority, former commissioner of Australian National Railways and former chairman of Australian Maritime Safety Authority; Richard Denton, company director, a partner in an accounting firm and director of the State Bank of NSW; and Patrick Geraghty, federal secretary of the Seamen's Union.

Four of them—Denton, Geraghty, Hurlstone and Kidman— had been appointed only in September of the previous year. The term of one board member, the Sydney lawyer Morella Calder, expired in June 1994. At the time she was suffering a serious illness from which she died in October 1994. Bolitho believed that he was surrounded by the most experienced and competent public and commercial sector business leaders and administrators. All supported ANL's position in what was to be an increasingly difficult relationship with the Commonwealth Government.

ANL For Sale

IN 1991 the sale of public assets, or privatisation as it was called, was on the political agenda. In the Federal Budget of that year it was announced that up to 49 per cent of ANL was to be sold. Also on the block for sale were other assets including Australian Airlines, which held 50 per cent of the domestic airline market, and a part of the Commonwealth Bank.

The Bolitho Board was fully in favour of selling ANL. International shipping was a ruthless and competitive business. Taxpayers' funds by way of government backing should not be exposed to risk, they firmly believed. But the Board agonised over how the public asset could be disposed of to maintain Australia's place in international shipping in the national interest. On 25 June 1992 the Bolitho Board wrote to the Minister for Industrial Relations, Shipping and Aviation, Senator Peter Cook, setting out a plan to achieve the government's publicly stated objective. The letter was accompanied by full documentation, valuations and advice.

The Board proposed a merger with Howard Smith Limited, an existing Australian shipper with a later float of the government's share in this enhanced enterprise:

> ANL should commence negotiations with an Australian, synergistic maritime company with the aim of merging assets and businesses to form a separate company owned jointly by the government and that operator. The intention is to create a company with as close to equal control and equity as commercially possible.
>
> When effected, this merger would form the largest marine oriented transport group in Australia with combined assets in excess of $800 million, enhanced earnings before interest and tax of around $45 million and net assets of approximately $350 million (based on published accounts at 30-6-91).
>
> Given the earnings of the combined assets and businesses and given the earnings growth forecast for ANL over the next 18 months to two years and a mild upturn in the economy, a public float of the government's shareholding in the combined entity at that time would be a highly profitable and achievable outcome

Helen James

Elizabeth O'Brien

John McLennan

Dr Robert Savory

Bill Bolitho

Tim Visscher

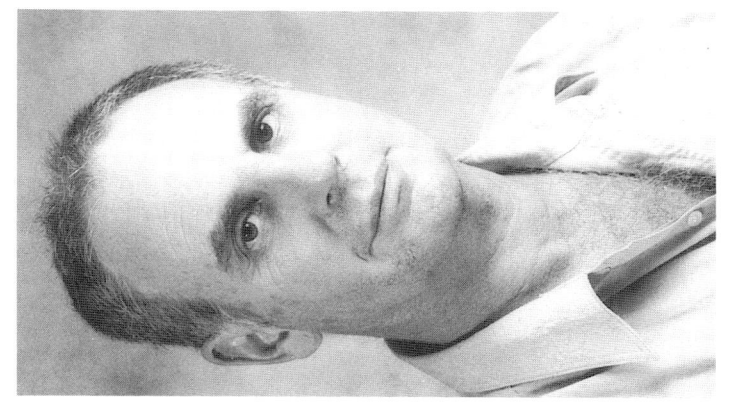

Dr Phil Nitschke

Phil Vardy

Jim Leggate

Alwyn Johnson

and clearly in the board's view, the optimum opportunity to maximise the return on its investment.

The Bolitho Board was aware that the Howard Smith Board was willing to contemplate such a merger and a window of opportunity presented itself. But neither the Minister nor the Cabinet acted on the ANL Board's advice and the opportunity was lost.

In the meantime the government's preferred methodology for the sale of the public's assets proceeded. The so-called sale process was to be undertaken, not by the entities to be sold, but by what was known as the Task Force on Asset Sales (TFAS) under the delegation of the Minister for Finance and the Minister for Transport and Communication. Bolitho contended in correspondence with the government that the sale decision itself was contrary to previous government assurances to ANL that a level of equity 'appropriate to ANL's commercial circumstances and its balance sheet' would be provided. The TFAS control of the sale process clashed with the responsibilities of the ANL Board under company law. What TFAS did, Bolitho later submitted to the Senate, was to undermine ANL's sale value, the stability of its internal industrial relations and the authority of the Board.

On 8 August 1991, Bolitho, on behalf of the ANL Board, wrote to the then Minister for Transport, Senator Bob Collins, complaining that a letter from the TFAS to eight merchant banks seeking proposals from them for a consultancy to sell ANL 'was bound to establish a fire sale mentality in the minds of potential vendors in which the true value of ANL would not be realised'.

The TFAS sale process was damaging to ANL's continuing efforts to maintain the A1 credit rating of its commercial paper, and as it was circulating widely in the commercial community it was bound to reach the maritime unions and cause industrial unrest. Bolitho complained that TFAS's action appeared to be in direct conflict with earlier discussions with Collins and Finance Minister Ralph Willis that the sale process would be negotiated between the parties and not pre-empted. The sale process was to drag on for the next three years under TFAS control.

The Bolitho Board had declared that it was not opposed to the sale of ANL but wanted to see that the timing of any such sale was designed to secure the best possible price for the asset. Timing was everything. It depended on competitive conditions in international shipping and ANL's profit performance. ANL was again struggling in the face of heavy undercutting from the Chinese state-owned shipping line which, unconcerned about commercial prudence, would cut prices to produce much-needed foreign currency.

The state-owned shipping lines of the centrally-planned economies of China and Russia did not meet any western accounting standards. Nor did they have to take account of the cost of the capital provided in arriving at reported profits. Also in the industry dynamic were the flag-of-convenience international ship operators operating tax free and largely regulation free out of tax havens. They used low-wage third-world crews and were free from the need to meet on-costs such as long service leave, superannuation, sick pay, payroll tax and other employee entitlements. A rule of thumb estimate by the Australians was that every substantial Australian flag ship had a wage bill of $2 million a year more than its foreign flag competitors. In the case of ANL, with about fifteen ships in the early 1990s, this amounted to a handicap of about $30 million.

A further factor affecting ANL's competitiveness was that being Australian-based, ANL encountered the appalling inefficiencies of Australian ports and the high cost of stevedoring charges at each end of every voyage. ANL's competitors traded over a wider range of ports and thus encountered these high Australian costs and inefficiencies less often.

The ANL Board figured that it was better to wait, rationalise ANL's routes and operations to withstand the competitive pressures, and keep on trading, confident that ANL's reputation for quality and reliable services throughout the world would see it through to more profitable days. ANL's forecasts of its profits and losses were often shot to pieces because of rapidly changing international trading conditions—a western world recession, in particular, as well as the tricks of its competitors unhindered by industrial and safety standards or financial accountability.

Bolitho was concerned that Board directors had legal liabilities in a situation where Government officers with no legal right in respect of ANL were endeavouring to exercise authority over the affairs of the company. 'While the Government continued to aver that the TFAS was acting only in an advisory role, in practice the opposite appeared to be the case,' he said. The ANL Board had legal advice, made clear on numerous occasions to the Government, of their onerous liabilities if they allowed government officers to usurp their authority.

However the Government continued, according to Bolitho, to act as if ANL was not a corporation subject to the Corporations Law, but a statutory arm of government.

In December 1992 the Minister for Shipping, Peter Cook, announced that the Government would sell 100 per cent of ANL conditional upon ANL's ships remaining on the Australian register and employees remaining on Australian awards; operations would continue to be in Australia and a majority of the Board would be Australian citizens. The Government promised that the ANL Board would be consulted.

Bolitho said: 'In practice the Board and management of ANL were excluded from this process and the Board learned from press reports in mid-1994 that at meetings in June 1993 and in February 1994 Cabinet had removed the conditions on the sale and decided to keep them secret. Certainly the Board and management of ANL were not aware of these decisions, but the TFAS officers appear to have been aware of them at an early stage and conducted themselves accordingly.

'It appears therefore that the ANL Board and management were working on the policy of the Government as it was known to them, while the TFAS officers were working on another and different clandestine policy known to them and not to ANL. However politically expedient this may have been, it was disastrous for the conduct of the sale process, the commercial activities of ANL and for relations between the Board of ANL and Government. It is hard to imagine a set of circumstances more likely to have an inappropriate outcome for the taxpayer.'

Bolitho believed that the Australian Labor Party and the maritime unions never knew about or agreed to the clandestine decisions made by the Federal Cabinet. In fact to put the policy to sell 100 per cent of ANL unconditionally without breaching ALP policy would require approval of the ALP's national biennial conference set for June 1994.

Minister Brereton

BOLITHO was later to learn from officials of the Maritime Union of Australia (MUA) that at a meeting of the MUA and the new Minister for Transport, (Laurie Brereton), the Minister had attacked the 'actions and omissions' of the ANL Board and that he would 'ratfuck the Board of ANL'. The MUA went on to mount a public campaign against Brereton to oppose any attempt to change the ALP platform, at one stage doorknocking every house in Brereton's Sydney electorate.

Over the years the ANL Board had often written to the Government warning of the potential for 'conflict, misunderstanding and damage to ANL and the sale process'. Bolitho believed that Mr Ted Harris, then chairman of Australian Airlines and the Australian Airlines Board, was facing similar problems with the Task Force on Asset Sales. At one stage the sale of Australian Airlines had to be aborted, Bolitho believed, because of this conflict of authority.

He said: 'The long, unfocused and unsuccessful sale process being carried out by TFAS was harming staff morale, inappropriate, commercially damaging to ANL, its profitability, viability and ultimate sale value. The TFAS never took the time or the trouble to understand either ANL's customer base or its competition and the relationship these factors bore to achieving a maximum sale value'.

In March 1994 Minister Brereton moved to change the articles of association of ANL to give himself ultimate control of the corporation. Decisions of substance had to be referred to him for final approval. At the time, Bolitho asserts, the ANL Board was unaware of secret Cabinet decisions relating to the conditions surrounding the sale of the shipping line. The Board was working diligently within the Government's publicly stated policy and believed that they had to stay at the helm of ANL to achieve the best results for the shipping line, its clients and employees and ultimately the taxpayers.

'Had the Board known that the true intent of Laurie Brereton and the government in respect of ANL was political in nature and not commercial, then when the articles were changed in March 1994 it is certain that some, if not all of the directors would have resigned. I certainly would have done so,' Bolitho said.

Laurie Brereton was an action man in the Keating Government.

He had a reputation for getting things done, for standing on toes until he got the desired result. It was apparent to Bolitho and other members of the ANL board that Brereton's desire to be seen to get a result with the sale of ANL had to be factored into their thinking— to get the best price for the sale of the asset. And in the best interests of the staff of ANL, whose livelihoods were at stake, Board members decided to stay at their posts, to influence the decisions the Minister would ultimately take under his new powers through the amended articles of association. But instead of close communication between the Minister and the Board there was nothing. Letters went unacknowledged and unanswered. It was apparent that Brereton perceived the ANL Board as in league with the Maritime Union of Australia which was giving him such a hard time politically. ANL management, with the Board's knowledge and approval, held quarterly meetings with the maritime unions at which industrial issues and progress in the sale of the line were on the agenda for discussion. The Board contended that this communication policy was responsible for the substantial reduction in industrial disputes at ANL but as relations with the government deteriorated Canberra saw it in conspiratorial terms.

Bolitho's credibility was to be tested and challenged at the Senate inquiry in 1995. On the key question of the ANL Board's knowledge of the Cabinet decision in 1993 to remove the sale conditions of an Australian flag (registration) and crews for ANL, a TFAS official had submitted evidence of notes of an oral briefing to a department official and of a meeting between then Ministers Collins and Willis with Bolitho and the ANL Board on 28 June 1993. The notes, which were said to have been cleared with the minister's office, reported alleged remarks by Minister Willis to the ANL Board that 'Cabinet had decided to remove any crewing constraint and put a 49 per cent limit on foreign ownership. Senator Collins said that these changes had been an ANL Board idea which the Government had acceded to'.

Bolitho was to submit in reply:

Neither the oral briefing recorded by the TFAS officer ... nor the TFAS record of the (Ministers and the ANL Board) meeting accord with my own or ANL notes.

Bolitho observed that neither the record of the oral briefing nor the notes on the Ministers/Board meeting had been passed to ANL for verification and agreement.

The statement attributed to Senator Collins that ANL requested the removal of the sale conditions specifying Australian flag, crew and awards is absurd ... at no time did ANL ever propose to Government that the Australian flag and crews under Australian awards should be removed. The suggestion is quite simply untrue.

It was my experience over many years in business and industrial relations that oral briefings and non-disclosed and non-agreed records of meetings written after the event tended to be neither satisfactory nor completely accurate and my clear instructions to ANL staff from the commencement of the sale process was to be aware of this problem and to keep exact and timely records of all meetings with Government in order to ensure that they had an accurate record of events available in the event of 'misunder-standings'.

ANL's records showed that on the 28 June 1993 meeting with Collins and Willis, the Government's latest thinking was for a 100 per cent sale of ANL. 'No mention was made of any changes to the conditions attaching to the sale despite a question to that effect.'

Bolitho said that he and the ANL Board only found out about the Government's secret intentions (made at a June 1993 Cabinet meeting) through a leak to the press reported by the *Financial Review* on 26 May 1994. At no time until the appearance of this leak was the ANL Board formally told of the far-reaching plan for the sale of ANL. Such changes would certainly have led to industrial difficulties for the government with the maritime unions had they been made aware of them.

The following chronology, taken from Bolitho's five submissions to the 1995 Senate inquiry and backed by 330 documents including formal correspondence, minutes and verified notes, details the path to disaster for ANL and the taxpayers of Australia. (It is interesting to note that the Government did not make available to the Senate Finance and Public Administration References Committee inquiry into the ANL affair its own full record, including Cabinet decisions.)

August 1993: Bolitho letter to Willis and Collins seeking 'clear written instructions' and 'precise confirmation' of the details of the Government's decision on the privatisation of ANL.
No written instruction given.

October 1993: Minister Collins invited to attend two-day conference of directors at Bowral to discuss Government's sale intentions.
Minister unavailable.

December 1993: Chairman ANL to Minister Collins: 'Failure to satisfactorily conclude the privatisation process, announced nearly three years ago, has been extremely expensive for the company both in terms of some millions of dollars of cash costs, executive time, market perceptions and loss of employee morale and must be resolved if the Board is to protect and preserve the assets and value of the company, the welfare of its employees and fulfill its obligations to clients. The Board is however unable to do so in a satisfactory manner until the Government has made and publicly announced its decision'.
No response received.

January 1994: Discussion between chairman ANL and new Minister Brereton. '... It was agreed that ANL and the Minister would work jointly together to develop a solution which would be acceptable to the ALP conference in September and would achieve the optimum privatisation outcome for both the Government and ANL.' Bolitho told the Senate: 'In my view the Minister never even attempted to carry out this agreement'.

February 1994: Federal Cabinet decided that due diligence would begin on ANL and expressions of interest would be sought so as to proceed with the sale after the September ALP conference.

March 1994: Minister Brereton wrote to ANL advising that the Articles of Association of the company would be changed.

14 March 1994: an article in *The Australian Financial Review* by Michael Dwyer revealed that Federal Cabinet apparently had decided in June 1993 to allow foreign ownership in ANL up to 49 per cent and *remove* the requirement that ANL ships were to remain Australian flagged, with Australian crews employed under Australian awards.

24 March 1994: ANL Board still not formally told of

Federal Cabinet's decision on the sale conditions although Senator McMullan had told the Senate on 14 March that previous sale conditions of June 1993 had been superseded by a Cabinet decision of February 1994. At a meeting between TFAS and ANL, Mr Kym Bills of TFAS had stated that Ministers wanted the sale 'unconstrained' and he believed the issue of the sale conditions would not be resolved until the due diligence first phase was completed, responses to expressions of interest were analysed and the ALP conference had reviewed the issue.

April 1994: After Bolitho's request for an urgent meeting to clarify position Minister Brereton met three ANL directors and later advised in writing that after the ALP conference the government would be in a position to be more definitive about the terms and conditions attached to the ANL sale.

May 1994: On 26 May an article in the *Financial Review* by Michael Dwyer leaked the Cabinet minute of February 1994 by which the change to the conditions of sale taken in June 1993 were to be kept secret.

June 1994: Opposition Leader Alexander Downer tabled a copy of the February Cabinet minute in the House of Representatives covering the Cabinet decision in June that conditions surrounding the sale of ANL were to be kept secret.

Bolitho submitted to the Senate that the correspondence record clearly depicted that even if the Government knew what it was doing at all times, it did not keep ANL appropriately informed.

22 August 1994

THE correspondence and minutes of the Board clearly showed a Board increasingly desperate and concerned about damage being done to the shipping line through the antics of politicians and leaks to the media.

On Monday 22 August 1994 the ANL Board assembled at ANL's Melbourne headquarters. Things, they were told, were moving in Canberra. The Minister would be on the line with the head of the

Transport Department, Graham Evans, to detail the governments next move. They were to get the sack.

Bolitho made a file note of his conversation with Brereton. It is Record No. 309 in his Senate submissions.

FILE NOTE: TELEPHONE CONVERSATION WITH THE MINISTER FOR TRANSPORT AT 1300 HOURS ON AUGUST 22, 1994.

BRERETON:
- Cabinet discussed at great length the ANL position this morning and in view of the critical financial position of ANL revealed by the Price Waterhouse and Salomon Brothers reports.
- Accordingly, Cabinet will be installing a new board.
- Neville Wran will be chairman with a small board to look at restructuring ANL over a six months period.
- Restructuring will be to salvage what is possible.
- Government will guarantee operations of ANL in an appropriate manner.
- Do not wish to have to amend the articles and invite you to resign over the course of the afternoon.

BOLITHO:
- Repeated the above back to be sure that it was correct.
- The Board of ANL has had its own valuations done both as a going concern, and in a liquidation situation. ANL is solvent at this moment and has a positive net worth.
- The Board has to this moment been perfectly justified in trading.

One by one board members were called to the telephone and told of the Government's decision to replace the Board forthwith. To some it came with a sense of relief. ANL had been struggling financially because of the downturn in international shipping and ruthless undercutting in its most profitable routes. As well, all their protestations to the Federal Government of collateral damage to the value of the asset had fallen on deaf ears. In many respects the problem was no longer theirs and that, in itself, was a relief. Brereton and Evans had been courteous on the telephone and the Board, realising that the Minister, as the shareholder in the company, had overriding powers, agreed to tender their resignations one by one. Indeed, had they wanted to bat on, the Minister could use his powers under the amended Articles of Association and simply terminate their appointments forthwith by letter. All Board members were intrigued by the reference to the Price Waterhouse/Salomon Brothers report on ANL. The Board had not been asked to make a submission to it. They had not seen it.

The Board members in Melbourne that day had a final drink and reflected that they had done the best they could to protect the public asset from a government whose actions had continually threatened to undermine its value. Little did they know their collective heads were about to be kicked in the political tradition of scapegoating.

A press report the following day detailed unquestioningly the Minister's line against the outgoing ANL Board. *The Sydney Morning Herald* article (23 August 1994) read:

> The Federal Government's dumping of the entire board of ANL yesterday reflected its frustration at a campaign by former directors to obstruct plans for a trade sale of the enterprise.
>
> When the Minister for Industrial Relations, Mr Brereton, announced the appointment of a new four-member board led by Mr Neville Wran and Mr Malcolm Turnbull to replace ANL's 10 directors, he said he was looking to the new board to provide a fresh start and develop a comprehensive strategic and financial plan for the enterprise.
>
> The Government's decision to replace the ANL Board was prompted not only by the financial mismanagement of the enterprise, but more so by the directors' concerted efforts to destabilise the asset sale process. Countervailing the plans of Government and Asset Sales Task Force, the board sided with the Maritime Union and hired a lobbyist to protest against the sale.
>
> Mr Bolitho—who served as chairman since 1983—is said by observers to have been a dominant and uncompromising chairman who, along with the board, ran the business and allowed its managing director, Mr McGuiness, little leeway to manage independently.
>
> An independent report by Price Waterhouse and Salomon

Brothers Australia, released yesterday when the Government announced it had shelved plans to sell 49 per cent of ANL put a negative valuation on the group.

Had ANL been doing well financially, the Government might have listened to the board, another observer said.

'It was a very strong board but not a good board—wilful is the word,' he said.

The only significant operation of ANL to be profitable was Australian Stevedores of which ANL has only a 25 per cent stake.

There, through the unattributed whispers of 'observers' to Canberra journalists was the defamation of ANL directors. Mismanagement was a particularly galling description. But that, as they say, was politics.

Bolitho and his Board had not been aware of the findings of Brereton's Price Waterhouse/Salomon Brothers report in advance of its release. Neither the Minister nor his department had sent them a copy, and never did. It was this report on which Brereton based his public claim that 'you couldn't give it away' when at his press conference that day he referred to ANL's financial position and its prospects for privatisation. It compounded the defamation of the Bolitho Board and the now resigned board members were privately furious.

In his public announcement of the appointment of the new board comprising Neville Wran QC AC, the commercial lawyer Malcolm Turnbull, Paul Merner, head of the Commonwealth's Maritime Transport Division and John Spark, a chartered accountant and company reconstruction expert, Minister Brereton had said:

The Minister for Finance and I commissioned a detailed due diligence report on ANL in March 1994 and consultants Salomon Brothers Australia and Price Waterhouse have undertaken a thorough financial investigation of ANL.

Their report was received on the weekend and indicates that neither a sale of 49 per cent nor of 100 per cent of ANL is practicable and that ANL's likely sale value has narrowed to within a range of negative $74.8 million to negative $117.8 million.

The statement went on:

In 1993–94 ANL is likely to report a loss before tax and abnormals of $23.5 million compared with the loss ANL budgeted in December 1993 of $2.4 million.

With increased competition from major new international container vessel tonnage on order to be built in the next couple of years, an increasing oversupply of tonnage will further worsen ANL's prospects in the longer term.

ANL's fleet is much smaller than it was in the early 1980s when it owned 23 of its fleet of 33 vessels. ANL now owns four of its fleet of 12 vessels. Of that fleet two operate in the north and east Asia trade, one each in South-East Asia and Europe and two across the Tasman. The remainder operate within Australian waters.

The Price Waterhouse/Salomon Brothers report had shown a 'negative' value for ANL of $75 million to $118 million. But the now former Board members were aware that the Australian National Audit Office which had the responsibility of examining ANL's accounts and certifying its financial statements as true and accurate, had declared the previous December that ANL was a going concern able to meet its debts 'as and when they fell due'. Yet Brereton was relying on this report alone to sink the Board and put ANL up for asset stripping and a fire sale. What was to follow stunned Bolitho and his former Board colleagues.

In the months leading up to the dismissal of the Bolitho Board there had been a powerplay inside one of ANL's strategic investments, the stevedoring company Australian Stevedores.

In 1994 Australian Stevedores was part-owned by Chris Corrigan's Jamison Equity (often described by *The Australian Financial Review* as a corporate cashbox) with a 50 per cent shareholding. ANL held 25 per cent of the company and the long established Australian company Howard Smith, with established interests in stevedoring, held the other 25 per cent.

Powerplay

ON 11 July 1994, forty-two days before the ANL board was sacked, Chris Corrigan and Jamison Equity had pulled a trigger which put the ownership of Australian Stevedores into play. The Board of Australian Stevedores (of which Bolitho was a member representing ANL's 25 per cent share) was deadlocked over Corrigan's refusal to accept an Australian Stevedores management recommendation for a three-year phase down of its Darling Harbour facility. In the boardroom debate Bolitho was seen by Corrigan as pro-union and not wanting to attack excessive costs through inefficient work practices. Corrigan wanted more immediate results.

Bolitho contends he did not want to protect the unions from justifiable change to reduce excessive costs and inefficient work practices. 'Just as in the case of the sale of ANL it was a difference of the means of achieving the ends, not the ends themselves, that was at issue. It was my view that the maritime unions had much more clout than Corrigan realised and that patient negotiation in good faith was in the long run a more productive approach than bringing on an almighty blue which we could not possibly have won with a Labor government in power and with an ACTU both dependent upon the support of the maritime unions and closely associated with the government through the Kelty/Keating accords. The subsequent events and the nationwide maritime strike support my views which were coloured by a lifetime in the industry and a close knowledge of the state of play in the industry and the unions.'

Significantly, the Howard Smith shareholders on the Australian Stevedores board supported the management phase down. Under the shareholders' agreement with Australian Stevedores, any deadlock at the board table could only be resolved by the parties agreeing to buy or sell each other's shares.

Confronted with the trigger in the shareholders' agreement, Bolitho and the ANL Board had recommended to Minister Brereton that the Government buy out both Jamison Equity's 50 per cent and Howard Smith's 25 per cent. Bolitho argued that between 1992 and 1994 major reforms of the Australian waterfront had been completed at massive taxpayer expense in redundancy payments to waterside workers to rationalise the industry. As a result of the taxpayer-funded reforms industry productivity had risen and costs had fallen. As well, the Australian and world economies had improved substantially coming out of the recession. Australian Stevedores was now in a strong profit position holding market dominance in the stevedoring industry.

On 22 August the ANL Board was sacked by Minister Brereton. The deadlock over the ownership of Australian Stevedores still had not been resolved.

On 30 August Chris Corrigan got agreement from Howard Smith to sell its 25 per cent stake in Australian Stevedores at the same time that Corrigan's Jamison Equity raised equity from Howard Smith by selling it a chain of hardware stores. The price agreed for Howard Smith's stake in Australian Stevedores was $28 million—Howard Smith later denied any link between the two transactions.

On 8 September the Wran-Turnbull Board, now in charge of ANL, formally made the same recommendation to Minister Brereton made by the Bolitho Board: Buy out the other 75 per cent of Australian Stevedores—Jamison's 50 and Howard Smith's 25. The Wran Board added a rider that in the event that the Minister decided against the buyout, selling to Corrigan's Jamison Equity was 'perfectly defensible and reasonable'.

Immediately Minister Brereton moved to authorise the sale of ANL's 25 per cent stake in Australian Stevedores to Jamison Equity. In a news conference Minister Brereton said: 'It was the unanimous view of all four ministers (Federal Cabinet sub-committee) that the Government should sell its share to Jamison Equity enabling Jamison Equity to move from its 50 per cent plus the 25 it's already secured from Howard Smith to a 100 per cent position. And this afternoon that sale has been concluded'.

The price? $28 million.

Eyebrows were raised when Laura Tingle reported on the front page of *The Australian* newspaper on 8 November 1994 that Chris Corrigan had to temporarily borrow $22.4 million from the struggling ANL to close the deal on 9 September.

Bolitho later told the Senate inquiry:

Simultaneously with the sale of their shareholding in Australian Stevedores to Jamison, Howard Smith purchased the Queensland hardware interests of Jamison to add to their own BBC chain. It is at least possible, therefore, that the $28 million may have been a balancing amount between the two transactions and unconfirmed reports put the sale price of the Jamison hardware interests in Queensland at $10 million.

If this is the case, then this places a value of $38 million on the 25 per cent of Australian Stevedores sold by the Minister for $28 million.

Thus irrespective of any detailed analysis or valuation we have a number of rough estimates of the worth of the 25 per cent shareholding in Australian Stevedores from a low of $31 million to a high of $44 million.

In all these circumstances, there is at least the possibility that the sale of the ANL shareholding in Australian Stevedores was sold at a value well below its true worth and as it was a public asset that possibility should not be overlooked in any examination of the transaction that may occur.

On 9 September the Maritime Union of Australia, according to officials, was tipped off by an informant that it was about to be 'bushwhacked' by Minister Brereton over the sale of ANL's stake in Australian Stevedores. Because of the industrial impact of the proposed sale the MUA called an immediate national strike which lasted for five days and cost shipowners and the Australian trading companies tens of millions of dollars in lost revenue. The strike also cost the Keating Government a reported $20 million in tax concessions to the industry.

Fight Back

IMMEDIATELY after the Board's sacking Bill Bolitho had agonised about what to do. He spoke to his former fellow directors including Morella Calder, who at that time was seriously ill with cancer at her Sydney home. Calder urged Bolitho to fight back for his own sake and for the reputations of the directors who had been struggling in co-operation with ANL management to keep ANL not only afloat but a viable sale prospect. Bolitho was later to reveal that it was Calder's urging which motivated him to fight back.

I really was pretty despondent and quite disgusted at the actions of the politicians and public servants concerned. I think it was the first time I ever really began to understand the depths to which the public process of democratic government had been subverted by the party political process and the self-serving ideology prevailing in the senior ranks of the public service, certainly in the central co-ordinating departments of Finance and Treasury. I was pretty well burnt out and felt I was probably not up to the enormous effort that I knew would be required to take on the full might and malice of the government and its bureaucracy.

I would, of course, have regretted not doing so all my life afterwards, but I believe that I might not have taken up the task if Morella, suffering from a painful and mortal illness and knowing that her end was near, had not roused herself to point me to what we both knew was a duty I owed to my colleagues, to the ANL management and staff and to the taxpayers who were to be the losers from the government's actions.

Bill Bolitho repaired to the farm to tap out on his word processor a statement which he planned to release to the media on Friday 16 September 1994. The statement first had to counter the very damaging claim in the Price Waterhouse/Salomon Brothers report that ANL had a very poor record of forecasting its revenues. By this time Bolitho had obtained a copy of the executive summary of the PWSB report from a newspaper journalist and painstakingly analysed its methodology in reporting ANL's problems to the Minister for Transport.

He produced a five-page report which was made available to the Canberra media. It received negligible publicity although it contained the very newsworthy concluding questions:

- Was the Minister's handling of the affair appropriate in all the circumstances?
- Was the sale of the ANL shareholding in Australian Stevedores for $28 million an appropriate action?

    These are questions of public importance concerning the disposal of a major public asset. They deserve a public airing and a public answer.

There was little mainstream media scrutiny of the questions Bolitho had so publicly raised. But there had been some awareness of the issues at stake from so-called commentators following the Board's dismissal on 22 August.

On 27 August 1994 Ken Davidson, an economics writer for *The Age* newspaper in Melbourne, had written in his column:

> It is difficult to think of an act of economic vandalism in the period since Federation that can rank with the cold-blooded destruction of the Australian National Line wreaked by the Minister for Transport, Mr Brereton.
>
> Before Tuesday I could not have imagined that any vendor, from a curbside stall, let alone a minister of the Crown responsible for a strategic community asset, would say about that asset: 'You couldn't give it away, that is the reality ... it's a pretty dismal picture'.
>
> Why would any vendor diminish the business that he is selling? Forget the cruelty to employees who are expected to soldier on in the face of destructive comments about the business that is still their livelihood, or the damage done to the commercial reputations of the sacked directors by Mr Brereton's carefully orchestrated public relations announcement of the ANL execution.

Davidson reported that the old ANL board was not shown the Price Waterhouse/Salomon Brothers report before it was sacked. The old board had read about it in the newspapers, particularly the headline-grabbing negative value placed on the ANL (negative $75 million to $118 million).

> This is a very different figure from the positive valuation of $50 million to $90 million put on the value of ANL's assets by the previous board in submissions to the Government.
>
> What is the difference? The main difference is that the ANL valuation includes, on the asset side, the full independent valuation of its ships and containers, whereas, according to the Price Waterhouse/Salomon Brothers report, the negative valuation was achieved after adding on to the assets side of the ledger (only) 70 per cent of the independent valuation of ANL's vessels, and 55–

70 per cent of the independent valuation of ANL's containers.

It is worth quoting what the executive summary says on this: Our broad valuation range principally reflects two variables. Firstly, there is a high degree of uncertainty attached to valuations of ANL's vessels (where we have adopted 70 per cent of the low and high range of independent variables) and containers (where we have adopted a range of 55–70 per cent of independent valuations). If these vessels and containers were valued at 100 per cent of the independent valuations, which we consider to be optimistic, the value of ANL would improve to (a range between) $35.3 million (negative) to $7.6 million (positive).

Why the 30–45 percentage points discount on the valuation? We are not told. Whose valuation is more credible? The valuations of an international shipping consultant that specialises in ship valuations for insurance purposes and whose reputation in this area is its major stock in trade? Or the valuations by non-shipping experts, whose core reputations are not on the line?

The Finance Department valuation also includes a negative $60 million as the cost of closure of ANL's head office and a further $69 million for redundancies.

The report admits 'no value has been allocated to ANL's trade shares in its various (shipping) conferences and consortia, given the extreme uncertainty as to value and transferability'. Really? I would have thought the ANL's conference shares, which determine its share of the international liner business to Asia, New Zealand and Europe, are the most valuable bits of the business to competitors in the event of an ANL asset strip and fire sale. And that the Government would get at least $30 million for these shipping rights built up over the past decade by the ANL management, which has made the ANL the biggest conference member in the Asian container trade.

If the cost of redundancies and head office closure are added back to a 100 per cent valuation of the ANL fleet and its containers, it is clear that the ANL has (or had, until Tuesday) a considerable positive net value as a going concern.

In 1983, the ANL was worth nothing. Since then the Government has injected a miniscule net $9.3 million of taxpayers' money into the business (not $120 million as claimed by the Government) and over the same period, ANL has net operating losses of $8.4 million.

Despite the crisis atmosphere cynically created by Mr Brereton, the most reasonable forecast is that the ANL could operate for a further three years without additional net cash injections from the Government and, as an operating entity, the ANL would continue to contribute a net $800 million a year savings on the current account of the balance of payments.

Ken Davidson's analysis was ignored. What should have been a front page story cranking up the political pressure on the Government and demanding answers and accountability was let lapse. Some journalists did pursue the consequences of Minister Brereton's action and the incident certainly raised questions about his ministerial capacity and record, but the issue died.

Then the Australian Senate came to the rescue of the Australian public and their assets—regrettably much less valuable assets, it could be said, than before. Its effort, although most welcome, would prove to be somewhat limp, allowing a triumph of mindless ideology over prudence and rational economics.

On 22 September 1994 the Senate voted to call for the tabling of all documents relating to the sale process 'having regard to the parlous financial state of the Australian National Line'.

The Senate also asked the Australian National Audit Office for an explanation of the different valuations of ANL—Price Waterhouse Salomon Brothers, the audited financial statements showing shareholders' funds of positive $157 million, and a valuation prepared for the ANL Board of between 'break even' and a positive $33 million.

With the ANAO's response now awaited with extreme interest by all parties, Bill Bolitho accepted a request from the author to a television interview. The broadcast on Wednesday, 6 December 1994 on the ABC's *7.30 Report*, was a fifteen-minute compilation of the main points in the saga and Bolitho's measured arguments that the ANL Board had been badly misrepresented by Brereton and that a valuable asset had all but been destroyed.

Bolitho gave a convincing display of his command of the facts with a grim-faced, determined presentation to the interview

grabs which were broadcast. He was asked about Minister Brereton's motivation for the dismissal of his Board.

Interviewer: Mr Bolitho, it would have been irresponsible of the
Minister to allow ANL to go on when he had this Price Waterhouse/
Salomon Brothers report, wouldn't it?

Bolitho: In the Board's view which I made clear to the Minister,
ANL was a going concern and perfectly entitled to trade. That was
also the view of ANL management, the view of our auditors and
the view of our financial advisers. I must make the point that the
Board of ANL had not seen the report by Price Waterhouse/
Salomon Brothers nor had, I understand, the Auditor-General. We
hadn't even seen the executive summary which had been widely
distributed to the press. In fact I think we got our copy from the
press. This was most unusual in my view ... discourteous to say
the least.

Bolitho dealt with the confusing question of the Price Water-
house/Salomon Brothers apparently damning report on the value
of ANL:

The Price Waterhouse/Salomon Brothers report seems to be based
on a liquidation, fire sale basis. If you took any major public
company in Australia and subjected them to the same liquidation
fire sale analysis you'd get the same result. They would all be gone.

Interviewer: What was your reaction to Mr Brereton's 'couldn't
give it away remark'?

Bolitho: Incredulity I suppose, concern, and curiosity. Incredulity
in the first place that a responsible Minister of the Crown could
make such a statement. Concern that the statement would actually
damage ANL and its sale value and curiosity as to why he did it.

Interviewer: Why do you think he did it?

Bolitho: I don't know. You'd really have to ask the Minister
that. There are a number of questions which need to be asked of
the Minister. That's one of them.

On the issue of the Ministerial direction, against advice, to sell
ANL's 25 per cent stake in Australian Stevedores, Bolitho

commented: 'This was a very valuable company. When I left (August 94), it was making about $2 million a month before interest and tax and I understand the projections for 94–95 are in excess of that. It was therefore a very valuable activity'.

Chris Corrigan also made an appearance in the broadcast report declaring that he had brought no influence to bear on Minister Brereton to ignore the advice of the old or new ANL board to buy (not sell) Australian Stevedores.

Corrigan asserted that the price of $28 million for ANL's 25 per cent stake in Australian Stevedores was never negotiable. 'After we'd agreed with Howard Smith, part of the negotiation with Howard Smith was that we would make an identical offer to ANL which we made and that was never negotiated.'

On the question of Corrigan having to temporarily borrow $22 million from ANL to complete the purchase, Corrigan replied: 'I'm never embarrassed to borrow from the government'.

In the broadcast Bolitho was asked why ANL did not just stay on for the ride with Australian Stevedores after the deadlock on that Board had been broken. Bolitho: 'I've no idea. Certainly there would have been no immediate rush to sell in my view. Had it been my choice and had I been there at the time I would have been happy to sit back and let the dust settle and see what pressures we could bring to bear to get the best possible price for the enterprise. Selling in such an enormous rush ... I really don't understand it'.

Bolitho asserted in the broadcast that ANL's stake in Australian Stevedores was worth 'every penny of $35 million'.

Interviewer: Mr Corrigan has made a corporate killing?

Bolitho: Mr Corrigan is a very competent corporate executive, a very good businessman and I am sure his board is rightly pleased with his efforts.

At the end of the interview Bolitho called for a public inquiry to examine all the circumstances of the sacking of the old ANL Board and the disposal of ANL's share in Australian Stevedores.

If as I understand the Auditor General's report to the Senate states

ANL was a going concern, was able to meet its debts as and when they fell due, was solvent, did have a positive net worth and was able to continue trading, it appears to me the Minister was not on very sound ground in dismissing the Board and making the statements that he did. If that is the case public unease would best be dealt with by a full open and judicial inquiry in which the Minister would have a golden opportunity to put his points.

Interviewer: Mr Bolitho, why are you speaking out now?

Bolitho: It has taken some months to let the dust settle, some months for reflection, some months to allow my anger to subside so that I can be measured in my approach to it. I believe that as the former chairman there is a very strict duty on me both public and private. I believe it places a duty on me to make sure that adequate public attention is given to what happened so that the public can be fully informed . . . and I have a private duty to perform to my colleagues. If in fact the Auditor General is reporting that we were a going concern, then the dismissal of my colleagues and the statements the Minister made has damaged their commercial reputations. I believe it is a private duty upon me to make sure that in so far as I am able I repair the damage done to their reputations. That's why I'm speaking out.

Neither Minister Brereton nor new ANL chairman Neville Wran was available for interview on the program.

The Australian National Audit Office, in a statement on 5 December 1994, said current and proposed legislation did not give the Auditor General the necessary freedom to provide Parliament with reports on the use of public money and resources by Government Business Enterprises (GBEs) such as ANL.

ANAO's only contribution to the public debate on the highly contentious questions raised by the Senate was this observation:

The actions and statements of those involved in the sale process can influence the perceptions of potential buyers which can result in a lower price for the asset. For this reason it is important that public officials involved in the sale of Commonwealth assets at all times act with discretion in order not to prejudice the Commonwealth's position.

The Senate, or at least a majority comprising the Opposition, Democrats and Greens, found this unacceptable and carried a resolution referring all outstanding matters to the Finance and Public Administration References Committee and ordered the Auditor-General to prepare a report taking into account the following issues and questions:

> Whether public officials (elected or unelected) associated with the proposed disposal of ANL have acted with prudence, discretion, integrity and propriety.
>
> Whether the actions of the Department of Transport, the Department of Finance (Asset Sales Task Force) and the boards of ANL, as individual organisations and collectively, have been effective in serving the taxpayers' best interests.
>
> What was the status of the Price Waterhouse/Salomon Brothers report in the sale process and was there any reason for preferring the PWSB valuation to other valuations?
>
> Whether the minister behaved with prudence, discretion, integrity and propriety by publishing the PWSB report and by making the comments he did when publishing the report.
>
> Whether the disposal of Australian Stevedores to Jamison Equity, against the advice of both the old and new ANL boards, was justified, whether the sale price was maximised, and whether the financing arrangements were acceptable on legal and com-mercial grounds.
>
> What were the circumstances leading up to the agreement with the Maritime Union of Australia, what was the nature of the agreement including financial arrangements, and whether the agreement was in the best interests of the Commonwealth.

In the political heat generated by the new publicity and the ANAO's inadequate report, Minister Brereton agreed to a formal request to the Auditor-General for an efficiency audit of the ANL sale process.

Bill Bolitho now had a public inquiry. He had to put up—or as the saying goes—shut up. He made a meticulous search of all the documents he had kept from his chairmanship and the notes ANL management officials had kept under his instruction.

He fired up the word processor in his study on the farm and constructed as detailed an account as possible, indexing the documents which would accompany his submission to the Senate. He carried out this work without secretarial assistance.

As the process unfolded, he submitted four additional written submissions to answer points raised by TFAS and Finance Department bureaucrats.

Bill Bolitho made his public appearance at committee hearings in Parliament House, Canberra, on 22 September and 20 October 1995. Minister Laurie Brereton did not appear before the committee.

The Finance and Public Administration References Committee chaired by Senator Robert Bell (Democrat, Tasmania) comprised senators Ian Campbell (Liberal, WA), Kim Carr (ALP Victoria), John Coates (ALP, Tasmania), Christopher Evans (ALP, Western Australia), Dominic Foreman (ALP, South Australia), Rod Kemp (Liberal, Victoria), Nicholas Minchin (Liberal, South Australia), Belinda Neal (ALP, NSW) and John Watson (Liberal, Tasmania).

Accountability

SUCH is the nature of party politics in Australia that the words used in the final report, tabled in the Senate on 16 November 1995, made no declaration of blame in the ANL affair. None of the questions the Senate had asked in instituting its inquiries was ever answered definitively. Thus was accountability of public officials abandoned.

On the question of differing valuations for the asset the committee sidestepped.

The committee agrees that the various valuations of ANL that are available are not necessarily directly comparable, in that they are based on very different assumptions. The committee does not intend to comment upon the validity of these assumptions, other than to say that there appears to be scope for disagreement among commercial experts. It does appear, however, that the relevance of any one valuation can only be determined within the context of the assumptions upon which it is based. In the view of *some members* of the committee, the 'fire sale' assumptions of PWSB may have had a negative influence in determining the value of ANL and its assets.

On the question of the Minister's now famous 'couldn't give it away' remark, the committee found:

> It is still not possible for the committee to determine the impact of the statements of the Minister on the potential market for ANL, and on the price realised for ANL and its assets. In the view of the *majority of members*, the statements carried the potential to have a negative influence on the interests of the Commonwealth and they question the prudence of the Minister's conduct in making statements which were potentially damaging to the sale process without providing the full documentation relied upon to support those statements. *Other members* endorse the Wran view that the market would make its own decision regardless of ministerial opinion, and note the release of the PWSB report by the Minister.

Inexplicably, the committee all but ignored Minister Brereton's sale of ANL's stake in Australian Stevedores to Chris Corrigan's Jamison Equity. Why the Senate committee should avoid the questions which needed exploring from this act of asset stripping, against the advice of both the old and new ANL boards, remains a mystery.

In any event, the senators all signed a final report which was critical of Minister Brereton and the process where ANL was scuttled by politics and Australian taxpayers confronted massive losses. Any sharply critical edge to the findings was qualified with the diplomatic language, 'some members are concerned' or 'in the opinion of a majority of members'. Press coverage of the committee's findings was negligible.

The committee reported in its executive summary:

> It is clear that the spirit in which the sale process was conducted was not one of mutual trust. It is not intended for the purposes of this report to assign 'blame' for specific events; however, it is the

view of the committee that the ANL sale process might fairly be described as characterised by confusion, uncertainty, delay, a lack of adequate documentation and a lack of communication and trust.

Given that a decision was made to sell ANL, the committee is concerned that the sale process has lasted for over four years. The committee appreciates the point made by Stephen Sedgwick, secretary of the Department of Finance, that, in the initial stages, the government may have needed to refine its options, and that this was the purpose of the scoping study. Nevertheless, the process was initiated via the scoping study in 1991. For a variety of reasons, the sale clearly has not proceeded in a timely fashion.

Some members of the committee are concerned at the at-times almost adversarial, rather than cooperative, nature of the relationship between the TFAS and the former ANL Board. For example, Mr Sedgwick was questioned as to the reason for the decision not to provide the PWPW (Price Waterhouse and Potter Warburg) report of 1992 to the Board. He advised that although he did not have a precise recollection of the reason: 'The circumstances which we were in were very similar to those of anybody who receives confidential advice, which they have paid for in the expectation that the advice would be provided to government. It does not seem to me that it necessarily follows that, simply because one party in a transaction has received some confidential advice, it needs to pass it over to any other party in a transaction. Frankly, I do not think that follows at all'.

As noted above, the committee received extensive documentary material from Mr Bolitho, which assisted greatly in gaining an understanding of the ANL sale process. In contrast, the Department of Finance, having been invited to give evidence at a public hearing, did not provide a written submission in advance of that hearing, and provided a submission only when specifically requested to do so by the committee. The committee was concerned at comments made by the Department of Finance with respect to the difficulty of locating detailed records of advice given to ANL.

It is apparent from the evidence that there were substantial difficulties in communication between the Minister, Government officers and the Board of Directors, which lasted for several years. The committee is therefore particularly surprised that greater efforts were not made by the Departments of Finance and Transport to document details in writing, in order to minimise misunderstandings. The committee was disappointed to find that written briefings of Ministers on key issues were not provided, notes of meetings were not available, and follow-up documentation was not maintained. In short, the documentation kept by the Department of Finance and Transport was inadequate.

The committee agrees with the point made by ANAO, that the Board should have been provided with the PWSB (Price Waterhouse/Salomon Brothers) report prior to its release.

The committee concludes that the sale process was protracted, decisions were not open and well documented, and certain individuals were not treated as fairly and openly as they should have been.

The committee recognises the inherent tension which exists for members of a Board of Directors of a corporation who are subject to the requirements of corporations law, and are also expected to comply not only with ministerial direction but also to be publicy accountable through the Parliament.

In speaking to the report in the Senate on 16 November 1995, committee member Senator Nicholas Minchin attacked Minister Brereton as 'utterly incompetent'.

I am amazed that he remains a minister in the government. It can only be as a result of particular friendships he has in New South Wales. His treatment of the former board, in particular, was disgraceful.

... It was clear to me and to other members from both sides of the chamber on this committee that Mr Bolitho is a man of great sincerity and integrity, a man who devoted many years of his life to building up this public asset. He took it over in the early 1980s when it was obviously in a very sick state and devoted a decade of his life—fulltime for what was a paltry part-time chairman's remuneration—to building up ANL. But ever since the government made the decision to sell the company back in 1991 it has been a downhill run for that company to the point now where we will get absolutely nothing back from the investment which people like Mr Bolitho made in the company.

It must be tragic for him, in particular, to see what has happened to the company he chaired. It must be particularly galling for him to see what occurred after August 1994 when Mr Brereton's good friend the Hon. Neville Wran QC was made chairman of the company for what was initially six months but was then extended to twelve months. He was paid $300,000 for one year's part-time work to chair this company. As we learnt, poor old Mr Bolitho got $40,000 per year to work probably eighty hours a week to try to resuscitate the company. It must be very painful for Mr Bolitho to see what has occurred in the twelve months since he was summarily dismissed. The total bill for the Wran board was $816,000, which is nearly 20 per cent of the best we might get for the company. It will probably end up being the same amount we will receive for the same company—an extraordinary amount of money doled out in one year to one board, two of whom coincidentally happen to be good friends of the minister.

This inquiry is a manual on how not to sell a government business.

No government members spoke on the tabling of the Senate committee's report—a deafening silence, given the vehemence of Minchin's attack and its reflection on the competence of Minister Brereton.

The Senate committee went on to recommend that the Department of Finance 'investigate possible options and models to develop a best practice model for the administration of any possible future Commonwealth asset sales'.

In November 1995 when this recommendation was tabled in the Australian Parliament, billions of dollars worth of public assets had already been 'privatised'. To the casual observer this recommendation might seem a little late in coming.

Major asset sales were started in 1987 and included the sale of the Tokyo Embassy, Williamstown Dockyard, Commonwealth Government Centre, Melbourne, Paris Head of Mission residence, the Defence Service Homes loan scheme, Australia House, Sydney, AUSSAT, Australian Airlines, Qantas, Commonwealth Bank of Australia and many government enterprises.

It was reported that the Board of Australian Airlines had similar misgivings about its relationship with the Task Force on Asset Sales as the Bolitho Board at ANL. The Keating Government ordered the 'merger' of Australian Airlines (which had 50 per cent of the domestic airline market) with Qantas, the international Australian airline, in 1992. The price listed for the asset was $400 million, although sources have told the author that some valuations estimated that Australian Airlines was worth $900 million to $1 billion. The Australian Airlines 'merger' went through without political controversy. Australian Airlines' domestic business was re-branded as Qantas, and together with the international business was subsequently privatised. One Australian Airlines Board member at the time complained to the author in 1995 that the Keating Government 'gave away' Australian Airlines and that the $400 million listed price was a 'book entry'. The board member declined to 'go public' with his claim.

For Bill Bolitho there was no real satisfaction in the Senate inquiry save the opportunity to place all his evidence on the public record.

There was some vindication in the inquiry's observations that the Task Force on Asset Sales was an inappropriate structure for the sale of government assets. But that structure prevailed until the Keating Government was defeated at the Federal Election of 2 March 1996.

Bolitho was impressed that the committee chairman, Senator Bell, a Democrat, was able to get agreement on those findings which were critical of Minister Brereton. The fact that no Labor senator rose to Brereton's defence was a fair indication of their acceptance of where the blame really lay for the ANL fiasco.

But apart from whatever Minister Brereton's motivations may have been from the time he assumed ministerial responsibility for ANL, what disappointed Bolitho most was the quality and behaviour of many of the public servants involved. He later told the author: ' They were less than truthful. They were inaccurate, biased and sloppy in their submissions. It was very depressing'. The contemporary standards of public administration in major economic departments of government had been brought into serious question. The public service had been neither independent nor objective in its advice. It had bent to a political imperative which was not, in this case, in the public interest. In short, the public service had been politicised. There had been a dereliction of duty.

ANL continued to trade and meet its debts as and when they fell due, as the accountants would say. In an article published in the industry journal *Ships and Ports*, Bolitho wrote that he had observed ANL executives Barry McGuiness and David Looker had finally extricated the company from the loss-making European trade without incurring the enormous loss provisions made for that exit by the Wran board of ANL in the 1993/94 accounts. The vessel involved in the European trade, the *Australian Venture*, had been sold for nearly $20 million. 'This is something like twice the price at which the Task Force on Asset Sales was prepared to sell the vessel to the government-favoured P & O.'

By 1996 individual sales of ANL assets totalled almost $50 million. The company was still in existence, with record 'liftings' and making money. Bolitho wrote bitterly that McGuiness and Looker, 'honest and competent executives', had since been dismissed from ANL.

Bolitho wrote:

The five year saga of the byzantine attempts of the government to destroy a valuable public asset in ANL for political reasons without being seen to do so and their bungling attempts to sell it at what is now clearly seen as below its true worth are to a large extent chronicled in the Senate inquiry into the sale of ANL.

It is my view that both the ANL saga itself and the inquiry into it reveal a climate in government and the public service where honesty and truth are little regarded and political interests and public service ideologies can and do take precedence over the public good.

Just as the weeds in my garden will eventually overwhelm the vegetables if not checked, so these bitter political and ideological weeds in government and the public service will eventually overwhelm the public good if we do not attempt to check them and it would appear to be more in the long term public interest for certain ministers and public servants to be summarily dismissed rather than honest and competent executives such as McGuiness and Looker.

Bolitho had stood up for himself, his colleagues, and the public interest, and he had delivered on his promise to the dying Morella Calder. He owed it to her, more than any other.

In a letter to Morella Calder's family in which he enclosed a copy of the Senate committee's report into the 'Proposed Sale of ANL Limited', Bolitho wrote:

Like most matters in Australian politics it is something of a compromise between the Coalition and Labor on the premise that 'we are not going to hurt each other too much are we'.

Nevertheless, although less critical of Minister Brereton and his action in dismissing the old Board than that despicable action warranted, the report, by criticising both Brereton and the public service conduct of the sale, justifies the former Board, and, in so doing, completely removes the unwarranted slurs that Brereton put upon the directors, including Morella.

The effort of defending the old Board against the whole weight of the Government and the public service including five separate submissions and two public appearances has been quite as significant as I knew it would be and I very much doubt that I would have entered into it in the first place had not Morella convinced me that it was my duty to do so. I am only sad that she did not live to see the outcome.

The fact that the Senate report repairs the reputations of the former directors of ANL dismissed by Brereton is therefore due to Morella and the impact of her honesty, courage in adversity and fine moral fibre upon me in making me do it. The report is in a very real sense a last tribute to a very fine human being and I hope that you will receive it in that spirit.

With every good wish and kind regard,

Bill Bolitho.

WHAT HAPPENED ABOARD THE *GRIFFIN VENTURE*?

'This is horrific. This is an Exxon Valdez *and this is a* Piper Alpha. *Massive pollution . . . total loss of life on the virgin coast of Western Australia—a recognised environmentally-sensitive area. This stuff can go down into Exmouth Gulf . . . who knows . . . who knows?'*—Tim Visscher, an officer aboard BHP Petroleum's *Griffin Venture*

O N 29 MAY 1994 there was an 'incident' aboard the FPSO *Griffin Venture*, BHP Petroleum's massive oil processing ship operating on the north-west shelf, 70 kilometres from Onslow in Western Australia.

Tim Visscher, then aged forty-four, a merchant naval officer with a Class 1 master qualification, held the rank of Second Mate. He had joined BHP Petroleum eighteen months before after a decade of experience on crude oil tankers and international container ships.

On 29 May Visscher came on deck at 6.30 in the evening to begin his shift. His job was to assist in tank clearing operations on agreed procedures set down at a 'toolbox' (safety) meeting chaired by the ship's Master.

That day's important task was to empty two of the vessel's seven huge crude oil storage tanks to allow for internal repairs to pumps at the bottom of each tank. The tanks contained crude oil with an atmosphere of liquid petroleum gas. The *Griffin Venture* processed oil and gas pumped from several undersea wellheads 200 metres below on the ocean floor for transfer to other tankers. It was said aboard that when operational, the *Griffin Venture* added around $2 million a day to BHP and its consortium partners' bottom line.

The *Griffin Venture* is what is called an FPSO—a Floating Production Storage and Offloading facility.

On the day of the 'incident' the *Griffin Venture* had thirty-seven crew on board and about 30 000 cubic metres of crude oil in three of the seven huge storage tanks.

The schedule of operational tasks on 29 May was designed to safely empty tanks one and three. Each tank had to be 'washed'— hot water pumped in to wash down the interior bulkheads to remove all residues of the crude oil. To make the tanks safe for human entry so that work could be done on the pumps inside each tank, the atmosphere in the tanks had to be gas freed. The operation to gas-free tanks is internationally acknowledged as the most hazardous that can be carried out on a tanker or FPSO. That means all traces of hydrocarbon and inert gas are removed and replaced with fresh air.

In the process, hydrocarbon levels inside tanks have to be reduced to less than 2 per cent per volume. Anything above 2 per cent is considered potentially dangerous—that is, if air is allowed into the tanks when hydrocarbon levels are above 2 per cent per volume, the mix of air and hydrocarbon gas could quickly become explosive.

All that would be needed would be a source of ignition—static electricity or a spark from an electrical or mechanical source. Such a situation could produce an explosion of massive intensity placing the entire vessel and its crew in jeopardy.

To reduce hydrocarbon levels inside a tank an inert gas (in this case boiler exhaust gas) is pumped in and the excess gases are vented to the atmosphere. In this way the levels of hydrocarbon gas are diluted until the percentage volume reaches 2 per cent. Gas detection instruments are used to monitor hydrocarbon levels at various stages of the operation to ensure that the level reaches 2 per cent or below before the tank is exposed to incoming air. The 2 per cent rule is published in safety manuals for oil and gas storage tankers the world over.

The instrument specially designed to check gas mixtures in oil and gas storage tanks is called a Tankscope. BHP Petroleum's work instruction specified that the Tankscope was to be used to measure hydrocarbon gases. The same work instruction also stipulated that the gas detection instruments were to be tested in accordance with internationally recognised procedures. To do the check a certified 'calibration' gas was required.

But on board the *Griffin Venture* on 29 May there was a problem. There was no certified calibration gas on board that day to check the accuracy of the Tankscope's readings.

Visscher had arrived back on board on 26 May. When there were discussions about the tank-clearing operation he inquired about the gas detection instruments to be used and was told by the First Mate that there were three LV analysers already on board and that a Tankscope was being borrowed from another of the company's facilities in the Timor Sea. The Tankscope was due to arrive by helicopter on 28 May, the day before tank clearing was to start. According to evidence at later enquiries, when he inquired if the correct calibration gas was also available to check the instrument he was told that it was on order, but because of freight problems it would not arrive on board until the scheduled gas-freeing operations were completed. Visscher indicated his unhappiness at this but was told that it was all right: there would be four instruments available to read the gas levels—three LV analysers and one Tankscope. When Visscher again told the First Mate that he was not happy the First Mate became abrupt and told him to raise his concern at the 'toolbox' meeting scheduled for later that day.

That meeting, followed by his evening shift, would lead to Visscher's moment of truth.

Stupidity, Bravado and Ego

VISSCHER was hardened to danger and he was as keenly attuned to safety as it was possible to be, given some previous life-threatening experiences.

He sometimes spoke with a slight stutter which, to the casual observer, might suggest a personality affected by insecurity. Such a perception would have been erroneous. Visscher made himself aware of facts and would adhere to them no matter what intimidatory pressures were applied to him. The stutter almost certainly resulted from his hard, almost brutal childhood and authoritarian parenting.

What was later to be called his 'obsession' with safety had its genesis in a terrifyingly narrow escape from death in another incident while he was in his twenties.

Tim Visscher is a direct descendant of Franz Joseph Visscher, the steersman or navigator aboard Abel Tasman's epic voyages of discovery of New Holland (later Australia) in 1634 on the vessels *Heamskirk* and *Zeean*. Franz Visscher's role in the discovery of the continent of Australia and the west coast of Van Dieman's Land (later Tasmania) is thoroughly documented (in the Mitchell Library in Sydney) and the Franz Joseph Glacier in New Zealand's South Island is named after him.

Many generations later Visscher's descendants settled in Australia. Tim Visscher's father was a fisherman at Wollongong south of Sydney. Young Tim was accepted into the Royal Australian Navy as a cadet at the age of fourteen and became an apprentice engineer. After six years he was discharged with the qualifications of a boilermaker and welder and was among the first Australians qualified to weld pipes offshore in the Bass Strait oil fields.

He got a lucrative job with a construction company working on the assembly of the Marlin, Kingsfish and Halibut offshore oil rigs in Bass Strait. With the proceeds of this work and his six years in the Navy, Visscher built a 60-foot steel fishing trawler—the *Illawarra Range*—at Port Kembla. At the time—1970—the boat cost $120,000. Today (1996) a vessel of those dimensions would cost close to a million dollars.

He took his investment to Queensland waters where from 1971 to 1979 he fished for prawns and scallops and made a fortune for the family company he established with his brother and parents. But it was an earlier incident in 1971 which changed Visscher's perception of life and safety forever.

After he left the Navy, Visscher trained for and was granted a private pilot's licence. He was just twenty-one. He was studying accountancy part time to broaden his skills. With his new pilot's licence he wanted to take three friends of similar age from the accountancy school on a sightseeing flight to Mount Kosciusko. Their chartered aircraft was a Cessna 172. They left from the Wollongong light aircraft field, Albion Park.

On the flight Visscher broke the rules. He was not trained or qualified to fly light aircraft through cloud and this international breach of procedure almost cost him and his passengers their lives.

En route to the Australian alps the Cessna flew over thick cloud. The applicable rule required Visscher to abort the flight if he could not obtain a visual position or 'fix' every thirty minutes. With what he later described as stupidity, bravado and ego, Visscher decided to break the rules—'just a little bit'. He decided to fly through the cloud to a lower level to get a visual fix on the Cessna's position. But soon he became completely disorientated. A crash seemed inevitable. The aircraft went into a frightening spin towards earth with Visscher and his three passengers screaming as gravitational pressure increased to nearly unbearable levels. Loose items flew violently around the cabin of the Cessna. All the perspex of the aircraft's windscreen and side windows shattered. Visscher pulled the aircraft up from its nosedive just in time, only to have the phenomenon repeated soon after. Having no bearing on the horizon and flying in heavy cloud, Visscher felt his aircraft spiralling into another uncontrolled nosedive. There was sheer terror as he and his passengers confronted their deaths. They screamed and screamed with wind and sleet tearing through the broken windscreen at their faces as the Cessna gathered pace and plunged to earth. Visscher, holding the controls and trying to read the altimeter, did not know what to do and for a fleeting moment thought the only thing to do was to pray. Then he managed to pull out of the terrifying dive and for a brief moment the four aboard saw a patch of treetops whisk past no more than ten metres below. The cloud base had descended to ground level. Sighting the treetops was to be their salvation. But first, there was another ordeal to endure.

Visscher made an instantaneous and radical decision. If he kept on going in the thick cloud he believed he would inevitably drive the Cessna into the surrounding foothills. He did not know how to navigate the plane out of its predicament. He and the others could barely see the green treetops just under the aircraft as they finally flew straight and level. Visscher made a decision then and there that he would have to land the aircraft on the treetops. To go on was madness and certain destruction. Visscher went into a landing pattern and brought the aircraft into the seemingly flat (30 metres) treetops. The Cessna almost glided to a halt at the top of the canopy with the tail making first impact, but as it thrashed through the tops of the trees its wings were ripped off and the aircraft disintegrated, spewing aviation fuel through the shattered windows, saturating the passengers, flooding the cabin and overflowing through the broken doors. The cabin of the aircraft containing Visscher and his three companions fell through the trees to the ground below. One spark and they would have been incinerated. Visscher was the only one with any injury, a split eyebrow.

When the Cessna came to rest, Visscher and his passengers disentangled themselves from the wreckage. They had crash-landed south of Fitzroy Falls. In the following hours a search was started but due to the persistent cloud it was two days before the wreckage was sighted. Eventually a rescue helicopter from the Naval vessel HMAS *Albatross* reached them and winched them up from a clearing 150 metres from the crash site.

The incident was to cost Visscher his unrestricted pilot's licence following the Civil Aviation Authority's investigation, and rightly so. A rescue photograph of the four at Fitzroy Falls made front page of *The Sydney Morning Herald*. The official investigation of the crash also took up five pages in the *Air Safety Digest* (No. 75) July issue in 1971.

He has never forgotten the words of the Air Safety investigator who interrogated him: 'Your courage in crash landing has without doubt saved your lives. However, you broke the rules, and may have killed three innocent passengers. With regard to the safety of your passengers you have no right—no discretion. You broke the rules and the sheer accident of your survival doesn't change a thing. By observing the rules you wouldn't have put the aircraft into a dangerous situation in the first place'.

For Tim Visscher it was a salutary lesson about the rules of safety. 'Through stupidity, bravado and ego I had placed the lives of three innocent people in jeopardy. The enormity of what I had done stayed with me every day. The preservation of human life is paramount. I had "totalled" an aeroplane but the human considerations are far more important.'

The preservation of human life was also paramount eight years later when Visscher's trawler, the *Illawarra Range*, caught fire.

Off to Court

THE VENTURE to fish for prawns and scallops in Queensland waters
had been a commercial success. The *Illawarra Range* became the
industry's top-producing boat. Visscher worked at it determinedly—
spending more than 300 days at sea each year. In 1977 he and his
crew of four produced 17.4 per cent of all scallops caught in the
state and many of his production records still stand. Through the
eight years that the venture existed he managed to retain almost
the same crew, about ten in all, 'young blokes' who would not stick
around if they thought they were being exploited. Visscher was a
good skipper, teaching them all he knew about making nets, catching
prawns and running a trawler—hard lessons he had learned from
his hard years working as a young boy on his father's boat, the
Lake Illawarra.

But the *Illawarra Range* was destroyed in 1979 off Yeppoon in
Central Queensland. The three crew were sleeping in the forecastle,
near the engine room, when Visscher noticed smoke and flames. His
first action was not to attend to the fire but to rouse the crew and get
them to safety. The fire was eventually extinguished but the *Illawarra
Range* was taking water fast and, despite their efforts, was sinking.
Visscher managed to get out a mayday on the trawler's radio before
scrambling with the crew onto a liferaft. After two days at sea the four
were rescued. Visscher had watched, devastated, as the boat he had
built himself and operated so successfully went down.

The family company filed an insurance claim but it was
contested by the insurer who only offered a partial payout of its
then insured value. The Visscher family sued and won in the
Queensland Supreme Court. The insurer appealed and the Visscher
family won again in the Court of Appeal. Visscher's action in not
attending to the fire before the crew had been awakened and their
safety secured was queried by lawyers for the insurer but was not
pressed. The insurer planned to appeal the case further, this time
to the Privy Council in England. To help fund the case Visscher
got work as the skipper of a prawn freezer trawler for the Lombardo
Marine Group in the Gulf of Carpentaria. But while he was away
at sea the insurer made an out-of-court settlement to the Visscher
family which was only marginally below the claimed payout. The

family company accepted the offer, much to Visscher's disgust, although he acknowledged they received costs for the litigation to that date.

Visscher toyed with the idea of building a large freezer trawler equipped with modern technology to stay at sea for long periods. However there were strains within the family at the time and this venture did not proceed.

Commercial Seafaring

INSTEAD he headed for Fremantle Technical College in 1981 and emerged with a certificate of competence as a Master of vessels under 300 tonnes. He was employed driving ocean-going dredges for the Westham Dredging Company before a downturn in the industry made him redundant.

He went back to school and funded himself through college again to gain a maritime qualification to work on foreign-going ships. In 1981 he married Sandra. Their marriage lasted five years and ended amicably.

Equipped with a Master Class III qualification he joined Associated Steamships in 1983 and after a year on coastal vessels he was assigned to the Belgian-owned *TNT Express* then under construction at the Samsung Shipyard in South Korea. On board the *TNT Express*, which travelled the world, Visscher was promoted from Fourth Mate to Third, Second and eventually First Mate. *TNT Express* was one of the last foreign-owned, Australian-manned container vessels. At the time the Australian Seamen's Union was picketing the Brisbane and Sydney offices of the Columbus Line to try to pressure the company to retain Australian crews on foreign-owned vessels.

In 1989 Belgian owners decided to replace the Australian crew on the *TNT Express* and Visscher was reassigned by Australian Steamships to oil tankers, in particular the *Mobil Flinders*.

In the Persian Gulf in 1991, with the fires from the burning oil wells of Kuwait in the distance, Visscher was seriously injured in an accident. During a night shift he fell down a stairway which was obstructed by a line inappropriately strung across it by the maintenance crew who were painting the area. Visscher suffered a fractured skull and spine and had to be repatriated ashore. It took twelve months to recover. When he got back to work Australian Steamships reassigned him to coastal work aboard the oil products tanker *Mawson*.

Track Record

SEEKING new challenges Visscher resigned from the company and took a job with BHP Petroleum as a Second Mate joining the FPSO *Jabiru Venture* operating in the Timor Sea.

When he went aboard the *Jabiru Venture* Visscher sensed immediately the standards were slack. The procedures were not as tightly supervised and regulated as they had been on the Australian Steamships vessels he had worked on. Visscher verbally reported his concerns about safety procedures to BHP Petroleum management aboard and to senior management in Darwin. In his own time he drew isometric plans of the *Jabiru Venture*'s pump room, underdeck and on deck pipelines. Such plans were required to be readily available but were not in existence in any useable format. These same plans were later incorporated into official company drawings and formed the basis of operational safety improvements on the *Jabiru Venture*.

He also drew to the attention of *Jabiru Venture* management his concerns over breaches of safe tanker practice which could have resulted in explosions. He found that his concerns were not being properly addressed so he told local Darwin shore-side management with the same lack of result.

He worked on without further complaint from March to October that year—four weeks on, four weeks off, twelve hours on, twelve hours off—until he was assigned to the *Griffin Venture* off the northwest shelf of Western Australia. By this time he was forty-four and had remarried.

He spoke of his concerns about the *Jabiru Venture* to the BHP Petroleum manager at Dampier who dissuaded him from putting in a written report to head office in Melbourne. Instead, on instructions, he submitted the report to the Dampier manager. Six weeks later the Darwin manager wrote to Visscher thanking him for his concerns and assuring him they would be independently assessed. Several months later and with no copy of the findings forthcoming Visscher heard that he was not to receive a copy. Apparently they were considered too hot and the company could not risk their ending up in the public domain. Much later, on 7 November 1995, Visscher received a letter from the Federal Minister for Resources which stated that as a result of ministerial intervention the Northern Territory Department of Mines and Energy had investigated practices aboard the *Jabiru Venture* and found that some practices were indeed unsafe.

29 May 1994

BUT nothing in Visscher's past and his now extensive maritime experience could equip him for what was about to happen aboard the *Griffin Venture*.

On 29 May 1994 he was to confront the most powerful corporation in Australia. And when an individual took on the corporation the individual would invariably lose. Everything Visscher had learnt about safety from his training, peers and hard experience would count for nothing against the corporate interests of BHP, no matter what the circumstances.

Visscher attended the 'toolbox' meeting aboard *Griffin Venture* on 26 May where the Master outlined the gas-freeing operation planned for 29 May. At this well-attended meeting of senior production, engineering and maritime staff, Visscher asserts he raised his concern about there being no appropriate calibration gas available to check the operation and accuracy of the gas detections instruments. He was talked down on this point by the Master and the Chief Engineer, the Master making the point that the calibration gas was not a requirement and that he knew more about gas freeing than anyone else employed by the company.

Gas-freeing operations began as planned during the early hours of 29 May. From the start Visscher was on duty and used the Tankscope to monitor hydrocarbon gas levels in 3C tank as it was being purged with inert gas. Under the Master's orders the pressure in the tank was kept artificially high by restricting the outlet gases from the tank. Visscher soon determined the development of a depressed hydrocarbon layer in the lower regions of the tank. He calculated from this that the operation would take much longer than planned. He went off duty at 8.30 am on 29 May.

When he came back on deck at 6.30 pm to resume work he went to the area above 1C tank at the bow of the 240 metre vessel. He was scheduled to relieve his workmate in the tank-clearing operations. According to Visscher's evidence at later inquiries his workmate told him that both 1C and 3C tanks had been hot water washed and that 3C tank had completed inert gas purging. 1C tank was nearing completion of inert gas (IG) purging. Visscher asserts that his workmate informed him that, as soon as 1C was purged, gas freeing of 3C and 1C would commence—the tanks would be exposed to the atmosphere with air being blown into the tanks by high volume fans.

'The officer I was relieving told me that the hydrocarbon gas concentrations in 3C was 0 per cent throughout the tank and that the hydrocarbon gas concentrations in 1C was 1 per cent at the top of the tank to 4 per cent at the bottom of the tank.' It was the industry rule that hydrocarbon levels in a storage tank must not be greater than 2 per cent by volume or the risk of explosion was increased.

The IG purging operations were taking longer than planned, adding to the pressure on board that day. As a consequence, it seemed that major departures were being made from the work instruction to allow oil production to resume as soon as possible. To allow the further IG purging of 1C and the subsequent gas freeing of both 1C and 3C, Visscher says he noticed that temporary purge pipes had been fitted to the tanks. These were not fitted with flame screens and were not electrically bonded to earth.

Visscher says that he also noticed that his workmate was not using the Tankscope in the monitoring of hydrocarbon levels but another instrument—an LV analyser. Visscher asked his workmate why he was using the LV analyser.

'He told me, "the Tankscope's no good". I said, "What's wrong with the Tankscope?" He said, "it's reading too much hydrocarbon gas".'

Visscher asked how he knew that the Tankscope was reading

too much hydrocarbon gas. (The only way of determining the correct operation of the gas detection instruments is by reading the appropriate calibration gas—a gas which was not then on board the *Griffin Venture*). Visscher's workmate replied that the Tankscope reading had been compared to three LV instruments and that all LV instruments read the same—each LV instrument indicated 6 per cent lower hydrocarbon gas than the Tankscope.

Visscher's evidence was that he was told at that time that the Tankscope had been discarded about half an hour after he went off shift earlier that morning, an action agreed to by the Master of the *Griffin Venture*, the First Mate and another Second Mate. At that time the First Mate arrived at 1C tank and Visscher expressed his concerns about the discarding of the Tankscope. The First Mate told him it was the correct thing to do and refused to discuss it further. Visscher then called the Master on the radio telling him that he was not happy about the gas detection instruments and asking for permission to check both types of instrument on an available 'makeshift' calibration gas. The Master replied, 'No, don't do that'.

Visscher was confronted with a dilemma. On board the *Griffin Venture*, as on all other BHP offshore vessels, the Master was in charge of all tanker operations. There was a strict chain of command, necessary for safety and good order aboard, and Visscher had been given a direct order by the Master not to check the operation of the instruments. But he believed common sense and any semblance of proper professional conduct had been discarded along with the Tankscope at 9 am—all in the name of cutting corners to get oil production back on line as quickly as possible.

A firm believer in the chain of command, Visscher had never before disobeyed an order from his superiors. However he believed the Tankscope had been discarded because the LV instrument was telling senior officers on the *Griffin Venture* what they wanted to see: low hydrocarbon gas readings in the tanks. He also knew the only way to obtain any sort of comprehensive factual data had to include checking of the instruments on the only calibration gas available. This would amount to a direct confrontation with the Master and could involve disobeying the direct order of the Master. He was also aware, too, that if the Tankscope was reading correctly, they were in all probability going to gas free the tanks in such a way that the atmosphere in the tanks would pass through the explosive range. This was to be avoided at all costs.

Visscher recovered the Tankscope with other discarded and previously used items of equipment near 3C tank. Collecting one of the LV instruments as well he went to the ship's workshop near the central control room and checked both types of instruments with the makeshift calibration gas. The analogue Tankscope indicated a hydrocarbon gas reading of 2.6 per cent while the digital LV instrument indicated a hydrocarbon gas reading of 3 per cent, indicating that both types of instruments were reading correctly on the makeshift calibration gas, which, according to the certificate of contention the gas canister contained 2.5% hydrocarbon gas. Visscher compiled sufficient data to disqualify the LV instrument and make a decision that in all likelihood the Tankscope would indicate the correct concentrations of hydrocarbon gas in the storage tanks. Visscher believes this decision, later proved to be correct, saved the *Griffin Venture* from possible destruction. At 8.15 pm, Visscher took the Tankscope on deck and measured gas from the top section of 3C tank using the Tankscope. This sample is taken by inserting a 1-metre length of hose attached to the Tankscope into a special sampling valve on the deck. The sample gas is then drawn through the hose and into the sample chamber of the instrument. A dial arm on the Tankscope indicates the level of hydrocarbon gas against a fixed graduated scale.

Visscher then took the Tankscope on deck and measured gas from the top section on 3C tank using the Tankscope.

The reading I got was 9 per cent.

Nine per cent! I thought ... this can't be. I checked the instrument. I repeated the samples. It was 9 per cent. This same tank, 3C, was thought by all to be ready to gas free as it was supposed to have 0 per cent hydrocarbon according to the LV instrument.

Faced with the alarming reading Visscher sought out the First Mate, physically showing him the Tankscope with the 9 per cent reading on the display. 'I told him: "If we gas free we will go through the explosive range ...".'

From that moment Tim Visscher was on a collision course with BHP.

According to Visscher, the First Mate reacted angrily and with personal abuse.

> The First Mate's reply was along the lines of, 'Yes Tim. You're right. We're wrong. If we had the calibration gas we'd know for sure wouldn't we?' Then a profanity and, 'You're real smart. You're a real smart fellow' ... and off he went. I called after him, 'that's not the point I'm trying to make, can you please come back and discuss this'. The First Mate kept on walking.

Desperately wanting some sort of positive decision to address his alarm, Visscher called the Master on the radio at 8.30 pm and asked him to come to 3C tank. The Master arrived a few minutes later, and according to inquiry evidence, the Master witnessed Visscher take a 9 per cent hydrocarbon gas reading from 3C with the Tankscope. While taking the reading Visscher explained to the Master the checks that he had just carried out on both types of instrument using the makeshift calibration gas.

Visscher said: 'I was then abused by the Master, along the lines of, "I told you not to do that. I ordered you not to do that. Can't you do what you are told." The Master then walked away from me'.

By this time Visscher was frantic. He had advised the two most senior deck officers on the *Griffin Venture* of a most dangerous situation and they had walked away. Was gas freeing going to proceed in spite of his objections? Was he powerless to stop it?

What happened next became a matter for hot dispute. Visscher's version is that only because he broke ranks and took his concerns to the Field Superintendant, the only other authority then aboard the *Griffin Venture*, was the gas-freeing operation called off that night. He believed he had no choice but to break the chain of command. He consciously refused to contemplate his fate thereafter. Taking another gas sample he walked fifteen metres to where the Field Superintendent was standing with the oil production supervisor. The time was 9 pm. Visscher briefed the Field Superintendent on all that had happened, showed him the Tankscope reading and concluded: 'If we gas free 3C the atmosphere in the tank will pass through the explosive range'.

The Field Superintendent agreed with Visscher that the Tank-scope reading was alarming and said: 'If you are not happy we will err on the side of caution, we will not gas free, we will continue inert gas purging until the appropriate calibration gas arrives. Only then can we be sure of the instrument readings and that it is safe to gas free'. Tim Visscher was at last relieved.

According to the Field Superintendent's later evidence to BHP Petroleum's own internal inquiry: 'In discussion with the Master, the Field Superintendent said that if there was any doubt about the gas-freeing operation it would have to stop. The Master agreed that he would not proceed with the next stage which was gas freeing. The first indication that the Field Superintendent had concerning problems with the gas analyser equipment was when Visscher approached him 29/2100'.

Later That Evening—29 May 1994

THE central control room on the *Griffin Venture* contains state of the art computerised panels which control all facets of oil well head control, oil and gas production, power generation and pumping crude oil to off-take tankers.

At 9.30 pm Visscher went to the control room. The Master was there with the LV instrument manual open on the control panel. According to Visscher, the Master indicated the manual and asked Visscher if he had calibrated the instruments with the correct calibration gas in accordance with the manufacturer's specifications and instructions. Visscher was dumbfounded. He had not calibrated the instruments. He repeated his earlier statement that he had made no calibration or alteration to the instruments and that he had simply checked them by running a makeshift calibration gas through the instruments and checking the reading. The Master then became abusive and finally the Field Superintendent approached both the Master and Visscher and broke up the argument.

The Field Superintendent and the Master retired to their cabins just before midnight. Visscher was left with written orders to continue inert gas purging 1C and 3C tanks overnight. The written orders also required him to equalise the fluid levels in the aft slop tanks, pump ballast, transfer crude oil cargo between storage tanks, perform loading and stability computer entries and to set level alarms on the crude oil storage tanks. The sailor normally assigned to assist Visscher was sent to bed by the Master. Visscher was left the deck watch alone.

30 May 1994

To prevent explosions in cargo tanks it is a requirement that the maximum oxygen content of the inert gas be no greater than 5 per cent.

Unknown to Visscher the oxygen sensor for the inert gas system had been problematic and *Griffin Venture* engineers had resorted to taking half hourly manual samples of the oxygen while inert gas was being produced. This is a clear contravention of the requirement that the oxygen content of the inert gas must be *continually* monitored. At 2.30 am Visscher was on deck monitoring gas pressures in the cargo oil tanks when he was called on the radio by the duty production operator stationed in the control room and advised that there was an alarm on the inert gas control panel. Visscher went to the control room immediately to investigate and, following normal procedure, woke the duty engineer by telephone, in this case the Chief Engineer, to attend to the problem. The Chief Engineer was also unsuccessful in resetting the inert gas alarm in the normal way and resorted to manipulating the electrical equipment inside the inert gas electrical control box. In this fashion the inert gas alarm was reset by the Chief Engineer at 3 am and purging of the tanks continued. Visscher made the following entry in the Log Book: '0300 I/G alarm. C/E called'.

Later in the morning the Master queried Visscher about the log book entry. In his evidence at an internal BHP Petroleum inquiry more than three months later, the Chief Engineer was to personally criticise Visscher. The Chief Engineer emphatically denied getting out of bed at three in the morning to attend the inert gas alarm.

At 7.30 am on the morning on 30 May, Visscher completed

gas samplings from 3C tank with the Tankscope. He recorded all of the readings in his notebook, then entered his readings in the log book. Provided the Tankscope was functioning accurately, the maximum reading of 2 per cent hydrocarbon gas inferred that 3C tank was now ready to gas free—but only just ready.

During the sampling another officer came on deck with the intention of taking gas readings in 3C tank using the LV instrument. Visscher allowed the other officer to take simultaneous readings with him and they compared their readings. During these comparative readings, with the Tankscope indicating between 1 per cent and 2 per cent hydrocarbon gas, the LV instrument indicated minus 1 per cent, minus 0 per cent and 0 per cent hydrocarbon gas. The minus readings on the LV instrument clearly showed that it was not indicating correctly and was in obvious error.

To further compare the instruments, Visscher and the other officer took a single reading from the bottom of 1C tank. The Tankscope indicated 8 per cent hydrocarbon gas and the LV instrument indicated 2 per cent hydrocarbon gas. Visscher commented to his colleague: 'How do you feel now? The LV indicates 2 per cent and you could gas free on that. There is 8 per cent in the tank and you would kill us all'.

At the completion of the readings Visscher went to the control room to enter the results in the log book. Meanwhile, unknown to him, the supply boat had arrived at about 8 am and unloaded two new Tankscopes as well as several canisters of the proper calibration gas. The proper calibration gas has a mix of 15 per cent carbon dioxide and 85 per cent nitrogen. Into this mix 8 per cent of butane is added.

One of the new Tankscopes was checked against the proper calibration gas and found to be functioning correctly. The First Mate and another officer then proceeded to take a full set of gas samples from 3C tank. This was a duplicate of the gas samples that Visscher had just taken as 3C tank had been dormant and isolated from 6.30 am when the inert gas purging was switched to 1C tank.

The results obtained with the new Tankscope ranged from a minimum of 1 per cent to a maximum of 2 per cent hydrocarbon gas. The results were entered into the deck log at 10.15 am. The readings from the second set of comprehensive gas samples from

3C tank were identical to the results obtained by Visscher a few hours earlier with the old Tankscope.

This proved beyond doubt that the old Tankscope was reading correctly and that 3C tank in fact contained 9 per cent hydrocarbon.

31 May

VISSCHER was getting 'feedback' from other sectors of the personnel on board warning him about his position. At 6 am on 31 May, Visscher had taken another set of comprehensive gas readings of 3C tank to check the progress of gas freeing the tank. This time the gas checks were for man entry into the tank, that is, gas samples to determine if the atmosphere in the tank was toxic free and suitable to sustain human life. The atmosphere had to be equivalent to fresh air. His sampling confirmed that the tank was in fact safe for human entry.

At about 6.30 on the same morning, unknown to Visscher, another deck officer tested the atmosphere in 3C tank. He found high readings of toxic gases and determined that the atmosphere inside would quickly kill any unsuspecting person entering the tank. Instead of re-checking the reading, this officer hurried to report his findings.

This new gas sample made a mockery of Visscher's 6 am reading and subsequent log book entry. This would prove Visscher's incompetence and provide sufficient grounds for his dismissal. The First Mate and Visscher were passing each other in the accommodation block when the other deck officer approached breathlessly and declared that no one was going into 3C tank that day. He reported the results of his gas sampling and concluded: 'Anyone entering 3C tank would perish'.

Visscher was speechless. What could have happened to the atmosphere of a tank he had just reported as being safe? The First Mate instructed Visscher to go back with the deck officer and recheck the readings in 3C tank.

The 3C tank is typical of all the huge storage tanks on the *Griffin Venture*. To take gas samples in the lower reaches of the tanks a sample hose over 24 metres in length must be used. On reaching 3C tank the other deck officer lowered the long sample hose into the tank and connected the hose to a special gas detection instrument that simultaneously measures low concentrations of dangerous gases as well as the absolute volume of oxygen. Sure enough, all the alarms on the instrument sounded in unison.

Visscher had observed the process in silence. He then said: 'Let me teach you something I learnt a long time ago. Let's wait for one minute and while we're waiting disconnect the sample hose from the instrument and let the internal pressure inside the tank purge all the resident gases out of the sample hose'. With the sample hose disconnected and purging the two men waited out the minute. All the following readings from the long sample hose confirmed Visscher's earlier samples and log book entry. The tank was indeed ready for human entry. It was the long sample hose which contained toxic gasses—not the tank.

Visscher's life on board the *Griffin Venture* had been made a misery from the time of the incident on 29 May. He would go to sit for his meal at a communal mess room table only to watch those already sitting get up to move to other seating.

Days without sleep followed the incident. Watching your back in an isolated and hostile atmosphere was an exhausting process.

Pressure Takes Its Toll

VISSCHER was scheduled to board an off-take tanker tied astern the *Griffin Venture* on 3 June. His duties were concerned with safety, which required him to remain alert. Without sleep for several days, he wrote a letter to the Field Superintendent and declared himself to be fatigued and applied to be repatriated ashore as soon as possible.

He wrote another letter dated 2 June 1994 to the Field Superintendent of the *Griffin Venture*:

> Dear Sir, I am of the firm view that tanker (gas-freeing) operations on the *Griffin Venture* are not being carried out in a proper and safe manner. It is my intention to request to the Company that I not be reassigned to the *Griffin Venture*. Yours sincerely, Tim Visscher.

He delivered his letter to the Field Superintendent soon after 6 am on 2 June. He was asked to reconsider and remain aboard. He declined.

He encountered the Master in the stairwell only moments after leaving the Field Superintendent's office and told him he had requested to be sent ashore. The Master replied without hesitation: 'You'll be on the next helicopter'.

At 6.45 am Visscher was in the ship's mess having coffee with two cooks who were among the only people still prepared to be seen in his company. According to his version the Master stormed into the mess room saying: 'I want to see you outside—now!'

He obviously had read the two letters. According to Visscher, outside the mess the Master screamed obscene abuse. Visscher protested. The Master finally walked away with the parting words: 'You can't prove a thing, you can't prove a fucking thing'.

At that time Visscher had never considered proving anything. But with the Master's words ringing in his ears he went to the control room and photocopied every relevant document that was to hand. The copies of the gas record sheets were a dog-eared mess. Visscher took the originals.

The First Inquiry

WHEN his helicopter arrived at Karratha Airport at Dampier Visscher was required to see the local manager of BHP Petroleum. He already had a copy of the two letters he had given the Field Superintendent on board the *Griffin Venture* that morning. Visscher pleaded to be allowed to sleep before answering any questions about what had happened. The manager replied reassuringly that it was all right, he wanted to hear the story immediately. He was going to investigate the matter.

Visscher then alleged that gas freeing had been going to take place on board the *Griffin Venture* when the atmosphere in the cargo tanks was going to pass through the explosive range. His actions had prevented this from happening. The manager took a careful note. Inexplicably to Visscher, the manager did not ask for substantiation, after Visscher asserted that he could back up his allegations with documentation—he had the gas records.

Visscher's flight home to Newcastle was cancelled and he was instructed to stay in Dampier for a few days. He was then advised by the Dampier manager that the Master of the *Griffin Venture* disputed his claims about gas freeing with an explosive tank atmosphere.

Visscher needed help from someone he could trust. He telephoned John Holland, a friend from his early childhood who lived in Brisbane and told him of the events of the previous week. Holland, an engineer and expert in corporate process, worked as the chief executive of a large engineering company. Visscher confided to Holland that he was thinking about resigning from BHP Petroleum and preserving what he could of his career. Holland was astounded at what Visscher had disclosed and questioned him at length about the details, finally saying: 'Tim, I think you're full of bullshit. We were both born and bred in Port Kembla and we both know that BHP doesn't do those sorts of things. They're a professional outfit and do things properly'. Visscher assured his friend that he was not exaggerating and the *Griffin Venture* could have been destroyed. Holland eventually replied: 'If half of what you say is true, they'll want you to resign and that will be the end of you and the end of the issue'. Visscher undertook to Holland not to resign until they had met face to face to talk things through.

On Monday 6 June the Dampier manager called Visscher at his motel and asked him to come into the office at 2.30 pm. When Visscher entered he found the assistant Marine Superintendent there too. This officer was a senior Master with the company. The Dampier manager then presented Visscher with the findings of his investigation.

1. All the people involved with the gas freeing had been interviewed.
2. He could find no evidence that gas freeing was going to take place at the time Visscher mentioned in his statement.
3. The Master of the *Griffin Venture* had declared that before gas freeing would have taken place, final hydrocarbon gas readings would have been taken.
4. The Master had declared that before gas freeing would have taken place there would have been a meeting and everyone

would have been in agreement that the operation was safe.

5. Visscher had over-pressured 3C cargo tank while taking gas readings on 1 June and the tank was not protected at the time.

Visscher was dumbfounded by the allegations that he had overpressured the tank and refuted the claim, suggesting this issue was a 'red herring' and an attempt to 'set me up'.

The Dampier manager concluded that his allegations of unsafe tanker practices were unsubstantiated and that his claims were groundless.

Visscher asked that he not be sent back to the *Griffin Venture*, saying that retribution would be made against him because he had broken the 'code' by taking his concerns about the 9 per cent hydrocarbon reading over the Master's head to the Field Superintendent. But the manager was not interested in further discussion and the meeting ended.

On Tuesday 7 June Visscher put all his evidence into a large brown envelope and mailed it to his solicitor. He worked at Dampier for two days and protested again that his position would be untenable if he was required to return to the *Griffin Venture*. He was reminded that he still had two weeks of his four-week tour remaining. He was asked if he was now refusing duty.

Visscher stated to the manager that he did not accept his findings clearing the *Griffin Venture* of unsafe practices but, realising that to be seen to refuse duty could be a breach of his employment conditions, he agreed to return. He rejoined the *Griffin Venture* on 9 June and was back on deck duty at midnight. The Master had completed his tour and was replaced. The next day Visscher telephoned the Australian office of the manufacturer of the LV Gas analyser. The product manager (Instrumentation) sent a fax addressed to the Master of the *Griffin Venture* which supported Visscher's judgement that in gas-freeing operations the Tankscope, not the LV analyser, should be used.

Visscher was given a dressing down by the Field Superintendent for having made telephone calls without permission.

During the morning of his second day back, Visscher wanted to drill some holes to mount a fire extinguisher bracket. The *Griffin Venture* had a system of permits to work which ensured that safety and procedure were complied with. The permits had to be approved and endorsed by all the relevant department heads and by the Field Superintendent. This was done. But when Visscher went to the workshop to get tools the Field Superintendent stormed in and in an intemperate outburst told him he was not to work outside his watch.

Visscher was shocked. He said he had a work permit signed by the Field Superintendent authorising the work outside his normal shift. He was instructed not to do the work.

Visscher cancelled and filed the work permit and went to his cabin to enter the details of the conversation in his diary. The Master rang through and asked him to come immediately to his room.

As soon as he entered he saw the Field Superintendent who said: 'This is a counselling session'.

Visscher was told that he looked fatigued. He replied that he had just spent a week in a motel at Karratha and felt fine. He was then asked if he had been drinking alcohol. 'No. I have not been drinking,' he replied. Alcohol is strictly prohibited on *Griffin Venture* and drinking is punishable by instant dismissal.

He was asked if he had been taking drugs. 'No. I have not been taking drugs.'

He was asked if he would like to go home. 'No. I do not want to go home. I will complete my tour.'

'Just say the word and you can go home and be with your wife tomorrow.'

Visscher declined. He declined again when he was told all his costs would be paid by the company. He was becoming distressed.

'You (Field Superintendent) and you (Master) want me off the *Griffin Venture*. You will never hear me ask to go home early. I'll finish my tour. If you want me off then you send me off and we'll address the issues as they arise.'

The Field Superintendent suggested that Visscher should consider his position with the company. Visscher replied: 'I will not be resigning from the company'.

Visscher returned to his room and recorded all the details of the work counselling session in his diary. He completed his tour on the *Griffin Venture* in an atmosphere of continuous hostility.

Duty

VISSCHER arrived home at Newcastle on 23 June and was suprised when John Holland answered the door bell. Holland took one look at his friend and made him sit down immediately on a table inside the front door. 'Tim, just sit there and take it easy. Your skin is grey. Your eyes are sunken. I have never seen anyone look so bad.' Visscher was almost incoherent from exhaustion and stress. It would be another hour and two cups of tea before Visscher left the table.

By three o'clock the following morning Holland had heard all Visscher's story and at the end of it he asked a simple question: 'What do you want?'

'I want the truth on the table. I want management to know what's happening out there and I don't want it to happen again.'

After going to Sydney to finish some business Holland returned to Newcastle two days later. Visscher had been asleep most of this time. The two then set to work to lay out a strategy:

1. What is the problem? 2. Is the problem solvable? Do we have the resources? 3. How can the problem be solved? 4. What are our strengths and where are we vulnerable? 5. What are their strengths and what are their weaknesses?

The following week Visscher received a telephone call from an FPSO in the Timor Sea. The 'word' on the grapevine was that the Master had thrown Visscher off the *Griffin Venture* and that Visscher had been altering the settings on the gas detection instruments. Visscher's name was being blackguarded through BHP Petroleum. Another call came from a colleague who had heard that Visscher caused unnecessary and costly delays on the *Griffin Venture*. Wanting more information, Visscher feigned applying for a job and started phoning other shipping companies. He was told that no one in the industry would ever give him a job because he had tampered with gas detection instruments on the *Griffin Venture* while carrying out a gas-freeing operation and that he could have caused an explosion.

Visscher was shocked when told that the basis for the 'bad word' on him was a report written by the Master of the *Griffin Venture*. On his personal undertaking of confidentiality for the source, Visscher was faxed a copy.

The report's cover, dated 8 June 1994, was headed with a BHP logo but gave no instruction limiting its distribution. It made several references to Visscher 'tampering' with the gas detection instruments on the *Griffin Venture* during a gas-freeing operation.

On 29 June 1994 Visscher faxed a request to the Marine Superintendent that he not be reassigned to the *Griffin Venture*:

> Gas freeing operations were carried out on the *Griffin Venture* on 29.5.94 to allow man entry into No. 1 and No. 3 cargo oil tanks. It is my view that the gas-freeing operation was not carried out in a safe and proper manner in that air was going to be introduced into the cargo oil tanks such that the atmosphere in the cargo oil tanks would have been well within the explosive range. My objection and intervention prevented the above from happening. The Dampier manager has investigated this matter and has determined that my objections were unfounded. I do not agree with his findings. I found that my subsequent service on the *Griffin Venture* was untenable. In view of the above, I request that I not be reassigned to the *Griffin Venture*.

On 9 July he faxed a letter to the Dampier manager of BHP Petroleum. He asked for copies of documents and said what he had heard. He also wrote:

> You have investigated this matter and all of the people involved with the gas freeing have been interviewed. After your investigation you have determined that my claims cannot be substantiated. You informed me of this on Wednesday 8 June, and asked me to rejoin the *Griffin Venture* and complete the remaining two weeks of my current tour of duty. I replied to you that I did not accept your findings and that my position on the *Griffin Venture* would be untenable. Over the last few weeks I have received feedback from several of our facilities that strongly indicates that my good name, both professionally and personally, has been defamed. I have spoken to a human resources officer on this point who advised that I bring my concerns to the attention of the Production Manager. I have decided to take the advice and will seek an appointment with the Production Manager. I will be in Melbourne on about Friday, 15 July.

The Dampier manager replied to Visscher's letter stating that due to confidentiality he was unable to supply a copy of the report. The manager also said he was unaware of any defamation and encouraged Visscher to provide any factual information to him for investigation.

Visscher wrote again to the manager saying among other things:

I do not see the need to keep your report confidential nor the need to carry out your investigation in confidence. My interview with you in your office on 2 June 1994, with the Production and Engineering Superintendent in attendance, was objective and made no personal references. The points that I raised and the allegations that I made relate directly to the safety of the *Griffin Venture*. As I said at this meeting, gas freeing was going to be carried out on the *Griffin Venture* such that the atmosphere in the cargo oil tanks would have been well within the explosive range. This would be a most dangerous situation and potentially catastrophic. As the person raising the issues I feel that it is reasonable that I be given copies of the reports and statements as requested in my letter to you dated 9 July 1994.

... If I do obtain substantial factual evidence [on the defamation matter] and if I do provide you with the evidence, I feel inclined not to do so in confidence. My view being that anything I have to say or write is objective and open and may be made known to any concerned party.

... I am joining the *Jabiru Venture* on 19 July 1994. I do not know the duration of my forthcoming tour, however, when I know of the completion date I will write to the Production Manager and request a meeting with him. It is my intention to advise the Production Manager of several safety issues including the gas freeing on the *Griffin Venture*. It is my view that I would be negligent in my duty if I failed to do so. I will also make it known to the Production Manager that I have been defamed.

Visscher returned to duty and on arrival in Darwin went to the local BHP Petroleum office as instructed where he met a hostile Marine Superintendent who remonstrated with him on his previous report on the *Jabiru Venture* and his involvement in the *Griffin*

Venture incident. Visscher was instructed not to put things in writing in future, later modified to making verbal reports to the Marine Superintendent first.

Visscher joined the *Jabiru Venture* as planned and in the following weeks sent faxes to senior management in Melbourne requesting the opportunity to make a presentation of the facts relating to the *Griffin Venture* incident.

After all the aggravation from company officials, Visscher was advised on 3 August 1994 that he was to attend a meeting in the Melbourne office of BHP on 10 August. Visscher contacted his friend John Holland and asked him to join him in Melbourne. He was going to make a presentation to BHP Petroleum's senior management. Also attending would be the Dampier manager.

They arrived at 10 am. The presentation was scheduled for one or two hours. Visscher read from his own hastily prepared notes and used an overhead projector to fill in details. It was a marathon effort. With time for questions the presentation ended just after 6 pm. Visscher and Holland were asked to leave the senior managers alone for twenty minutes so they could confer in private. When they resumed, the Production Manager proposed that an independent inquiry of experts be set up to investigate and report on the issues and that Visscher be involved with the selection of the investigators and setting the terms of reference.

Visscher was straight-faced when told by the officials that his request for a copy of the personal work counselling report aboard the *Griffin Venture* was unnecessary. There was no work counselling report, he was told. What happened at his meeting with the Master and the Field Superintendent was an 'informal meeting to address concerns about your welfare'. But Visscher had in his attache case a letter he had received in the mail the day before. This was a copy of a work counselling report clearly marked for internal distribution to his personal file.

The meeting ended soon after and when they were in private Holland reflected: 'Well, now I believe everything you've been saying. I had some reservations but now I have none . . . they've been swept aside'.

In denying the existence of the work counselling report it appeared that the company was covering up. Holland and Visscher resolved to fight on. They were still relying on BHP Petroleum to come to terms with the facts they had presented. They still held hopes that the company would address those facts in its own interests as well as those of its staff and its reputation for putting safety at the highest of corporate priorities.

Visscher and Holland left Melbourne the next day. Back in Newcastle, Visscher equipped the downstairs area of his house with a rebuilt computer, high speed photocopier, fax and filing system and learnt to touch type.

The Second Inquiry

TWO days after the Melbourne presentation he wrote to the Production Manager recommending a candidate for selection as investigator in the independent inquiry. Visscher's recommendation was in turn passed on to the Dampier manager who rejected it. Two subsequent nominations were also rejected. After Visscher received the terms of reference of the second inquiry it became apparent to him that the Dampier manager was in charge of its organisation and administration. The Dampier manager also referred to the forthcoming inquiry as a 'review', a reference Visscher objected to. Visscher also objected to the involvement of the Dampier manager in the second 'independent' inquiry. Although the terms of reference were expanded to accommodate some of Visscher's points, the Dampier manager continued to organise and administer the inquiry.

Visscher was unsuccessful in his efforts to have one of the terms of reference removed from the outset. It read: 'This review is to be used, not to lay blame . . .'

The second inquiry consisted of two experts, a tanker Master from an internationally renowned English consulting company specialising in maritime/tanker safety and an engineer from BHP Engineering. The inquiry started taking evidence on 2 September 1994. All of Visscher's evidence was tape recorded. Visscher was pleased that the investigators agreed that the Tankscope was the correct instrument to use to determine the level of hydrocarbon gas in the cargo oil tanks of the *Griffin Venture* and that they accepted his argument that there was 9 per cent hydrocarbon gas in 3C tank when it was previously thought there was 0 per cent.

The experts inspected the tanks and facilities aboard the *Griffin Venture* in pursuit of their objectives to 'examine the process used to control a hazardous operation in terms of procedures, work instructions, documentation, meetings, adherence to procedures, and the roles and responsibilities of all personnel concerned in the operation'.

On 11 October 1994 Visscher was instructed to attend the Sydney office of BHP Engineering to be shown a preview of The Report on Tank Operations on the *Griffin Venture* prepared by the two-man investigating team and then to attend a meeting with the Dampier and Darwin managers of BHP Petroleum. John Holland was there at his side and they met the BHP engineer who had conducted the inquiry. The managers from Dampier and Darwin were scheduled to arrive from Melbourne at 1 pm.

On instruction from the Dampier manager, Visscher was only allowed two and a half hours to view both the report and the statements of evidence. Holland was not permitted to view the documents with him. Visscher was allowed, however, to take notes.

He was devastated by what he saw. The foremost conclusion of the report of the second inquiry was that 'the *Griffin Venture* was not placed in jeopardy by the tank operations in May/June 1994'.

And the reason given in reaching this conclusion was that 'Visscher had misjudged the signs that appeared to indicate that gas freeing was about to commence when in fact there was no intention to commence gas freeing at the time'.

To Tim Visscher this was a cover-up. An inquiry required by Federal legislation (*The Petroleum–Submerged Lands–Act No. 118 of 1967* was administered by a State authority, the West Australian Department of Minerals and Energy WADOME) to address safety issues had not arrived at the inescapable conclusion that safety procedures had been breached and that as a consequence the vessel was in jeopardy.

Many of those interviewed by the review panel did not support Visscher's version of events. There were lapses of memory, for instance, about a key conversation Visscher said he had had with a workmate. There was the worrying declaration that 'the Field

Superintendent said there would be no gas freeing until the span (calibration) gas was on board. This statement was verified by the Production and Engineering Superintendent who attended the toolbox meeting'. The review team noted: 'When questioned, other attendees could not remember this statement being made'. Visscher's clash with the Master of the *Griffin Venture* and his breach of the 'golden rule' of taking his concerns to the Field Superintendent were comprehensively covered. Where there was no consensus on events between the parties, the review team highlighted the evidentiary differences or the lack of recall by particular witnesses.

Many of the findings and observations of the review team were supportive of Visscher's safety concerns. The review agreed that tank cleaning and gas freeing aboard a production and storage vessel 'is the most hazardous period of tanker operations'. It also found 'The situation was not under tight control and the potential for an incident was apparent'.

The review criticised the quality of the gas monitoring procedures. In the most hazardous operation on a production and storage vessel, the keeping of vital records which would enable any decision-maker to order operations safely were criticised: 'This is indicative of the very poor, if not abysmal, recording of the tank gas sample test results'.

On the evidence from crew interviewed, exhaustion of personnel was noted: '... a period of 27 hours or more must have been worked by ... (the Master and the First Mate). In anyone's terms this is far too long to be involved with critical operations and to be expected to make sound decisions in a rational manner. Our comment should be taken in light of the fact that the *GV* is a floating process plant ...'.

Significantly the review was confused over the equipment. 'The most commonly used analyser for this (gas monitoring) purpose is the MSA Tankscope. The *GV* was not provided with a Tankscope ... it was decided to obtain a Tankscope from the *Skua Venture* (another production and storage vessel).' The *Skua Venture* Tankscope was calibrated in the Timor Sea well before delivery to the *Griffin Venture*. Standard procedure was for the operator to calibrate to ensure the accuracy of the readings. No span gas was on the *Griffin Venture* for this purpose.

The review team admitted to being unsure about the correct use and limitation of LV equipment: 'There seems to have been an arbitrary decision made as to which analyser, Tankscope or LV, was correct. We do not condone this but realise the confusion which existed regarding these analysers'.

And there was this general finding: 'We conclude that without both the proper instruments and span gas the tank operations should never have proceeded... '.

On the intention to gas free that night Visscher was devastated to read the review parted company with his submissions: 'It is our opinion that T. Visscher has apparently misjudged the reason for the spading and purge pipe installation at 1C and 3C. It is clear that this operation was to enable production to re-start and was not a sign of the intention to gas free'. And: 'We do not find any evidence to suggest that gas freeing would take place at this time'.

The review team had therefore rejected Visscher's judgement instead of asking whether a reasonable person in Visscher's position in relation to this most hazardous operation would conclude that there were enough indicators of an intention to gas free to act decisively in the face of antagonism from his colleagues. To Visscher the failure of the review team to look at it this way seemed odd, to say the least, and a flaw to put it more seriously.

In its executive summary the 'Report on the Tank Operations on the *Griffin Venture*' concluded:

- the *GV* was not placed in jeopardy by the tank operations in May/June 1994;
- there were serious personality clashes between various members of the marine staff;
- there was a lack of understanding of how to operate and use the gas analysis instrumentation due to poor operating manuals and lack of training;
- the 2nd Mate was correct in drawing attention to the perceived safety problems with the tank operations;
- the 2nd Mate misjudged the signs that appeared to indicate that gas freeing was about to commence when in fact there was no intention to commence gas freeing at the time;

- there were excessive hours worked by the Master and the 1st Mate on the *GV* during the tankwork programme;
- there was no production pressure applied to rush the task;
- there was poor communication between marine staff throughout the tankwork operations;
- design of the IG system in the tanks may have led to difficulties in purging and gas freeing;
- recording and documentation was abysmally poor during the operation;
- there appeared to be difficulties with the marine department working as a team with the process organisation;
- there was no evidence of H_2S release putting the staff in jeopardy.

The report made general recommendations to tighten procedures, documenting of gas analysis, communication and training.

Visscher was flabbergasted that the review team could not clear up the key question for all BHP's offshore oil processing activities: What was the right equipment for this most hazardous operation?

He knew the review team had before it a letter from the Australian representatives of the manufacturers of both the LV analyser and the Tankscope specifically declaring that the Tankscope should be used and not an LV analyser in these operations.

And the observation about the intention to gas free was devastating: 'From the available evidence we concluded that the *Griffin Venture* was not placed in jeopardy during the tank operations in May 1994. Assuming the 9 per cent hydrocarbon reading was correct ... the only operational danger would be to gas free. We do not find any evidence to suggest that gas freeing would take place at this time'.

At the meeting, the Dampier manager asked Visscher for his views of the report. Visscher replied that he did not agree with all the evidence. He drew the Dampier manager's attention to references in the report that stated he had tampered with the gas detection instruments. The manager said that he would have that section of the report reworded. Visscher was asked if he felt the report had adequately addressed his concerns about having been defamed.

He replied that the report did nothing to address those concerns. He still wanted his good name restored, he still believed that BHP

Petroleum had defamed him and that the company should come up with a solution. The Dampier manager, in consultation with the Darwin manager, suggested that Visscher should speak to one of the company's solicitors in Melbourne about the defamation issue. Visscher agreed with this proposal. He now believed that the second inquiry was perverse.

He and Holland had an even greater challenge ahead of them. BHP Petroleum was appearing to address the concerns he had raised by the expenditure of significant resources in a formal inquiry. But the result was, in Visscher's view, a cover-up of what really happened. If that was allowed to stand, the corporate culture would not learn from the exposure of its mistakes. Those mistakes could easily happen again with possibly devastating consequences for BHP, its staff, its public standing, its shareholders and the environment it was statutorily obliged to protect.

Visscher flew to Melbourne on 20 October 1994 and in a meeting with BHP solicitors the company offered to publish an apology or retraction of any defamatory inferences about Visscher's role in the *Griffin Venture* incident. It was proposed that a suitable form of words, agreed to by Visscher, would be published in industry and trade union publications.

Visscher returned to the *Jabiru Venture* but was injured. His left leg and ankle were hurt in a fall and he was repatriated ashore. He became aware from his now extensive network of sources in the company of a 'witch hunt' to try to find the person or persons responsible for sending documents to him.

Back home in Newcastle he found a message on his fax machine. It was a draft of a confidential letter withdrawing any suggestion that Visscher had tampered with gas detection instruments on the *Griffin Venture*. The fax was unsigned but the name printed at the bottom was that of the Master, *Griffin Venture*.

The fax referred to 'the Report on Tank Operations on the *Griffin Venture*', which had been circulated to company offshore facilities, so he contacted the Dampier manager and asked for a copy. When he received it he found it was no different from the draft copies he had read in October.

Considering the draft of the letter he'd been faxed, Visscher was extremely disappointed. He decided there was no alternative but to have his concerns addressed in another forum. He made the following response:

Solicitor
BHP Petroleum
cc Managing Director and CEO BHP

I am in receipt of your faxed confidential draft copy transmitted on 7 November 1994. My understanding from our 'without prejudice' meeting held in your office on 20 October 1994 was that the Master of the *Griffin Venture* was going to make a written apology and retraction of his defamatory statements about me so that my good name could be properly restored.

It was also discussed in your office that the above apology and retraction would be published in trade and trade union magazines and publications.

The defamatory statements made by the Master have been circulated to the extent that my personal life has been adversely affected and my professional career may be in ruins.

I have co-operated with the company in all respects in an endeavour to have my allegations of defamation addressed 'in house' and in a consultative and negotiated manner. Your faxed confidential draft is far short of the response that I had envisaged and fails to indicate any common ground whereby a statement may be developed that would satisfy or address the degree of defamation and hurt that I have suffered and continue to suffer. This has been my last attempt to have this matter resolved in an amicable environment. The company gives me no alternative. I now elect to have my claims of defamation determined in a different forum. All further correspondence on this matter should be addressed to my solicitor.

On 9 January 1995 Visscher wrote to a local member of the Federal Parliament and requested help to have an official inquiry established into the safety of operations of BHP Petroleum. On 13 February he was advised that the member did not have sufficient time to consider the information which had been passed to him. On 14 February Visscher faxed a detailed letter to the Federal

Minister for Transport about the *Griffin Venture* incident. He did not receive any response. On 22 February he contacted Senator Dee Margetts from the West Australian Greens. Her response was immediate. On the same day he contacted the author. A meeting in Sydney was immediately scheduled to assess Visscher's evidence.

In the meantime John Holland had been keeping in contact with BHP officials in an attempt to head off a public confrontation. Holland had spent considerable time with a very senior BHP executive who had taken copious notes.

Since July 1994 Visscher had been receiving leaked documents, information and verbal reports from a variety of sources within BHP Petroleum. One caller equally concerned about the organisation's operational safety said: 'Our hopes are riding with you. If you fail on this, what chance have any of us got.' This was a persistent comment from within about BHP's corporate culture where careerism was the over-riding imperative, not BHP's often published commitment to the highest safety standards.

On 26 February 1995 Visscher believed that he had put the last piece of the puzzle together. He had laid out the factual basis of the second inquiry which had concluded that the *Griffin Venture* was never placed in jeopardy. He believed this was a lie and he set out to prove it.

On 28 February he was contacted by the office of Senator Margetts and given an outline of what the senator intended to say about the *Griffin Venture* incident in the Senate the following day. On 1 March this question was put to the Minister representing the Minister for Transport:

Is the Minister aware of an incident that occurred on board the *Griffin Venture*, a FPSO operated by BHP Petroleum off the Western Australian coast between Barrow Island and North West Cape in late May 1994 which could have caused the vessel to explode, endangering the lives of the thirty-seven men on board and potentially causing a major environmental disaster? If so, what action is the Government taking to investigate this incident to ensure that the procedures that led to this potential disaster are not repeated on this vessel or any other similar facility operating off the Australian coastline?

Senator Bob Collins, in response, announced that a joint Federal/State inquiry would be set up to investigate the incident. This was to be the third inquiry into the incident aboard the *Griffin Venture*.

That week ABC TV's *7.30 Report* broadcast a fourteen minute story on the incident including an interview with Visscher. BHP declined to provide a spokesman to answer the claims on camera. The program said the incident 'raised serious questions about BHP's work and safety practices and internal accountability methods'.

On the program, Visscher had put his perspective of the issues to be faced: 'This is horrific. This is an *Exxon Valdez* and this is a *Piper Alpha*. Massive pollution. Total loss of life on our back doorstep on the virgin coast of Western Australia. . . a recognised environmentally sensitive area. This stuff can go down into Exmouth Gulf. Who knows? Who knows?'

Visscher put the issue succinctly when he said that on 29 May 1994 he may have been the only friend of the Board and shareholders of BHP. Had he not intervened the cost to the company could have been astronomical. Visscher had pleaded in his televised interview: 'We've got to clean this one up. We've got to clean it up as an issue . . . clean it up as a point of fact . . . and not clean it up with respect of cleaning off the beaches and cleaning the seabirds and explaining to coronial inquiries. That clean-up's a lose. This clean-up's a positive.'

Visscher's extensive documentary evidence was laid out on a table in the televised report. It outlined the claimed flaws in the second inquiry report's findings. Through the documents Visscher asserted that there was ample evidence that gas freeing was going to take place. More to the point, he said, the intention at all material times was to gas free on the evening of 29 May.

There was the written work sheet which scheduled gas freeing for 29 May. The tank clearing operation had already begun without the right calibration gas being on board. And there was a leaked copy of the Master's report so critical of Visscher's action that night: 'No gas freeing was carried out as a result of Mr Visscher's actions'. The Master's statement made no sense unless gas freeing had been planned.

As well Visscher insisted he was told by his workmate that tank

3C was almost ready for gas freeing and he saw purge pipes had been installed for what he believed to be this purpose. But the review team had relied on statements by other crew members that no decision had been taken to gas free.

In the televised interview Visscher declared: 'I went in succession to the First Mate, the Master, the Field Superintendent, with an instrument in my hand that says that tank over there, the one we're going to gas free, has got 9 per cent hydrocarbons in it ... and I have stated to these three fellows if we gas free that tank will go through the explosive range. Wouldn't the reply be to me ... "So what Tim, we're not going to gas free. We're going to wait until the calibration gas arrives". That would have been the reply. What was the reply? In two cases abuse and ridicule and insult and the third case, a decision that we won't gas free'.

The second review, he noted, was equivocal about his conduct. It said he was right to have reported his 9 per cent reading but: 'We do not condone his actions in disobeying the Master's orders not to test the instrument'.

The Federal/State Governments' inquiry was underway in late March 1995. To avoid duplication, pool expertise and ensure a timely report, there would be a joint investigation by AMSA (Australian Maritime Safety Authority) and WADOME. Visscher's high speed photocopier ran hot as he sent copies of all his submissions and supporting documents to the investigation.

The two officers carrying out this third inquiry were an official from WADOME and a marine incident investigation officer from the Department of Transport representing AMSA.

Visscher became sceptical about the outcome of the third inquiry when he faced hostile questioning while he was giving evidence and was accused of 'wanting BHP's dirty washing to be hung out on the line'. He rejected the charge.

On 19 May 1995, after further reports reached him of slanderous statements circulating within the company, Visscher was called to Melbourne head office for a meeting with the President of BHP Petroleum and the Manager of Safety and Environment. The purpose of the meeting was to discuss 'the way forward'. Half way through his now oft-repeated presentation of the *Griffin Venture* incident the president declared: 'Okay, I've heard enough'. Visscher and Holland were told the General Manager of BHP himself had issued a directive to get the matter resolved. The president said that the way forward was to 'start afresh' and that he wanted Visscher to consider a possible appointment to Vietnam where the company conducted operations. Visscher agreed to consider the president's proposal. They agreed to meet again the following week. When they did Visscher and Holland submitted a lengthy statement which demanded that BHP make full disclosure of its deficiencies and failings to now underline its commitment to maintain ethical standards.

The submission sought from the company an acknowledgement that the *Griffin Venture* was placed in jeopardy by negligence and asked the company to make a public statement to that effect.

> If the company is unable or unwilling to comply with the above, the issues can be resolved by the company publicly and practically supporting Visscher in his campaign to have an open and public inquiry into the *Griffin Venture* incident. Thereby people will be compelled to give sworn evidence which will be subjected to scrutiny and the truth determined and made public.
>
> As Australia's leading corporate citizen and the manager of some of our major offshore oil reserves, BHP have a duty to publicly demonstrate that they are conducting their business in a professional, safe and accountable manner. Therein the essential ingredients are honesty and integrity. If BHP Petroleum cannot demonstrate honesty and integrity, particularly with respect to self regulation, should the company remain in the oil business?

At the meeting the president of BHP Petroleum was firm. There would be no public inquiry. It was acknowledged that the second inquiry no longer applied. The third inquiry, about to be tabled in the Federal Parliament, was now the valid document.

The Third Inquiry Report

ON 30 May 1995, one year after the original incident, the AMSA/ WADOME report was tabled in the House of Representatives and the Senate. It contained both bad and good news for Tim Visscher.

Findings:
- the *Griffin Venture* was not placed in jeopardy on 29 May 1994;
- without Mr Visscher's intervention, gas freeing from No 3C tank may have proceeded;
- had gas freeing commenced with a hydrocarbon vapour content of 9 per cent in the tank, the tank atmosphere would have entered the flammable range;
- had the gas freeing operations commenced, the possibility of an explosion occurring was unlikely, due to the absence of a source of ignition; and
- while there was no evidence of an intention to specifically cover up this incident, there appears to be a general reluctance by local management of BHP Petroleum to advise Head Office of issues which may reflect adversely on their management.

The investigating officers identified two acts which were considered as unsafe, namely:

- discarding of a Tankscope instrument in favour of LV instruments on the basis that the Tankscope instrument was reading 'too high' (these instruments are used to measure hydrocarbon concentrations in tanks) was an unsafe act;
- the decision to deviate from the Temporary Work Instruction, without discussing possible safety implications at a toolbox meeting, was against the procedures agreed under the *Griffin Venture* Safety Case and is an unsafe act.

Minister David Bedall announced that the Federal Government's response was to request relevant State and Territory Ministers to audit all existing offshore oil production facilities to see that previous internal BHP safety recommendations had been universally implemented. He announced he would refer the issue of excessive hours worked aboard the *Griffin Venture* to the Director of Public Prosecutions to determine if there was a prima facie case to prosecute BHP Petroleum.

Visscher was insistent that 'there was a source of ignition' and evidence he had presented to the third inquiry on this point seemed to have been ignored. He had testified that the source of ignition was in the unbonded and 'earthed' temporary purge pipes he had seen across the deck from the cargo tanks to the vessel's sides to take gases being purged from the tanks to overboard. The temporary purge pipes consisted of several lengths of sheet metal ducting. The sections of metal ducting were supported with plastic drums and joined together with 'duct' tape, a plastic tape which does not conduct electricity. The section of purge pipe thus constituted isolated conductors accumulating large voltages of static electricity. At frequent intervals sparks from the static electrical build up would occur at the joints between the pipes. Visscher asserted that the initial ignition would occur in the purge pipes which carried gases being exhausted from the tanks. The exhaust gases were a mixture of all the gases in the tank. That meant that when the exhaust gases became explosive, all the gas in the 17 000 cubic metre volume of the tank would be explosive. An explosive path from a detonation in the purge pipe would cause the entire volume of the tank to explode with an explosive force equivalent to 2000 lbs of plastic explosive.

In spite of this evidence the third inquiry had declared there was no source of ignition, therefore the *Griffin Venture* was not in jeopardy.

Visscher and Holland discussed the third inquiry report at length. Visscher's requests to make a further presentation to the Board of Directors of BHP was rejected. Holland wrote to directors individually. Visscher made a lengthy video presenting again all his factual evidence. The Board of Directors did not respond, individually or collectively.

Visscher and Holland declared that the fight was not over.

The AMSA/WADOME report did not clear the matter up. Visscher insisted that the *Griffin Venture* was in jeopardy. AMSA/WADOME had advanced the findings on the question of gas freeing from the 'would not' of the BHP review team to a 'may have'.

It had declared that the *Griffin Venture* was not in jeopardy. 'The possibility of an explosion occurring was unlikely, due to the absence of a source of ignition.' This was akin to saying, absurdly, that the vessel was not in jeopardy because it had not blown up.

Where was the intellectual and logical rigour in this? It was a bureaucratic and political Catch 22.

Why couldn't the regulatory authorities bring themselves to declare that the *Griffin Venture* was in jeopardy because of very slack procedures and that BHP's publicly stated commitment to the highest standards of safety was PR rhetoric? Why torture the words when the indicators of unsafe acts were now on the record?

They had to prove that there was a source of ignition on 29 May 1994.

Visscher was by now something of a hero with some BHP Petroleum employees. Although he had earlier been approached by his union to take over his case, Visscher had decided to press on alone, expending all available leave entitlements and exhausting any remaining shreds of goodwill towards him from within the corporation. Employees from within the company now regularly telephoned him at his Newcastle home and he was soon aware of all company moves in his case. Many personnel from the *Griffin Venture* had now moved on to other jobs. Because of the original terms of reference 'not to lay blame' there had been no personal consequences or personal accountability for any action they may have taken on 'the most hazardous operation' which could be performed on a tanker.

Visscher and Holland sent the videotaped presentation to key federal politicians. It is doubtful many endured its three-hour length and technical detail. With his sources within the company now actively helping him, Visscher flew to Western Australia and other parts of Australia to personally interview others who had been aboard the *Griffin Venture* that day. Because of slack safety procedures he had perceived from the moment of his arrival aboard the *Griffin Venture*, he was certain he could produce the evidence about a source of ignition.

On 17 October 1995 the West Australian Minister for Mines was asked by the Hon. J.A. Scott: 'During the various inquiries, was WADOME made aware by BHP Petroleum... of the configuration of the temporary purge pipes set up for gas freeing operations? The Minister's answer: 'Yes'.

Was this configuration earthed according to present standards and/or regulations? The Minister's answer: 'Yes'.

In the Senate, Dee Margetts extracted from the Government an additional report produced to answer Visscher's videotaped claims. This report found that Visscher's allegations about the assembly of the temporary purge pipes were untrue. The report maintained that internal metal 'non-fixed or bolted' sleeves were used to join the sections of the purge pipes together and that these metal sleeves would provide electrical bonding to earth. Other documentation stated that Visscher's allegations had been subjected to extensive investigation.

The report did state, however, that if the temporary purge pipes were assembled as Visscher had described, the investigating team would agree that the temporary purge pipes could produce a spark. Significantly, it stated that if the temporary purge pipes were assembled as described by Visscher without the metal joining sleeves, it would constitute an act of wilful negligence.

The safety bible, *International Safety Guide for Oil Tankers and Terminals* declared: 'Earthing and bonding minimise the dangers from ... accumulation of electrostatic charge' and '... earthing and bonding to guard against static electricity are often associated with moveable equipment and must be established whenever the equipment is set up'. ISGOT is the internationally recognised minimum safety standard. It was often said in the industry: 'To go outside ISGOT you must be very stupid or very smart.'

Visscher noted a reported comment of the *Griffin Venture*'s First Mate, the person in charge of setting up the temporary purge pipes: 'Those directly concerned with rigging the portable (temporary) purge pipe at 1C and 3C were the First Mate, a Second Mate and the IRs (crew). The First Mate told the inverview team that the flexible pipes had to be secured to the purge pipe with (duct) tape. Then the tape was used to join each section of the flexible pipe together. The flame arresters then had to be taped over the ends of the flexible pipes.'

The First Mate was specific, the sections of purge pipes were joined with tape. There was no mention of metal joining sleeves. Yet the AMSA/WADOME investigation had not confronted what Visscher believed was obvious evidence of a likely or probable source of ignition.

On 30 November 1995 Senator Margetts tabled in the Australian

Senate six statutory declarations gathered by Visscher from workers who were on board the *Griffin Venture* at the time of the incident.

Margetts said the declarations 'totally contradict the evidence provided by BHP Petroleum to the joint State/Federal investigations into this incident'. She urged the Federal Government to establish an independent judicial inquiry into claims of wilful negligence by BHP Petroleum on the *Griffin Venture*.

Margetts said the six statutory declarations confirmed Visscher's claims that the purge pipes were incorrectly assembled and therefore could have produced the sparks necessary for an explosion. 'The statutory declarations demonstrate that BHP Petroleum have wilfully misled the three joint State/Federal investigations that have been conducted.'

For Tim Visscher the struggle to make BHP confront the truth was far from over.

He had written increasingly stinging letters to the corporation accusing it collectively of a cover-up through the September 'review' report. He accused BHP directors of having failed to act in a proper manner when acquainted with safety problems aboard the *Griffin Venture*, with a duty of care. He called on BHP to support a full, open judicial inquiry into the incident.

'Is BHP Petroleum a fit and proper corporation to have an operating licence/permit in offshore oil exploration? The practice of continued cover-up would suggest a negative answer.'

Would it take an explosion and loss of life to bring genuine accountability for breaches of safety by both the company and the safety regulators? On 19 June 1996, Ian Howarth reported in *The Financial Review*: 'Mr Baugh (Mr Michael Baugh, president of BHP Petroleum) acknowledged yesterday that he had always believed Mr Visscher's version of events.'

Visscher rejected the job offer in Vietnam. The issue remained alive in the Federal and West Australian Parliaments as this book went to press.

THE COURAGE OF
THE WHISTLEBLOWERS

A S YOU CAN SEE from the stories in this book, any responsible citizen can become a 'whistleblower'.

Confronted with worrying circumstances, individuals can react differently. But most, it seems, have a vague awareness of the personal risks and consequences in questioning corporate authority. To some, exposing a questionable practice can be perceived as an act of the grossest disloyalty.

Self-preservation is a strong instinct within organisations. Careerism within an organisational culture is predicated on 'covering your arse,' as well as not making an 'arse' or a nuisance of yourself. This applies to bureaucracies within the private as well as public sectors. This mentality or mindset within organisations is well known and individuals confronted with or coming into possession of worrying knowledge almost automatically take account of the consequences of actually raising their concerns. They might do so innocently at first, expecting or hoping that those in authority within the organisation will reward their honesty. When that does not immediately happen, when there is an intriguing delay or they find their position is undermined, sometimes with malice, they quite naturally can become angered by the response to their concerns. With worldwide media and movie attention on prominent cases of whistleblowers, public consciousness has been raised as never before. But that does not make it easier for those whistleblowers who may not be Daniel Ellsbergs or Karen Silkwoods.

Writing in the book *Corruption and Reform* (University of Queensland Press 1990), John McMillan, who teaches administrative and constitutional law at the Australian National University, described the great popular interest in whistleblowing ... 'partly because of the spectacle of a person publicly being disloyal to the organisation to which he or she belongs, and partly too because whistleblowers have often focused public attention on a hidden membrane of corrupt behaviour'.

McMillan says their moral courage has bestowed international fame on many whistleblowers including Ellsberg 'who released US Government documents that reported how the public had been misled over the Vietnam War; Clive Pointing, a British civil servant who gave to an Opposition member of Parliament information showing that the government had misled Parliament about the sinking of the Argentine ship, *General Belgrano*; Frank Serpico, who testified to the Knapp Commission that his New York police colleagues had been corrupted into crime; Stanley Adams, who exposed that his employer was illegally fixing prices in the European Economic Community; Karen Silkwood, who was killed in a mysterious car accident on her way to provide to a journalist evidence of falsified nuclear safety records by her employer, Kerr-Mcgee; Ernest Fitzgerald, a US Defense Department employee who gave testimony to a US Congressional committee of a $2 billion cost overrun on the Lockheed c-5A transport plane; in Australia, Phillip Arantz, who was sacked from the New South Wales Police Force after disclosing the deliberate inaccuracy in published government statistics on crime clean-up success'.

Since McMillan's analysis there has been an Australia-wide movement for the legislative protection of whistleblowers. But legislative structures, it is argued by some, can be manipulated or used as a device of further 'damage control'. In short, the whistleblower may only get 'protection' if he or she keeps the information they possess confidential to the whistleblowing receipt authority. Whistleblower protection legislation is more than welcome as a 1990s contribution to ethical practice in public and private sector institutions. The effective operation of the legislation in its various (and sometimes deficient) forms will be subject to academic analysis and criticism in the years to come.

But as we have seen with police corruption, accountability structures themselves can become part of a pattern of institutionalised cover-up, or what Jim Leggate, the Queensland Mines Department official, has helpfully described as 'regulatory capture'—the capture of the agency meant to enforce the rules by the vested interests meant to abide by them. Those directly involved in the administration of whistleblower protection legislation have a challenge ahead of them to make sure that protection of the whistleblower and exposure of the wrong doing or maladministration is achieved. If they are having trouble in reaching that objective because of external or internal pressure they can always do what many whistleblowers themselves have had to do: hit the phones to the media, while taking full account of the risks and consequences of 'going public'.

According to McMillan the fate of whistleblowers in the United States shows the devastating personal consequences for those carrying out their civic duty.

Of a group of 233 whistleblowers studied in the United States (up to 1990) 90 per cent lost their jobs or were demoted; 27 per cent faced lawsuits; 26 per cent faced psychiatric or medical referral; 25 per cent admitted alcohol abuse; 17 per cent lost their homes; 15 per cent were subsequently divorced; 10 per cent attempted suicide and 8 per cent went bankrupt.

The question of future employability after the whistleblowing incident is a key issue now that the phenomenon of whistleblowing is well known. It remains hard, if not impossible, for organisations to restore the whistleblower to previous or higher status. **Dr Robert Savory** who confronted BHP's manganese subsidiary on Groote Eylandt was not embraced by the company after his warnings of massive fuel leaks had been vindicated. His efforts eventually received only grudging acknowledgement. Savory was saved from hopelessness and unemployment by a government department in another jurisdiction after media exposure of his plight. As he said, it was hard to get a job after you had been sacked by the biggest company in Australia.

Tim Visscher, the second mate aboard the *Griffin Venture*, is still with BHP Petroleum but in employment limbo. It is almost as if the company does not know what to do with him although, again, there has been acknowledgement of his safety concerns.

It remains doubtful if **Bill Bolitho**, the former chairman of ANL, will ever be offered another government board appointment after he publicly exposed the wrecking of the value of the national shipping line by political and bureaucratic incompetence. He may not want one ... but would any government offer?

John McLennan, the Westpac letters whistleblower, remains in demand as a consultant for aggrieved bank customers. His experience and qualifications would equip him for a return to the inside of the banking system but he is certain not to be asked.

Helen James, a senior official within the Civil Aviation Authority, has returned to academic work after she exposed a mentality of cover-up and damage control in a regulator whose primary duty was to guard the safety of the travelling public. After internal ostracism her ultimate act was to do the corporately unthinkable—go public. Instead of being acclaimed as a protector of public safety she was formally charged with disloyalty and, except for political intervention following publicity, would have been robbed of her accumulated work entitlements. Her prospects of returning to an operational role will only rest with the judgement of an enlightened employer.

Alwyn Johnson, the senior Tasmanian banker, has paid a high price for having alerted that State's political masters to a bank out of control. He has not been able to return to his field of expertise—a personal and industry tragedy when one considers that prudential judgement should be foremost in the minds of banking leaders, financiers and government.

Jim Leggate was eventually forced to accept a job outside mining where he had been an aggravated thorn in the side of a bureaucracy which refused to enforce its own legislation. Leggate's experience is indicative of the contempt which can be shown by a regulatory regime to laws enacted by Parliament. Only the Parliament could confront that contempt but its members refused to stand by its enacted laws or to change them and instead opted for rhetorical and ultimately empty assurances.

Elizabeth O'Brien became an urban activist when she realised that authorities meant to oversee public health were not effectively doing so. Whilst the children of Australia were in grave danger of intellectual impairment through lead fallout she had to organise, infiltrate or confront the authorities in spite of the fact that they had access to all available scientific information. Her whistleblowing was met with patronising remarks about her emotive reaction concerning her own child and her alleged economic ignorance. She is rarely asked to speak to industry bodies to give her invaluable insights into the health risks of lead fallout.

Dr Phil Nitschke, a young, irreverent medico, simply wanted to point out that nuclear preparedness had to be taken seriously. His insistence and activism divided the community, producing personal smears on his character and more serious consequences. Eventually he had to leave his hospital. If being a team player means that you have to keep your mouth shut and do what you are told rather than contributing to the team's efforts to solve problems, there was no place in such a team for Nitschke.

Phil Vardy suffered the fate of most whistleblowers—loss of the work he loved and crushing personal pressure as a consequence of accusations he felt morally obliged to make. Although he was vindicated by an aggravated process of exposure and inquiry which took years, nothing will restore to him the loss of idealism, trust and hope in science's search for the truth. Everyone has suffered.

Whistleblowers rarely survive within their own organisations. The culture shock their actions produce leave deep scars. Authority within organisations cannot, it seems, tolerate being questioned. Organisation leaders demand loyalty, confusing it for unquestioning personal obedience rather than a loyalty to the stated aims and objects of the organisation. The whistleblower's exposures of incompetence, maladministration or corruption may eventually result in the destruction of careers—managers or supervisors may be disciplined, transferred or sacked. But there appears still to be no future in their jobs for whistleblowers who have done what is right and proper in alerting the organisation (if ultimately necessary by 'going public') however embarrassing that may be for the particular organisation.

This was brought home to the author with his own organisation, the Australian Broadcasting Corporation. John Millard, once a reporter with The Investigators, a consumer affairs television program, had gone public in 1994 with concerns about alleged back-door sponsorship of some ABC television programs against the provisions of the ABC Act and ABC Board editorial policies. The programs included popular 'infotainment' shows like *The Homeshow* and *EveryBody* run on ABC TV in the early 1990s.

Millard was eventually vindicated through an independent inquiry (by Mr George Palmer QC) which found there were irreconcilable differences between the ABC's so called co-production guidelines and the expectations of external bodies which funded those productions. When *The Investigators* was axed by ABC Television management in late 1995 Millard found there were no places available for him to continue his career in ABC television. This was in spite of the fact that he was no longer with *The Investigators* and had been working for another features program pending negotiations on his next assignment. ABC management claimed he had agreed to return to *The Investigators* before the announcement of its unfortunate demise. Millard was faced with the prospect of being edged towards the door and an uncertain future given his unasked-for whistleblower status. Management had made a commitment to make genuine efforts to place all affected staff but no other programs seemed to want John Millard. Following staff and union agitation in his support, ABC managing director Brian Johns established an inquiry by an industrial lawyer (Mr Phillip Coleman) to examine Millard's and his union's claims that his treatment by the ABC amounted to victimisation. In the meantime ABC Radio found work for Millard.

In July 1996 Coleman found that Millard had been victimised for his whistleblowing activities.

Coleman's words restored Millard's status as a credible professional journalist after he had been blackguarded as 'mad', with a 'bee in his bonnet' and 'difficult to work with' in a whispering campaign of unsubstantiated denigration.

It seems to me extraordinary, considering Mr Millard's ten years of experience as a television reporter and producer, with an unblemished employment record, a manifest dedication to public broadcasting and the ABC, a successful career, having won a number of awards and an enthusiasm and passion for his work rarely found, that ABC management decided not to renew his contract for 1996.

After careful consideration of all the relevant evidence I have come to the conclusion that Mr Millard's activities in relation to the ABC's complaince with its editorial policies had an effect on management's decision not to extend Mr Millard's employment at ABC Television.

Brian Johns offered John Millard a job back in ABC Television, but, on legal advice, took no disciplinary action against the managers named in the Coleman report.

From actively participating in the support of John Millard within my own organisation it was disturbing that restoration of this whistleblower was not accompanied by necessary accountability. This was most revealing for an organisation which often used whistleblowers in its current affairs and documentary programs to expose malpractice, incompetence or corruption in other organisations and produced lectures about human resource best practice, non-discrimination and equal employment opportunity. The national broadcaster has a long way to go. As one ABC Board member commented: 'Love thy whistleblower'.

In December 1996, the ABC Board approved ground-breaking public interest disclosure and grievance procedures for its staff as a direct consequence of the John Millard case.

The Psychodynamics of Whistleblowing

WHISTLEBLOWERS go through a personal hell. Most often it is self-created, coming as it often does through proactive measures.

The author's spouse, Elizabeth, a psychiatrist, has contributed observations on some of the psychological aspects of whistleblowing from case histories contained in this book.

There were common factors in a number of the subject whistle-blowers. Most seemed to come from families or had grown up in an environment where there was a clear sense of morality, of determining right from wrong. It may have religious or secular origins. There clearly seemed to have been passed on to the individuals a standard of behaviour or ethics. There were often formative childhood experiences such as shifting around frequently, lots of different schools and racial groups, which made them more self-reliant and less dependent on their immediate peer group for their sense of personal identity.

As well as childhood factors there were, in some cases, later experiences where the individuals had stood up to an authority figure at some stage and found that they were treated with more respect. This tended to cement their own feeling of personal integrity and effectiveness. And it strikes one how effective these people are *before* the crisis. When actually faced with the crisis, a combination of these life experiences seemed to have led them to what they considered to be correct actions. On these occasions they did not meet with support but instead suffered hostility and denigration. In attempting to defend themselves from what immediately became both personal attacks and a questioning or challenging of their integrity, they had to establish the rightness of their concerns. When that happened a mixture of disbelief and outrage produced a response of resourcefulness, concern and a full consideration of their own positions. They then tried to redress the problem appropriately.

As they continued to meet opposition and efforts to cover up they seemed to struggle with feelings of anger, helplessness and disbelief. Where less self-reliant people might retreat, the hostility and denigration only served to strengthen their resolve. But it became apparent in most cases that the individuals could not put all that energy into that part of their lives without it beginning to take away from other aspects. Then you begin to see the breakdown in their relationships, the negative and damaging effects on their own emotional stability and self-confidence. The more of themselves they have to invest the more they have to lose, psychologically, professionally, financially. That's when they may appear to become fanatical or obsessed to significantly narrow their vision. But they cannot give up the task or they lose their self-respect.

One gets a sense that while they may be vindicated by findings, inquiries or reports, that cannot compensate them for the personal cost involved. They are, in fact, traumatised by the experience.

Public recognition of the psychological costs of their stance as well as financial, social or occupational recognition, legislative protection and whistleblower support, may help them work through the trauma.

The trauma of whistleblowing comes from the attack on a person's self-esteem, self-identity or self-worth. The authorities which attack them seem invariably do so in a highly personalised way. There are accusations of emotional instability, mental illness, drunkenness or obsessive behaviour. They can be framed, victimised, harassed, intimidated and coerced. No holds are barred in the effort to discredit or destroy the whistleblower. That is why it is so damaging personally and emotionally. Although they have grown up with a sense of self worth, not necessarily reliant on the approval of others and coping with dissonance in their lives, the intensity of the attack upon them can have long-term effects.

The experience may strengthen them and make them even more self-reliant. But one discerns that few escape without some evidence of emotional scarring.

Whistleblower Protection: the Early Days

IN a critical analysis of whistleblower protection legislation William de Maria, a University of Queensland lecturer and founder of the Whistleblowers Action Group, wrote in *The Alternative Law Journal*, (Vol 20, No 6, December 1995) that protection for whistleblowers who went to the media was a big 'no-go area' for legislative draftsmen in Australia and New Zealand.

Only the NSW statute offers protection for media whistleblowers, and that protection is so highly conditional that its effectiveness remains to be seen.

De Maria argues that the media is often the last resort for the whistleblower. With his kind permission his analysis of government reluctance to protect media whistleblowers is reprinted here.

Media exposure is often the shove governments need to get them acting in the public interest. Fanny K (a pseudonym), a Queensland whistleblower, offers a good example of this. As a worker in the Basil Stafford Centre, a government facility for intellectually handicapped people, she claimed to have witnessed countless instances of patient abuse. She went through official channels from early 1986 to November 1990, seeking action from the authorities to stop the abuse, injury and loss of life occurring at the centre. No notice was taken of her and she was subjected to threats and victimisation, including tampering with the brakes of her car. She finally went on the Hinch TV program and the Hayden Sargeant radio talk-back show in Brisbane. The media pressure sparked government interest and put the Criminal Justice Commission into a corner: a public inquiry was now the only way out. The government went into damage control mode soon after the inquiry started and peremptorily closed the centre.

This case also led a chastened Queensland Government to slip a provision into the new Whistleblowers Protection Act 1994 (Qld) that was not in any previous draft, nor part of the pre-legislative consultative process. The 'Fanny K Clause' as it is referred to by the Queensland Whistleblowers Action Group, allows anybody to disclose a substantial and specific danger to the health and safety of a person with a disability. Without Fanny K's fortitude and a responsive media (in this particular case), this clause would never have been included. The Goss Government cites this and kindred provisions as offering sufficient protection to whistleblowers to make contact with the media unwarranted, but it is interesting to note that a proposal to bar CJC whistleblowers from contacting the media was considered before the tabling of the Whistleblowers Protection Act 1994, but abandoned as too controversial.

The argument always trundled out by government against media whistleblower protection is the risk of damage to innocent reputations by unsubstantiated media stories. While no doubt this argument has some merit, the main problem for government with disclosures via the media is that the whistleblower is 'off the chain'. Broken loose of the tight, cautious, prolonged and above all semi-secret agency procedures, the exasperated whistleblower makes media contact with stories that are usually innately newsworthy—although this is not to say that they are always followed through by the media.

The whistleblower-media relationship is virtually unresearched and seems to be different each time a whistleblower makes media contact. Conflicts between sensationalism and investigative journalism; snapshot coverage and sustained reporting; and victim-focused versus system-focused stories swim below the surface, usually out of the sight of the whistleblower.. Such conflicts are resolved by media management against the public interest more times than is realised. The fiercely free media, exposing wrongdoing wherever it finds it, is largely a myth that we and whistleblowers hold on to along with the myth of accountability and integrity in government. Bar some spectacular cases such as the Fanny K case, the government does not have much to worry about with the media, which is driven more by economic considerations: will the largely conservative media consumer 'buy' the whistleblower's story, and therefore buy the newspaper or item in the electronic news?

De Maria's analysis goes to the heart of the legislative and media problems associated with whistleblowing. No individual can completely rely on legislative protection or media solidarity with their cause. The process of whistleblowing is fraught with danger. Those embarking on it should be starkly aware of all the consequences.

From the case histories in this book it is obvious that those genuine whistleblowers who have endured their personal ordeals and been vindicated, albeit covered in 'blood' through intimidation or harassment, have equipped themselves for the fray.

What has impressed the author in their stories has been their intelligence, hard work and tactics. It is hard work being a whistleblower. To be obsessed can be a help if it brings with it a determination to win, to pay attention to every fine detail in the evidentiary trail. But to be obsessed to the point of paranoia or illogicality will diminish or destroy the whistleblower's case.

Authority will invariably try the line of least resistance when confronted with a whistleblower. If quiet reassurance will not work, delay, obfuscation or ignoring the problem will follow. If the problem does not go away and the whistleblower persists, rejection and recrimination may result. If that does not dissuade the whistleblower from prosecuting what has now become a quarrel, full frontal reprisal can be the next step.

Australia is fortunate to have such public consciousness in this democracy that reprisal is most often limited to denying the whistleblower meaningful employment—either by outright sacking or harassment to the point of resignation. In some other countries disloyal and dissenting people would be treated with much harsher methods up to intimidatory assault or even murder. In the subtler methodology apparent here, there is a process designed to 'ratbag' the whistleblower. He or she is depicted as 'mad', 'obsessed' or a 'zealot'. To a casual observer this may appear to be the case. The whistleblower often harms his or her support potential by haranguing non-involved people, appealing to their own sense of morality or conscience or guilt to the point of personal insult. When this happens, potential supporters can run a mile. What is really required, of course, is a factual description of the issues at stake in a non-threatening way. Once appraised of the facts most people of humanity and conscience are prepared to satisfy themselves of the circumstances and then are only too happy to lend practical and moral support. Whistleblowers in the full flight of self-righteous anger can quickly stuff whatever support that may be available to them by playing the martyr. Their 'dreams' of martyrdom are quickly realised. But it is an unhappy, bitter and soul-destroying isolation which inevitably follows from the whistleblower made illogically obsessed by his or her circumstances. Friends, wives, husbands, children and genuine supporters are put through the fires of hell in their support of the whistleblower engulfed by the righteousness of the truth. What is needed, obviously, is a broad support base and objective assessment by family, friends, supporters and constructive critics to plan tactics and strategy.

People who find themselves in situations where they feel obliged to blow the whistle now have a ready-made support system in Australia. It is not through the legislative mechanisam enacted by various Australian parliaments. Whistleblowers Australia Incorporated operates on Edmund Burke's philosophy: 'All it needs for evil to prosper is for people of goodwill to do nothing'. This voluntary association has been in operation for some years now and has within its membership many Australians who have themselves blown the whistle and suffered the consequences. All Attorneys-General and their officers in Australia know of the existence of the whistleblowers support network. Their newsletters and writings are monthly adding to the debate about accountability and ethics of public and private sector organisations in the nineties.

Whatever else you do ... take a note. Those whistleblowers with a meticulous note of what they have experienced are the ones most likely to achieve vindication when some other body examines the truth of what they are saying. Whenever you feel your own credibility is going to be called into question it is time to start taking notes and compiling a documentary record of all your involvements, including personal, and telephone conversations. If the truth is what is at stake you have to demonstrate that you possess it in word, thought and deed.

In some cases whistleblowers have purloined documents they know to be sensitive in order to prove their claims. This may even involve illegality. After all, the documents are the property of the organisation. To take sensitive documents is to steal from the organisation no matter how damning the documents may be. This is a moral and tactical judgement. Much resourcefulness is required when ethical concerns would dictate that the end does not necessarily justify the means.

As public consciousness is raised about the moral imperative of blowing the whistle on misconduct, corruption and maladmin- istration within organisations perhaps judges will no longer side with the organisation and its 'damage control equals cover-up' mentality.

Unethical, immoral and even illegal behaviour is a constant in everyday social and commercial life. The society is often saved by those within it who are not prepared to act unethically.

Those individuals who have found themselves in situations where they blow the whistle display a profound courage and moral leadership. Many do not know it at the time, they do not know the risks, or are downright foolish. But if the facts are clear there is little any but extreme tactics can overcome.

Whistleblowers have a unique place in our national life. But rarely are they invited to Government House for a cup of tea or decorated for the bravery they have displayed. Bravery awards are usually for physical bravery in the face of danger. This is a deserving criterion. But of equal if not more significance is the person who makes an organisation face its own hypocrisy or corruption or maladministration. The truth should lead to honesty and appropriate reaction. Obviously this is not always the case. But the people who have the courage to set aside their own self-preserving interests, to set aside the painful but probably short-term embarrassment or exposure, are the great change-makers.

They are the ones who can make a difference. Without them modern society would be lost to the barbarity of market forces, of political expediency, or damage control, of cover-up, and of institutional and corporate lying and mediocrity.

Whistleblowers Australia Inc.
PO Box M44
MARRICKVILLE SOUTH
NSW 2204

PREMEDITATED DECEPTION

'We get into these situations without realising the total end cost and we estimate that it will be one battle at a time and that the sequence of battles will be short and successful. Inevitably, it's a long sequence of battles which are bitter, bloody or pyrrhic.'
—Phil Vardy, Sydney 1995.

I T WAS 1977. Phil Vardy was fresh out of university. He had been offered an exciting job as research officer at Foundation 41. He was thrilled. It gave him the chance to work for someone he admired—Dr William McBride.

It was also a great personal relief. He had a career at last. He had prospects. Phil Vardy had been confined to a wheelchair as a result of a motorcycle accident a few years earlier. This job was everything he could want.

Phil Vardy was born in Murwillumbah in northern New South Wales in 1949. His father, Alan, served in the Air Force during the Second World War in Europe and North Africa. His mother, Jean, and Alan instilled in young Phillip a firm idea of right from wrong. After the war, the family moved around a lot because of Alan's Air Force job. They lived at RAAF facilities at Newcastle, Brisbane, Wagga, Ipswich, Elizabeth in South Australia, Melbourne and Brisbane again.

Young Phil Vardy had to make new friends in seven primary schools and three high schools throughout his school years. He claims he was not very bright at school, achieving only average marks. He was a reserved boy, not the life of the party, but through application and hard work rather than a natural brilliance he achieved good matriculation grades. He was an avid, but poor musician on recorder, guitar and accordion. Through his adolescence, Vardy had been a member of the Scout Movement which he believed was a major influence on his sense of duty. Although he was not overly religious, he went to church and at sixteen he was confirmed after catechism classes in the Anglican Church.

In the year the Russians put the Sputnik into outer space, Vardy started a slow tertiary education at the University of Queensland, taking on a science curriculum. In 1970 he joined the Bureau of Meteorology as a trainee weather observer. This gave him an opportunity for adventure and in 1971 he was accepted for a twelve-month tour of duty at Australia's Antarctic Davis base. He was only twenty-one. It was, he said, one of the best years of his life. Back at university the following year, he struggled to complete a science degree.

In 1973 came the accident which broke his back. He had finished a vigorous game of squash at the university and at about 6 pm was riding his motor cycle back to the Union College where he boarded when he failed to take a bend. The bike hit the gutter and Vardy slammed into a tree. He was rushed to Royal Brisbane Hospital by ambulance. The prognosis: the accident had rendered him paraplegic, T7 complete—spinal cord severed at the level of the seventh thoracic vertebra. He spent seven months in hospital. But he was encouraged by the fact that he could still do many things, even though he was confined to a wheelchair. He went back to university to resume his studies and recommenced tutoring in histology, a job which involved microscopes. The disability forced Vardy to focus more intently on his studies and he eventually achieved a Bachelor of Science degree with first class honours.

A year after the accident he met a therapist Gail Yost and they were married a year later. It was a joyous event. While he was still an honours student Phil Vardy saw an advertisement placed by the School of Pathology, University of New South Wales for a job as Foundation 41 Research Officer. He applied and flew to Sydney for an interview. The quiet almost aloof man he saw on the interview panel was Dr William McBride. 'I thought, gosh ... this is *the* McBride of Thalidomide ...'

Vardy got the job and he and Gail moved to a flat at Randwick in Sydney. The next happy event in their lives was the arrival of son Scott, delivered by Dr McBride.

Foundation 41

FOUNDATION 41 had been founded by the great Dr McBride in 1972. Its charter was to study the first forty-one weeks of human life from conception. McBride had become world famous as a young obstetrician when he drew attention to the drug thalidomide, which caused horrific birth defects around the globe in the early 1960s. As a result of his timely warning, McBride had been feted and applauded. His reputation had reached truly heroic proportions in Australia by the 1970s. Riding this wave, McBride had established Foundation 41.

Following his success with thalidomide, Dr McBride was keen to search out other drugs which caused birth defects. Many of the experiments conducted in the laboratories of the Developmental Biology Unit at Foundation 41 were directed to this end.

Vardy was assigned to do experiments with a range of substances, including the pesticide 2,4,5-T. But after some time he became concerned about some of the experiments. Some were very badly designed and lacked proper protocols. Vardy started to have doubts. He began to wish that Dr McBride would spend more time doing work he was obviously good at, like public relations and running the Foundation. He wished McBride would leave the research to the professional scientists employed by Foundation 41. Under closer scrutiny McBride's personal gloss began to wear off.

By 1980, McBride had come to the conclusion that the morning sickness drug, Debendox or Bendectin, was a possible teratogen (drug which causes birth defects). McBride went public with his fears. In February 1980 he gave evidence against the drug at a major trial in the United States.

In August 1980, McBride directed Phil Vardy to carry out tests with scopalomine, also known as hyoscine, a drug from the same family as an ingredient of Debendox. Vardy was reluctant to do the experiment. He was about to move laboratories and had committed all remaining stocks of rabbits to other experiments. 'But Bill was adamant; he wanted the experiment done. We went ahead with it. We obtained twelve rabbits. Six were injected with hyoscine and the drug was put in the drinking water of the other six. There were no controls,' he said.

'The results of the intraperitoneal part of the experiment were most disappointing. Three animals proved to be not pregnant. Two died. That left only one. The results of the oral dosing were a little more interesting in that one of the six, rabbit No. 71, produced a malformed litter.'

This was a rather insignificant result from a poorly designed experiment and Vardy soon forgot about it. Once he had given McBride a summary of the results, Vardy and his assistant, Jill French went on with their work.

Two years later, in June 1982, a parcel arrived at the offices of Foundation 41, addressed to McBride, Vardy and French. Since McBride was overseas, Vardy opened the parcel to find reprints of an article he had never seen before. The article bore his and French's names as co-authors. It had been published without their knowledge, in *The Australian Journal of Biological Sciences*.

'As I read, it quickly became obvious that things were not right with the paper. The things which particularly upset me were that two animals had been added that I had no knowledge of and the dosages for many other animals had been changed.'

Vardy asked a secretary at the Foundation for the lead-up file concerning the paper. He was horrified when he read the contents. 'It was overwhelmingly obvious that I had in my hands proof of a scientific forgery.'

The file that Vardy read contained progressive alterations to the results of the experiment. Through six separate drafts, the paper was changed so that it finally bore little resemblance to the original experiment. Not only had McBride added two extra rabbits, but he had also included controls that had never been used in the original experiment and changed the drug doses so that they were fairly consistent. McBride had also claimed that the foetuses were sectioned (sliced to enable internal examination), although Vardy found the exact same foetuses intact in jars in McBride's office. All the changes to the drafts and results were in McBride's handwriting. These changes altered an insignificant and meaningless experiment into an indictment of a safe drug. (Debendox is rated by the US Food and Drug Administration as one of the safest drugs.) Vardy was horrified by what he had found. 'It was a deeply bitter blow to find that Bill had done that. He lost his moral authority and his credibility.'

Vardy now faced the dilemma of all whistleblowers. Should he forget about what he had seen and get on with his job? Or should he take a stand? He was distressed about his discovery for a number of reasons. It was hard to believe that Dr William McBride, with such an international reputation, could stoop to such action. By putting Vardy's name on the article, McBride had implicated him in the fraud. On the other hand, by bringing all this out into the open, Vardy risked destroying the good work done by Foundation 41. At stake was his own job and the means of supporting his family. The collapse of Foundation 41 would also result in his colleagues at the Foundation losing their jobs.

'And I was deeply afraid of Bill McBride suing me. I had to throw away an opportunity of a PhD on full salary in an interesting area of science, for an alternative which was not at all attractive.'

After weighing up all the facts Vardy sought legal advice. When McBride returned from overseas Vardy confronted him with fraud allegations. McBride flatly denied having altered the data. He tried to persuade Vardy that the work on Debendox was vitally important. The conversation ended in a stalemate. Vardy then took his concerns to Professor Bob Walsh, a senior member of the Foundation's Research Advisory Committee (RAC). Walsh advised Vardy to look for another job.

But Vardy did receive support from his colleagues who had their own concerns about the research being done at the Foundation. The staff wrote a letter to the RAC asking its members to look into the allegations of fraud.

In the meantime Vardy had more talks with McBride but finally felt he had no alternative but to leave the Foundation. Vardy's colleague Jill French, whose name also appeared on the disputed article, also resigned from the Foundation because of her disgust at the article and the way she was treated. It took her almost a year to find another position.

But before Vardy left, the RAC held an extraordinary meeting to discuss the allegations. Vardy was given no notice of the meeting and was caught totally unprepared, with no time to marshall either his thoughts or his documentation. There were three members present, including the chairman of the RAC, Dr William McBride.

Vardy explained his position. He refused to hand over his evidence saying: 'I'm not willing to have this information disappear and the matter swept under the carpet'. The meeting heard from the other research staff but then ended inconclusively.

After being given his holiday pay Vardy wheeled himself out of the door at Foundation 41 into unemployment.

In what was called a 'major restructuring' all the research staff who had written to the RAC were retrenched, although that decision was overturned after a notified industrial dispute went to the Industrial Commission.

Phil Vardy's worst fears were then realised: the incident was swept under the carpet where it stayed for another five years.

The Research Advisory Committee asked McBride to write to the *Journal of Biological Sciences* and retract the acticle. But all McBride did was write to the editor seeking to retract a table contained in the article. No one followed this up.

Vardy found a job dissecting human tissue at night in an effort to help support his wife and young child. The experience at Foundation 41 had devastated him. Eventually he took up a teaching position in Tasmania. His wife had a speech pathology practice in Sydney and was unable to join him, putting further strains on their marriage.

While he was in Tasmania Vardy discovered that McBride had not withdrawn the journal article. In fact he had done more work and published a note reinforcing the claims in the original paper. Vardy and French then wrote to the editors of the *Journal of Biological Sciences* withdrawing their names from the article. But even that caused no reaction.

Some time before this a journalist, Bill Nicol, contacted Vardy for his assistance with a book he was writing on McBride. Vardy agreed to an interview but Nicol could not find a publisher at that time. Again the matter seemed destined to die.

By 1987 Vardy had returned to Sydney. There he was approached by Dr Norman Swan, a radio journalist who was researching William McBride. In spite of many misgivings Vardy agreed to talk to Swan although he kept doubting whether he was doing the right thing. 'It was as though I was holding the tool for justice to be done and other people wanted me to play the card, to put the key in the lock, to put the bullet into the gun so to speak. I was reluctant in that process.'

Swan aired his findings on the ABC Radio 'Science Show' which looked at the broad issue of scientific fraud and detailed the actions of Dr McBride and Foundation 41. The report was broadcast on Radio National on 12 December 1987.

'It was a Saturday. Gail and I had separated but she had asked me to come home to handle any press when the 'Science Show' broke. She didn't want to be there not knowing where I was. So I did that and we listened together. I was scared and pleased. It was such a good program. I couldn't help but be moved by its content. I realised how far Norman had gone—he had researched thoroughly and put all the pieces together. It was interesting to see it through his eyes, the way he could see the big moral picture, whereas I could see only this one small piece because I was tied up in it.'

There was instantaneous uproar. Initially the allegations, broadcast nationally, were denied by McBride and Foundation 41. The denials were accompanied by considerable mud slinging and personal abuse, much of it directed against Phil Vardy. Vardy felt exposed and frightened. He was sure that McBride would sue him.

But some months later, to its credit, Foundation 41 agreed to an independent inquiry into the 'Science Show' allegations. It was to be headed by no less a figure than Sir Harry Gibbs, the recently retired Chief Justice of the High Court of Australia. The inquiry took three months. The result: Dr William McBride was found to be guilty of scientific fraud.

Phil Vardy's reaction was one of relief. 'It is great when a neutral umpire assesses the situation and comes down on your side.'

McBride resigned from Foundation 41 but again became a director after the Foundation's board was overthrown following an internal faction fight.

In 1989 the Complaints Unit of the New South Wales Health Department laid a total of 15 charges against McBride. Nine of the charges related to McBride's treatment of some of his patients and six related to his research on Debendox. The hearing lasted for a record 198 days. The Medical Tribunal which heard the charges released its final decision in July 1993. In a three to one majority it found that McBride had engaged in 'premeditated deception'.

The tribunal struck McBride off the medical register. It found him not guilty of almost all of the medical charges.

The tribunal's report said:

Dr McBride's character mirrors the classic tragic character—the person of eminence in public life whose good deeds and interest in human welfare command respect and admiration but who is brought down by a fatal flaw in character.

The tribunal also said:

His acts demonstrated a course of conduct of premediated deception in the field of medical research and indicate a serious flaw or defect in his character, a trait of dishonestly.

So, finally, Vardy could feel completely vindicated in his actions and was free to lead his own life again. But at what cost? Most of his worst fears had been realised. Both he and his colleagues had lost their jobs. His marriage was destroyed. His trust in a man he had admired was smashed. He had lost the chance to do a PhD on full salary. Foundation 41 was forced to close. Science had been dragged through the mud.

Would he do it again, knowing what can happen to those who blow the whistle?

'To look back now on the total experience, its cost and its sequelae, it certainly makes you think about whether you would go down that track again and cause that sequence of events. Because inevitably everyone has their price and you tend to think, well, maybe it wasn't worth it in the end. That's my feeling now. But if truly confronted with another case of scientific fraud, that's another question, and the answer has to be ... yes.'

Dr Phil Vardy has managed to put some of his life back together again. He completed a PhD at Macquarie University. He has a new job and is now able to say that the McBride episode is finally behind him. He says he had no idea the struggle would last so long and be so tough. He is much wiser now. 'This event does violence to your identity. A new identity emerges through the trauma. You have to be prepared to take risks ... huge risks. The adverse

consequences are clear—broken marriage, loss of home, unem-
ployability as well as damaged sense of self.'

Now with the trauma behind him there are other things in his
life that are important, including heading up Sailability Australia,
an organisation which facilitates sailing for people with disabilities.

But his experience at Foundation 41 has marked Phil Vardy
irrevocably as an Australian whistleblower. Public confidence in the
integrity of scientific research was greatly enhanced by the courage
of this particular whistleblower.

FREE SPEECH IN DARWIN

'People need to be able to speak on issues that are important and where they can see the wrong thing being done.'—Dr Phil Nitschke

Dr Phil Nitschke reported for work at the Royal Darwin Hospital. It was 24 March 1993 and little did he know that the events which were to follow would turn his life upside down and lead to his public vilification. He was about to become a whistleblower although, until that time, he had never heard of the term.

Nitschke had completed his PhD in physics before he decided that medicine was his real vocation. He was in his thirties when he embarked on a medical degree and since he had been living in the Northern Territory he returned there to do his internship at Royal Darwin.

Because of his background and his strong personal beliefs, Nitschke joined the Darwin branch of the Medical Association for the Prevention of War and also became the hospital's designated resource officer for radiation safety. Nuclear-powered ships sometimes visited Port Darwin and any city permitting nuclear-powered ships to enter its precincts must by law have a radiation accident safety plan.

The hospital sent Nitschke to a conference on radiation injuries and on some training courses. He submitted a detailed analysis to the hospital on ways in which their inadequate nuclear protocol could be upgraded. His suggestions were largely ignored, as were his attempts to raise the awareness of other staff about the dangers of a nuclear accident.

In March 1993 Nitschke had been working full time as a resident at the hospital for four years and was in the Accident and Emergency Department. 'When I got to work that day, I was surprised to see a notice on the board inviting staff to a one hour briefing session on the management of trauma casualties for radiation contamination. Apparently, the USS Houston, which is a nuclear-powered ship, was due in port the next day. But I was the Radiation Safety Officer with the hospital and no one had even raised the matter with me. This was the first I knew about it and I was very angry because I knew the hospital still didn't have a legal Nuclear Accident Disaster Plan and they were trying to get away with a one-hour briefing session, which wasn't even compulsory, except for accident and emergency staff. It was run by the environmental health officer for the Territory and all they did was show a video made in America. The whole thing was a joke'.

Please Explain

NITSCHKE was so angry about the incident that he issued a press release criticising the lack of any protocols to deal with nuclear accidents. The release went out on behalf of the Medical Association for the Prevention of War. The media knew they were on to a story and gave Dr Nitschke air time.

The reaction from the Royal Darwin Hospital was swift. Within 24 hours he was called into the office of the hospital general manager, Dr David Douglas. He was given a week to explain why he should not be suspended for having violated the Public Service Act by speaking to the media. Douglas claimed that the hospital did in fact have an appropriate protocol and was quite able to handle any emergency.

Nitschke's colleagues rallied behind him and, after a flurry of press releases and public posturing, the Department of Health and the hospital held a meeting with representatives from the Resident Medical Officers' Association. The result, on 16 April, was a public apology for Phil Nitschke, a commitment to revise the inadequate protocol dealing with nuclear contamination and an acknowledgment that they had overlooked Nitschke's expertise on this issue.

'It was everything I would have asked for,' Nitschke said. 'I was more than happy with the apology and pleased that they were finally going to address the matter that I'd been telling them about for ages and, as far as I was concerned, life could just continue on in the same old way.'

But Phil Nitschke had still to learn that you do not brawl publicly with the authorities and escape scot free. In July he gave a lecture to the Menzies School of Health Research on whistle-blowing and its impact on health, in which he made a reference to his own experience earlier that year and another instance to do with needle exchanges. A news item about the speech was broadcast on local radio and the hospital asked Nitschke to explain his actions. The medical superintendent at this time, Dr Pauline Wilson, accepted his explanation.

Job On the Line

IN July that same year, some three months after he had received his apology from the Health Department and resumed his role in the Accident and Emergency Unit, interviews were held for contracts for the next year's employment. This was a fairly routine procedure. So routine that he had almost forgotten they were being held. Nitschke was confident that his current position would be upheld, especially since he had requested to again be placed in accident and emergency, a ward where most people hated to work.

On 20 July, the day before his scheduled interview, a Senate Standing Committee visited Darwin to gather evidence for its inquiry into accident preparedness. Dr Nitschke appeared before it and gave evidence under privilege.

A news item about the Senate inquiry's public hearing on the local radio station that evening mentioned that Dr Nitschke from the Medical Association for the Prevention of War had given evidence.

That same night the Minister for Health and Community Services, Mike Reed, issued a press release in which he condemned Nitschke over his 'attacks' on the hospital. 'If Dr Nitschke doesn't like the situation, I have no doubt that RDH will be able to scrape by without him.'

A month later Nitschke was astonished to receive a letter from the hospital telling him that he had been unsuccessful in his application for a position as RMO for 1994. It was from this point that the nightmare of whistleblowing really began.

Nitschke asked for the reasons his contract had not been renewed, especially as he was part way through his obstetrics and gynaecology diploma. He was simply told that his behaviour was deficient. Backed up by his colleagues who were furious at the way he was being treated, Nitschke pressed for a further explanation and the hospital set up an inquiry into the selection procedures. But by September the situation had become volatile.

Patients circulated petitions against his dismissal and doctors at the hospital threatened to strike and refused to co-operate with the inquiry. Allegations of a personal nature started to surface, with vague complaints about Nitschke's personal and professional conduct being floated. The Nursing Federation issued a statement saying that the nuclear issue should not be confused with the incompetence one. Suddenly Nitschke found himself labelled as a bad doctor, something which had never been raised before.

The personal costs were starting to take effect. Never one to walk away from a fight, Nitschke threw himself wholeheartedly into his defence. But his partner, who also worked in a senior position at the hospital, found the situation almost unbearable. A popular, professional woman who always got on well with everyone around her, she was automatically assigned a position in this battle and friends of many years standing were suddenly on the opposite side of the fence. Many of her colleagues stopped talking to her and in the end she could no longer bear to go to work. The hospital was divided in a major way and there were many innocent casualties. At home Nitschke was so preoccupied with his own troubles that he had little time left for hers and the relationship became very tense.

The federal body of the Australian Medical Association also became involved in the battle, defending Nitschke's right to speak out publicly without fear of intimidation or retribution. They appointed Dr Peter Arnold from the federal executive of the AMA to hold an independent inquiry into the affair.

By early November both the internal hospital report and the AMA report were completed. The hospital, which had looked into the selection processes of junior medical officers, stuck by its guns and found no anomalies, stating that the decision had been unanimous, that the general manager had not unduly influenced the process and that Nitschke had only been excluded from round one of the selection process but may have been offered a position in round three, if all positions had not then been filled. The AMA report, on the other hand, found that there had been confusion in the process, that it was not a unanimous decision as claimed, that the general manager had influenced the decision and that Dr Nitschke's job application 'was mishandled'. It recommended that he be given his job back.

In another twist of events, threatened legal action by three separate people meant that this AMA report was never published and at this point, the AMA extricated itself from what was proving to be a complex and sticky issue and had nothing more to do with it. A planned meeting between Nitschke and Dr Brendan Nelson, president of the AMA, in early 1994 failed to eventuate because of a misunderstanding over dates.

On 12 November Nitschke was verbally offered his old job back in Accident and Emergency in spite of the fact that he was now halfway through his Diploma in Obstetrics and Gynaecology and wished to complete his qualification. At about the same time, Nitschke approached Senator Bruce Childs from the Senate inquiry to see if there had been a breach of privilege when he appeared before the Senate committee in July and if that had been a factor in losing his job.

Malodorous

IN late November a new campaign began with the *Northern Territory News* splashing headlines across its front page detailing accusations by a nursing sister against Nitschke. These accusations led to the following charges being laid: that he wore malodorous sneakers, that he swore in front of patients, that his dress standard was poor, that his body odour was offensive to pregnant patients, and that his manner was uninterested and uncaring and his examinations incomplete.

By this stage Nitschke was reeling from the shock of it all. He had always considered himself a good doctor and one who got on well with his patients. He could not work in an area where people felt like this about him so he just left work only to be told he was in breach of his contract. A new inquiry was set up to examine these charges and staff and patients from the Obstetric Unit were questioned about his behaviour—both professional and personal. To Nitschke it felt like a gross invasion of his life.

At the end of January the inquiry was complete and he was shown but not given a copy of it. In spite of having been cleared of all the charges except one of swearing in front of a patient, which he admitted to, he was told that he could not return to the obstetrics ward for practical reasons. It would be detrimental to the ward because of the ill feeling that had been generated by the dispute. Nitschke also discovered that there was no place in the Northern Territory where he could complete his Obstetrics Diploma. So on 3 February, less than 11 months after the USS Houston sailed into Port Darwin, he left home to complete his obstetrics training in South Australia.

Even now the ordeal was not over. His relationship with his partner was damaged even further by their forced separation and when he finally returned to the Territory he was unemployed. He did some locum work at Palmerston Hospital but the media quickly found out and he knew that there was no future for him in the public system. He also had to attend two hearings of the Senate Privileges Committee, one in Canberra and one in Darwin. He decided to represent himself—a 'big mistake because the Department sent ten people and hired a QC. It was much harder than I expected and I felt pretty well demolished by some of it'.

When the report was released in June 1995 it found that he had indeed been discriminated against but could not establish, beyond reasonable doubt, that the reason for this had been his appearance before the Senate inquiry and therefore no finding of contempt could be made. The report went on to say that 'it would be especially worthwhile if a remedy were to follow from those who have punished Dr Nitschke for exercising what should be his right as a citizen, as a representative of a community organisation and as an informed professional, to state publicly his medical opinions'.

Through the whole depressing experience there were a few rays of light. Soon after his dismissal in August, he met Dr Jean Lennane from the Whistleblowers Association and she warned him of the different ways in which whistleblowers can be treated. 'That was tremendously helpful, because there is no way I could have anticipated the personal consequences and to know that what was happening to me was not unusual helped to make it easier to cope with.'

Nitschke also received a lot of support from fellow doctors. On one occasion two huge banners saying FREE SPEECH? were hung from the roof of the Royal Darwin Hospital. When guards tried to gain access to the roof to remove them, they found that the keys had been broken off and glued into the locks. Many of his fellow doctors were also very supportive and seven of them resigned in sympathy with him. The general public was also sympathetic. 'I had people coming up to me on the street and offering their support— that is very sustaining.' Nitschke also says that a doctor who blows the whistle is treated a bit easier that some others. 'You don't get dragged before a psychiatrist and doctors usually don't have too much trouble finding another job.'

Ultimately, he feels that his actions were justified. 'People need to be able to speak on issues that are important and where they can see the wrong thing being done.'

The Royal Darwin Hospital now has a credible nuclear protocol in place and doctors are properly trained in correct procedures. The fact that he was offered another job means that the hospital acknowledged that a wrong had been done and Nitschke has now set up in private practice from where he continues to speak out on issues that concern him.

In particular in 1996 he came to national prominence when confronted with the difficulty of lawfully implementing the Northern Territory's unilateral euthanasia legislation. After meeting the requirements of the legislation, Nitschke attended upon a patient, Max Bell, a Broken Hill taxi driver who was suffering terminal cancer. Nitschke defended the patient's right to die, speaking in media interviews that were to be broadcast and published across the world. However Nitschke and Max Bell were unable to get the signature of another specialist doctor required by the legislation. Mr Bell died, without the aid of euthanasia, on 2 August 1996.

By the following month, Nitschke had successfully gained the required signatures for another patient, a retired Darwin builder, Bob Dent. On 22 September 1996, Mr Dent became the first Australian to legally choose to die under the Northern Territory's unilateral euthanasia legislation.

THE MAN WHO
SAVED THE BANK

'Your position is redundant and you are redundant.' —Paul Kemp, managing director of the Tasmania Bank to Alwyn Johnson, 3 July 1991.

T HE 1980s in Australia were the profligate decade. Entrepreneurs were feted and banks fell over themselves to lend them money. It was the era in which politicians scrambled to be photographed with the movers and shakers. Who could forget the famous photograph of Hawkie, Richo and Last Resort Laurie (the Prime Minister Bob Hawke, Senator Graham Richardson and Laurie Connell, chief executive of Rothwells Merchant Bank) in a row boat off the West Australian coast on a fishing trip. This was indicative of the times. The deals, the connections, the takeovers, the stunning acquisitions were dominating the media and the glossy business magazines which were claiming full knowledge of what was going on.

But the 1990s suffered the whirlwind as the country's financial system began to collapse under the strain of the excesses.

Ten banks experienced major losses while the State banks of Victoria and South Australia teetered on the brink of ruin and had to be rescued by the munificence of Australian taxpayers to the tune of around $6 billion. Soon afterwards the Labor governments of those states were drummed out of office by an irate public.

In the uproar that followed it was not generally realised that the Tasmania Bank very nearly went the same way.

This is the story of the man who saved the bank from ruin in the nick of time, and the way in which his loyalty was repaid.

Alwyn Johnson was a career banker. He began working in a bank when he was seventeen and steadily worked his way upwards. He was born in Horsham, Victoria, in 1949. He had three elder sisters, and his father was a carpenter. After a happy childhood with all-round sporting experience and diligence at school work, Alwyn joined the then CBC Bank and began what was an unblemished career. His philosophy in dealing with bank customers was to satisfy himself that the customer always had the ability to repay the money the bank was lending. He was well aware that heavy financial pressure on any individual could have devastating effects. You could lose your home or your marriage. 'I had to make decisions with the customer in mind as well as the bank,' he said. In his mid-thirties he was manager of underwriting in the treasury department of the National Australia Bank and one of an elite group, hand-picked to be fast tracked on the promotions list. But this also meant that he was at the beck and call of the bank. He lived in a house provided by the bank and was expected to move whenever and wherever they wanted.

Alwyn and his wife Julie had always wanted to live in the country, with land around them and a permanent home where their children could grow up safely. They did not want to leave Australia— this would have been the next career move for Johnson. They fell in love with a property just outside Launceston in Tasmania and decided that this was where they wanted to build their dream home. The only problem was finding a job there. This was not an easy task in the banking industry in rural Tasmania. Johnson applied for a number of jobs and, just as their house was nearing completion, he was offered a position as manager of corporate lending at the newly formed Tasmania Bank. This bank was an amalgamation of the old Launceston Bank for Savings or LBS, as it was affectionately known, which had been operating since 1834, and the Tasmanian Permanent Building Society.

It was a wonderful start to their new life and the Johnsons were overjoyed. Alwyn Johnson started work on 18 February 1988, just two weeks after the new managing director, Don Adams. It was a new beginning for everyone and Adams, who had come from the State Bank of New South Wales, was keen to make his mark. He appointed a former colleague, Neil Moore, as head of a new division called Wholesale Banking. Its role was to move the Tasmania Bank into the big league, lending money in the corporate world, rather than just helping the mums and dads of Tasmania to purchase their homes. It was a bold move, fraught with difficulties for a small bank with limited funds.

The Wholesale Banking Division started off with a staff of twenty, but soon found that Tasmania was too small for its ambitions and turned its attention to the mainland where it offered syndicated loans to property developers and entrepreneurs, including Warwick Fairfax who was launching a takeover bid on his family company.

Meanwhile, Johnson was promoted to chief manager of lending and was also appointed a member of the bank's Credit Review Committee. This committee's role was to examine and endorse all proposed loans before they were sent to the Board for approval. It was here that he became aware of the activities of the Wholesale Banking Division and he knew, from his long experience in banking, that these activities were dangerous and misguided.

Johnson was so concerned about the amounts and numbers of loans being made that he spoke to the managing director, Don Adams, asking what would happen if one of these big loans went bad. Adams replied that they would have to cross their fingers and hope that nothing went wrong.

As the months went by Johnson became more perturbed. The new managing director was popular with most people at the bank and at the Credit Review Board Johnson was the only person continually to query the proposed loans. He was seen as a bit of a wet blanket. Over the first two years of its life the Tasmania Bank increased its staff by around 39 per cent and its expenditure by 72.5 per cent. The bank moved its executives into new and more sumptuous offices and acquired two new Volvos, one for the managing director's wife and another, complete with chauffeur, for the managing director himself. This last addition caused some amusement to the good burghers of Launceston.

In November 1989, some twenty months after he had joined the bank, Johnson was so concerned that he drafted a letter to the Premier and Treasurer of Tasmania, the Honourable Michael Field, outlining all the problems that he could see at the bank and warning of impending disaster. But Johnson did not send it because he knew that there were still no obvious danger signs and his warnings could be discounted. So he left it in his drawer at home. Johnson kept hoping that the bank's auditors would discover the problem, but the 1989 Tasmania Bank annual report was published with no mention of 'shaky' loans.

Each night Johnson came home and recounted the latest 'disaster' to Julie. Finally she could bear it no more and she typed up his draft letter on their old typewriter. Then they spent several weeks revising and discussing it, weighing up the consequences and considering what might be the different outcomes. The one thing they never considered was that Alwyn might lose his job.

On 9 June 1990 Johnson sent his anonymous letter to the Premier of Tasmania. The letter comprised nine pages of precise detail about the problems within the Tasmania Bank which could spell its demise and produce a massive financial burden for the government and people of Tasmania.

The Premier took the letter seriously and immediately called in independent auditors to investigate the claims. He also appointed the secretary of Treasury and Finance, Dr Michael Vertigan, to the board of the Tasmania Bank. Neil Moore, head of the Wholesale Banking Division, resigned from his position and returned to Sydney. The managing director, Don Adams, was given a copy of the letter and there was a concerted effort within the bank to discover the author.

A month went by and Johnson waited for some action. The same sort of loans were still being approved by the Board, even though Vertigan had a copy of his letter detailing exactly these problems. Johnson knew that some loans had already failed but the Board was not being told. So on 8 August he wrote another letter to Premier Field telling him that there would be a run on the bank unless urgent action was taken and the Wholesale Banking Division closed down.

At about the same time he was sent to a conference in Sydney and shared a taxi with the auditor who was preparing the report on the Tasmania Bank for the Board. Johnson went to see the auditor after the conference and revealed himself as the author of the two letters to the Premier. He then assisted the auditors in the preparation of their report.

The auditor's report was tendered to the Board meeting in October, a meeting which lasted for three days instead of the usual few hours. At the end of it Don Adams was given the choice of resigning or being sacked. He chose to resign.

The Board then asked the auditors if they knew who had written the letters to the Premier. They admitted that they did but would not disclose Johnson's identity. So the Board asked that a message be passed to the unknown person, thanking him. The assessed losses to the bank were large, but they were not a lethal blow.

After news of the boardroom drama broke in the media there was a minor run on the bank. The problem was debated at length in the Tasmanian Parliament and the Premier claimed to have acted quickly when he received information about the bank, so that the net loss was only around $8 million, instead of possibly hundreds of millions. In fact, the total loss grew to more than $18 million.

After these dramatic events everything seemed to settle down. Alwyn and Julie had a second son and the position of managing director of the Tasmania Bank was advertised. Johnson applied for it. But the Field Government was growing increasingly nervous after the close call and began secret negotiations to sell the Tasmania Bank.

In March 1991 staff members were called into the boardroom and told that their bank was to be merged with its small rival, the SBT or Savings Bank of Tasmania. Paul Kemp, general manager of SBT, had been appointed managing director of the Tasmania Bank and he would hold both positions until 1 September when the two banks would merge to become the Trust Bank. The Premier announced that there would be no sackings as a result of the merger.

A few days later the Launceston *Examiner* carried a front page story giving the names of four senior executives already appointed by Kemp to positions in the new bank. Johnson's name was not among them.

Johnson had never met his new boss and had been concerned that he might be passed over for a senior position. After talking it over with Julie he decided to write to Kemp, introducing himself and detailing his expertise. In the letter he informed Kemp that he was the man who had saved the Tasmania Bank by writing to the Premier. He listed events that he thought would have occurred if he had not taken that course of action. Johnson sent the letter by registered post. Kemp did not reply. Johnson tried to ring Kemp. He was never available. Johnson then realised that he was persona non grata. In spite of his experience and qualifications he was not appointed to any of the executive positions on offer and he began to fear for his job.

Alwyn Johnson was also growing increasingly concerned about the merger, which was looking like a recipe for disaster. For a start, SBT was an even smaller bank than the Tasmania Bank and it was against all good banking practice for a small bank to rescue a larger one. In addition, no one had carried out the due diligence checks which would have shown that SBT had some bad loans and was not in a really strong position itself. But the merger was approved by the Governor of the Reserve Bank, Bernie Fraser, and by the Prime Minister, Paul Keating.

Johnson began to think about protecting himself in this uncertain situation. In early May he telephoned Dr Michael Vertigan at home, identified himself as the author of the two letters to Premier Field and asked for a meeting. A few weeks later Vertigan agreed to see him in his Hobart office on a Saturday morning. Johnson explained that he had revealed himself to Kemp and was now concerned for his position. He also outlined his concerns about the upcoming merger. Vertigan undertook to tell Premier Field about their conversation but took no steps to help Johnson.

Shortly after this the Tasmanian MP, Dr Bob Brown, appeared on ABC TV's *7.30 Report* talking about whistleblowers and the need for legislation to protect them. Julie saw the item and told her husband about it. This was the first time either of them had heard the term 'whistleblower' but it seemed to fit what Johnson had done. Johnson spoke to Brown, identifying himself as the Tasmania Bank whistleblower and Brown agreed to see him at once. Brown then took up Johnson's case, speaking to the Premier on his behalf. Premier Field did nothing.

At the bank a massive restructuring was taking place prior to the merger and staff members were being offered voluntary redundancies. Johnson was not interested in the offer because he had a mortgage and a young family to support. He continued to worry about his own future as well as the bank's.

On 1 July Alwyn Johnson faxed a confidential letter to the Governor of the Reserve Bank, Bernie Fraser. The letter explained that this was the second time he had come forward to alert authorities to problems within an Australian bank. He outlined the events of the Tasmania Bank and drew attention to the situation with the SBT-Tasmania Bank merger, emphasising that this bank would not be government guaranteed. He said that the new management was even more incompetent than the old one and asked for a meeting with Fraser to explain his concerns, requesting that they meet before Fraser talked to the managing director so that he could give him all the facts.

Johnson was surprised when Bernie Fraser rang him personally, but disappointed when Fraser said he had been assured by Paul Kemp that there were no problems with the new bank.

The following day Alwyn Johnson was sacked.

On 3 July Kemp was seeing senior officers at fifteen minute intervals about their redundancy payouts and Johnson was also given an appointment. He was the only officer who had not applied for redundancy. When he entered Kemp's office for the first and only meeting he was to have with him, Kemp handed him a letter of redundancy saying: 'Your position is redundant and you are redundant'. He then handed Johnson a second letter and said: 'We will enforce this letter to the hilt'.

Johnson would not give Kemp the satisfaction of seeing how upset he was. He replied formally: 'I'd like to wish the Trust Bank all the best for the future'. He left Kemp's office. The other person in the room, Philip Spinks, then escorted Johnson to his office, waiting while he packed up his belongings, took him to his car and waited while he removed his possessions from the vehicle and then took the car keys.

Johnson went to a public phone to ring his wife to tell her what had happened. Julie had been expecting the call and after the anxious conversation with Alwyn she went into their beautiful garden. 'It no longer looked the same. It was as though a dark cloud had covered it. Everything was clouded. Everything was different after that phone call. It was awful.'

The letter that Kemp had handed Johnson threatened him with legal action if he criticised the bank. It said:

The bank has been advised that you have made contact with various individuals and bodies in order to provide what can only be described as scurrilous misinformation regarding the bank's affairs.

The only people Johnson had spoken to were Bernie Fraser and Michael Vertigan, to whom he had turned in their professional capacity as financial watchdogs.

Johnson spent that evening with others from the bank who had taken the redundancy offer. They were not quite sure what had happened to him and he was still reeling from the shock. 'When you get dismissed from the bank you've just saved, it's the most dreadful thing you can ever imagine.'

The next morning Johnson started to have chest pains and Julie rushed him to the doctor who prescribed medication to calm him down. For weeks afterwards Johnson was in shock. He could not talk to anyone or see anyone. He had delusions that the police were going to search his house and that he had done something wrong. His condition worsened. He got a fever, then pneumonia. For months he was very ill. Julie coped well initially but, as Alwyn started to recover, she too succumbed to the stress and became ill.

The effect on their family was traumatic. Their eldest son, Alwyn, had just started attending a private school but now they could not afford the fees and he had to return to his old school. Their youngest son Matthew was not yet twelve months old and Julie had been looking forward to full-time motherhood. Now she had to get a job night nursing which meant that Alwyn looked after the baby. With one stroke the family was changed forever.

Alwyn began looking for another job but was also seeking some political help to redress the wrong which he believed had been done him. He had saved the government, after all, from the possible collapse of the Tasmania Bank, a debt that had been acknowledged by the bank's Board and by the Premier.

In Victoria, the State Bank had aleady collapsed and the same was occurring in South Australia. Premier Field said in Parliament, however, that the government did not intervene in the staffing policies of the banks and that he had been assured by the bank that Johnson's dismissal had nothing to do with writing the letters. After the Field Government lost the 1992 election, the new Liberal

Government took no responsibility for the actions of its predecessors, despite representations on Johnson's behalf by prominent federal Liberal, John Howard.

Johnson had also approached his union for help. In August 1990 he had shown the secretary of the Bank Employees Union, Mel Cooper, copies of his two letters to the Premier. Cooper had shared Johnson's concerns about the bank and raised them with Michael Field. Just days before his dismissal Johnson spoke to the union again, telling them that he was worried about his position. The union took no action on his behalf. After his dismissal he received a letter from the secretary of the Finance Sector Union telling him that he was no longer eligible for membership.

After ten months of unemployment Alwyn Johnson found another job, out of his field of expertise. It paid a fraction of his former salary.

When the media took up his case the Trust Bank claimed that he had taken voluntary redundancy, then tried to discredit him, saying that he was incapable of holding down any position at all in the bank. These claims were quickly disproved. Johnson finally found a legal firm to take on his case on a pro bono basis and they found a barrister who commenced legal action against the Trust Bank. The case was listed for hearing in the Hobart Court in September 1994 but was withdrawn at the last minute. The bank issued a statement saying that the proceedings against it had been withdrawn and the bank was entirely satisfied with the outcome. Johnson obviously was not.

The Senate inquiry into Whistleblowers took up Johnson's case and numerous senators have raised his situation with the Reserve Bank, the Trust Bank and the Tasmanian Government. The Alwyn Johnson case has been debated in the parliaments of Tasmania and the Commonwealth on numerous occasions.

Since his dismissal he has been a consistent campaigner for whistleblower protection legislation for both public and private sector employees. In 1996 and 1997 he was pressing the Commonwealth Attorney-General, Daryl Williams, to bring in such legislation with its over-riding impact on all jurisdictions. He argued that with white collar crime and fraud estimated to cost $16 billion a year to both the private and public sectors, whistleblower protection could be one very effective weapon for the community.

Alwyn Johnson pays tribute to his wife Julie for her tactical, emotional and bread-winning support through his ordeal. What started as an act of concern for his bank has resulted in a personal upheaval. Asked if he regretted the action he had taken in the retrospective light of these devastating personal consequences, Johnson says, 'I deeply regret losing my job. Would I do it again? . . . I'd have to say—yes. Who'd want to be a senior executive of a bank which collapsed.'

Alwyn Johnson is still in limbo. Five years after he alerted the government, quietly and confidentially, to the problems in the Tasmania Bank. Julie is forced to continue working in order to help maintain the family. He has lost his career, his superannuation and his self-esteem. For doing what he saw as his public duty he has been vilified and ignored with no meaningful acknowledgement by the community's representatives of just how important his actions were.

A LAW UNTO THEMSELVES

'Legislation, as enacted by Parliament, should be implemented at least to the letter of the law.'—Senate Select Committee on Unresolved Whistleblower Cases 1995.

J IM LEGGATE is a big supporter of mining. It is an industry which creates wealth. The resources from the earth, discovered, extracted and sold to the world, contribute massively to human wellbeing.

Australia is particularly blessed. It is a vast continent, rich with minerals in seemingly inexhaustible quantities. Leggate knows that Australia needs the mining industry.

Leggate's experience in the industry has also produced a knowledge of the damage which occurs when mining is not carried out correctly or responsibly. He is concerned that such a big industry does not appear to have the proper checks and balances. And Leggate is a man who should know.

Jim Leggate has worked as an environmental scientist in the mining industry for more than twenty years and, from 1983 to 1986, was responsible for protecting the magnificent and fragile Kakadu National Park in the Northern Territory from any ill effects which might be caused by the Ranger uranium mine. This was in the early years of the government of Prime Minister Bob Hawke when Australia's environmental movement was looking for reasons to force the closure of the mine.

Jim Leggate was a forester by training. He was born in Rhodesia (later Zimbabwe) in 1937. His father, Jim senior, was a government doctor working in difficult areas of public health including the country's leper settlements. Jim Leggate and his wife Josephine had settled in Rhodesia in the 1920s and brought up their children in the privileged position then enjoyed by the white colonists. Nevertheless, their staunch Anglicanism and humanitarian values instilled in the young Jim some sense of social responsibility, even if he did not realise it at the time.

The Leggates saw that Jim received a good education sending him to Cape Town University where he won a scholarship in science and forestry to Oxford University, England.

After graduation and ten years working in the Solomon Islands for the British Colonial Service, Jim Leggate emigrated to Australia in 1969, becoming an Australian citizen soon after. He married Joan, a Queenslander, and together they brought up four children.

He began work in the field of environmental science when he was employed to begin rehabilitation of the bauxite mine at Weipa in far north Queensland. The mine was expanding at the rate of 2.5 square kilometres a year and Leggate had to manage a massive tree planting program that would cover the scars left by the mining. He later carried out a similar job in the sand mining areas of New South Wales and then moved into coal mining where he coordinated environmental impact studies and helped in the formulation of mining policy. By the end of this intensity of experiences, through the application of practical measures to help build an ethos of care for the environment which had delivered such wealth, Jim Leggate knew as much as anyone in Australia about the industry and its practices.

He had seen at first hand the terrible scarring and environmental ruin irresponsible mining could inflict. He also believed that with goodwill and commitment, almost all serious impacts of mining could be eliminated within a few short years ... if the correct procedures were followed and if mining was done with proper care.

Over the many years Leggate worked he earned the respect of his peers and the recognition of the mining industry. He gave regular papers on the subject of 'environmental mining'. And in 1982 he became chairman of the Environment Committee of the Queensland Chamber of Mines.

In 1986 Leggate joined the Queensland Department of Resource Industries as an ecologist. Part of his job was to ensure that the mining industry in the great State of Queensland complied with that State's mining laws. When a mining company was granted a lease, it had to agree to certain 'mandatory' environmental conditions about how it would carry out its operations and how it would rehabilitate the site, both during the mining and at the end of the operation. These were contractural and legally enforceable.

Under the Mining Act Leggate, a government ecologist, was authorised to enter any mining concerns and investigate their compliance with the environmental obligations stipulated by the lease. But he soon discovered that his powers of enforcement were non-existent. All he could do was to write a report about what he found and pass it on to his superiors in the department for further action.

As he went about his work, Leggate found that the Mining Act was being breached on a regular basis by almost all the companies he inspected. Some of the infringements were minor. Others were major. But of greatest concern was the fact that few companies were accomplishing ongoing rehabilitation of their sites. Unless the Queensland Government stepped in and insisted that they improve their results, Leggate could see big problems down the track. He feared that when mining was completed and a company left a particular site the problem would remain and it would be up to the taxpayer to finance the clean-up. In some cases, where mining had been carried out for twenty or thirty years, the damage would be massive and the costs enormous.

About this time there was a gold rush occurring in Queensland. Leggate was concerned when he saw new gold mines opening up, old ones being re-worked and major environmental problems, being totally ignored. Acidic tailings waste was accumulating rapidly, leading to potentially huge problems, and one gold mine closed down, leaving the clean-up to be carried out by the government—at public expense. Leggate suggested that the Minister, Martin Tenni, use a 'show cause' notice under the Act, to make mine lessees meet their obligations. This legal device meant that the lessee could be asked to show cause why the mine should not be closed or a fine imposed for breaching the mining laws. But the Minister apparently thought this was going too far.

From his agitation about the wholesale flouting of lease obligations to environmental protection Leggate was soon seen as a thorn in the side of Minister Tenni's government, then headed by Sir Johannes Bjelke-Petersen. At one stage Tenni described the government ecologist as a poor ambassador for the public service. Leggate responded that, for his part, he was only trying to do his job. If he stopped officially reporting the catastrophes that he was witnessing, then he could be seen to be negligent in his statutory duty. But if he continued to do so he was seen as a nuisance by his political masters. At one stage Jim Leggate was sent on a public relations course by the department and was taught how to smile while answering the telephone.

If he had few supporters within his own department, he had even fewer in the government. Mining industry executives told him that he was being 'over-zealous' because the Premier himself was always telling them not to worry about all this nonsense of cleaning up. Their job was to mine as well as they could, pay the government its rail freight and forget about the greenies.

But Leggate persisted with his reports and his internal complaints to the department and as time went by Tenni responded, at last realising that there were definite problems. The Minister called for a Code of Practice for the mining industry. Leggate was asked to work on it. After so much aggravation it looked as if things might improve.

The political climate in Queensland was about to change for the better. The days of Bjelke-Petersenism under the National Party were numbered. The Fitzgerald inquiry into police and political corruption had exposed the Bjelke-Petersen regime and discredited it. The Nationals were swept from office by the people of Queensland and in late 1989 a new government under the leadership of a young Labor Party lawyer, Wayne Goss, came to power. The Fitzgerald inquiry had identified institutional failure in Queensland's public service during the Bjelke-Petersen years and recommended new legislation to protect whistleblowers as a cornerstone of sweeping reforms.

The Goss Government immediately set about implementing Fitzgerald's recommendations, including whistleblower protection legislation. Under the legislation new bodies, the Criminal Justice Commission (CJC) and the Electoral and Administrative Review Commission (EARC), both had the power to investigate whistle-blowers' allegations and offer them 'protection' if they were genuine.

Other reforms were not implemented so quickly. Queensland

had a new Minister for Mines, Ken Vaughan. Leggate noted that Vaughan stopped all work on the new Code of Practice for the mining industry that Tenni had authorised. Vaughan told the Queensland Parliament that there already was one in place. Vaughan also said that the regulatory approach to the mining industry was the wrong one. Leggate started to become very concerned at this.

In 1990 Jim Leggate's job was reclassified to that of Principal Environmental Officer. He had to apply for it. His application failed and he was told it was because he was too legalistic. He felt sure that it was because he was too honest in his assessments. By now there were several other environmental officers in his department and they all saw the problems within the mining industry that Leggate was seeing. He was not alone. Leggate now felt that he had no alternative but to fight. He had carried out his statutory duty. But instead of official recognition of having carried out those duties, he was being bureaucratically disempowered.

On 14 January 1991, more than a year after the election of the Goss Government, Leggate filed what is called a 'grievance' about not being appointed to the new position. Five of his departmental colleagues also lodged a joint grievance protesting that Leggate should have been appointed Principal Environmental Officer. The grievance got Jim Leggate nowhere. And the bureaucratic run-around which followed was incredible.

Leggate compiled a list of forty-four mines in Queensland which he asserted were violating their lease obligations. He delivered this list by hand to the Director General of Mines, Paul Breslin, in February 1991. Leggate believed he could have included more material but felt that he had made his point. As far as he knew this information was never checked or investigated. His grievance was determined on the basis of departmental staffing procedures instead of his allegations of possible collusion between the department and the mining industry.

Another senior job was advertised in his department and again Leggate applied. Again he was unsuccessful. Again he lodged a grievance. It was dated 27 August 1991. But this grievance could not be resolved because the earlier one was still outstanding. Catch 22!

Leggate was growing increasingly frustrated and concerned. He needed to tell someone who was in a position to take some action about his worries. He could see a massive environmental problem looming for Queensland in the years ahead and no one in the Department of Mines would listen. He felt that the Fitzgerald inquiry had been hinting at exactly his situation when Commissioner Tony Fitzgerald QC had talked about institutionalised problems. Leggate was confident there were now sufficient protective measures, with the draft Whistleblowers' Bill before Parliament, to stop him being victimised for drawing attention to the truth. So he decided to take action, but only within the limits of the draft Bill. This required him to only take matters up to designated authorities. In short, he could not 'go public'.

He started by writing a report to the Queensland Ombudsman. This outlined his personal situation and the broader concerns which surrounded it. A preliminary meeting with the Ombudsman's staff confirmed that he had a case, but months later he was told that it was outside the Ombudsman's jurisdiction because Leggate was not personally affected by the wrongdoing he reported.

Leggate then sent the same report to the EARC, who were interested. But some time later the chairman, Tom Sherman, left to take up a job as the chairman of the National Crime Authority. Leggate's case was passed by the EARC to the Public Sector Management Commission which, under Fitzgerald reforms, had replaced the Public Service Board. This commission was reviewing the efficiency of each government department in turn, but on the basis of their dealings with their clients. In the case of the Department of Mines the 'client' was taken to be the mining industry and not the people of Queensland. Leggate's complaint was based on the assertion with supporting evidence that the Mines Department had too close a relationship with the mining industry and was ignoring its responsibilities to its true client. His complaint apparently was deemed by the Public Sector Management Commission to be outside the parameters of its review of the department.

Leggate had now taken his concern to three separate bodies. But no one was able to deal with it. He was caught in a nightmare of bureaucratic buck-passing. But the identified problems were still there and were growing all the time.

In the creation and transmission of documents during this process, Leggate kept his department informed about his actions and tried to follow proper channels. His agitation to the bureaucracy was making him very unpopular. But it appeared that it was to no avail. Leggate now decided to raise the stakes and take a bigger risk.

The Queensland Minister for Environment was in the process of drafting an Environmental Protection Act and Leggate wrote to him as a private citizen and enclosed copies of all his reports. He sent the same correspondence to the Director General of Mines, Paul Breslin. Leggate was officially reprimanded for having written to the Minister and Breslin told him he had breached his duties. Leggate later heard that the information had been taken to the Goss Cabinet but the ministers collectively took no action. But at the same time the information was leaked to the press. Some journalists chased the story but press coverage soon died.

Included in the 'leaked' report were examples to demonstrate the scope of alleged non-compliance practices in the Queensland mining industry.

1. Comalco Ltd's Weipa bauxite mine, Cape York. Alleged breach of Commonwealth Aluminium Pty Ltd Agreement Act (1957). The company for many years has mined more land than it was permitted to mine, under Section 19(d) of the Act, in relation to the amount of rehabilitation it has completed. It appears that, to date, the government has not provided confirmation as to whether the steps being taken to regenerate the mined areas are sufficient to satisfy Section 19.
2. Collinsville Coal Company (MIM). Alleged breach of special conditions of Mining Lease 1009, and alleged breach of Clean Waters Act, Section 23 and Section 31.
   There is a lack of progressive rehabilitation using topsoil which breaches Special Condition 2.4, and possibly special conditions 1.3 and 2.3 also. Mining has continued for several years after the lease expiry date, pending its renewal and the tightening of conditions.
3. BHP Ltd's Moura coal mine. Alleged breach of provisions of the Thiess, Peabody, Mitsui Coal Pty Ltd Agreement Act (1962–

1965). Section 31(d) of that Act requires the company to submit annually its proposals for regeneration of mined areas for approval by the Minister. Up to 1990 no such submission appears to have been made. The submissions that have been received since 1990 apparently have not yet been approved. This mine is a huge open cut, at least 25 km in length.

4. Placer Ltd's Kidston Gold Mine. Alleged breach of special conditions attached to Mining Lease 3347. The lessee has mined more land than it was permitted to mine under special condition 16, without having progressed its rehabilitation. This discrepancy has been as high as 800ha. This is the second largest gold mine in Australia and has generated a huge mass of acidic tailings waste.

5. Horn Island Gold Mine, Torres Strait. Alleged breach of special conditions attaching to Mining Lease 5948. The government permitted the lessee to mine in breach of special condition 18 which required acid-forming waste to be buried. Clean-up of this mine which is now defunct is at public cost.

The new Minister for Industry Resources, Tony McGrady, issued a media release claiming that Leggate's report was not an 'official' one and trying to play it all down. Leggate believed that McGrady was muddying the waters by claiming that the new policy would fix up all the problems when Leggate knew the government already was making deals which would weaken it. Leggate was outraged at McGrady's public statements and wrote to him, bluntly pointing out his errors. McGrady initially agreed to meet with him, but then cancelled the meeting.

The battle lines were well and truly drawn now and Leggate was forced to fight on several fronts. In August 1992 he lodged a complaint with the Criminal Justice Commission, claiming that McGrady and Breslin were in breach of public trust. At the same time he was trying to carry out his duties as an environmental officer. But he was severely hampered by the fact that the Queensland Mining Council had apparently written to all its members urging them to ignore Leggate. When he attended a meeting in his official capacity all the industry delegates walked out.

At the end of August he was told by the CJC that there was

no suspicion of official misconduct in the department. He presented them with new information and was interviewed about his complaints. In November 1992 they informed him that because their jurisdiction only extended to potentially criminal matters, his complaint fell outside their office and he should take his case to the Ombudsman. He was back where he had started.

During the latter part of 1992, fed up, tired and frustrated by the way in which the department was isolating him, Jim Leggate decided to take a week's leave. Before he went he was told that there was a vacancy for him in the Forestry Department, but he told them he did not want to consider a transfer at that time. The only department he wanted to transfer to was Environment and Heritage but he had been unsuccessful in arranging such a transfer there. He did not immediately accept the job in Forestry because he felt he could do more good where he was. However, when he returned to work the mining industry no longer trusted him. He was told there was no longer a job for him in Mines.

He could see that the mining industry was being allowed to breach all the rules with no protest from the only body capable of controlling it—the Department of Mines.

In the months that followed Jim Leggate found a term which, to his mind, described the relationship between the Department of Mines and the mining industry it was meant to regulate—'regulatory capture'. It seemed to describe the way in which the very authority that was meant to regulate and control the industry for the public good, was actually facilitating the mismanagement of mining sites.

Jim Leggate had almost reached the end of his options. He took the job in Forestry—he had little choice—and worked there for three years, reluctantly but productively. But he was effectively isolated from the area in which he had the most knowledge and expertise.

He had been to almost every regulatory and accountability body he could think of to draw attention to this problem which was costing the state, on his estimate, more than $1 million a week. He even appealed to the Commonwealth Attorney-General on the grounds of the validation of mining grants by the Native Title Bill and the environmental performance of mining companies in

Queensland with overseas exports and finance. But the all too familiar reply was that his major concern—the environmental one—was outside federal jurisdiction.

In 1994 the CJC agreed to include mining in its inquiry into the improper disposal of liquid waste in Queensland. Jim Leggate gave evidence under oath but his allegation of suspected misconduct by the Director General of Mines was largely ignored. However the inquiry did find that there were problems within the mining industry and recommended a full inquiry into mining activities. The Minister for Resource Industries, Tony McGrady, admitted that some of the problems that Leggate raised were real. 'Some mines had a pretty abysmal record in environmental management—but things are being done about it,' McGrady said. But by 1996 no further inquiry had been carried out. The recommendations of the Criminal Justice Commission have been ignored.

Leggate later told the Senate inquiry into unresolved whistle-blower cases that he disagreed with the Minister's statement that things were being done. On the contrary, he believed that the problem was growing on a daily basis and that no one had the courage to take on the mining industry. In spite of all the legislation passed by Parliament it was a law unto itself. Leggate estimated the cost of outstanding rehabilitation in Queensland alone is more than $1 billion and that many of the problems which have occurred in New Guinea from the mining at Ok Tedi were being repeated in Queensland too.

As a result of Leggate's concern for a cleaner and more responsible mining industry he had lost his job, was locked out of the industry he had devoted almost two decades to and had been let down by colleagues he had respected. None of his former colleagues had been prepared to publicly agree with his prognosis. But over all these disappointments Leggate was most angered that he was not able to carry out the Parliament's wishes, enacted through the Parliament's legislation, to protect the environment from within the government itself—the Department which had the power to identify the problems and do something about them.

Leggate has also been left wondering whether his fate would have been different if there had been no whistleblower protection in Queensland. And how is it, with so many regulatory bodies, there was not one capable or willing to confront the mining industry and safeguard the public interest?

Jim Leggate's vindication will come. The problems he has sought to expose regrettably have had cumulative, devastating and costly effects.

In 1995 the Senate Select Committee on Unresolved Whistleblower cases acknowledged Jim Leggate's contribution while seeking to umpire the dispute between Leggate and the Queensland Government over his employment.

> The Committee acknowledges the endeavours by the Queensland Government to address the environmental problems caused by mining. Further, the Committee considers that the implementation of this policy did play a major part in the problems experienced by Mr Leggate. It appears that Mr Leggate had difficulty reconciling his personal views with this policy or its rate of implementation. As well, according to the Government, it was Mr Leggate himself who initiated the question of his transferring to another section. Mr Leggate was also offered and accepted a position in the Forestry Division of the Department of Primary Industries, suitable to his experience and qualifications and with no loss of remuneration or conditions. However it appears that these problems arose because Mr Leggate attempted to implement the provisions of mining legislation as enacted by the Queensland Parliament and attempted to bring breaches of legislation to the attention of the relevant authorities. The Committee believes that Mr Leggate was acting only as required to do so as a responsible public sector employee. Legislation, as enacted by Parliament, should be implemented at least to the letter of the law. If problems arise with legislation it is the role of Parliament to amend the legislation; it is not the role of the public sector to implement 'administrative arrangements' to circumvent the letter of the law or to ignore alleged breaches of legislation.

The committee found that most, if not all, of Leggate's frustration and difficulties started when he did not receive any satisfaction with his disclosures of improper practices within his own department.

In order to take his claims further, it was necessary for Mr Leggate to link his personal issues of victimisation to his broader allegations. The issues of improper practices which he raised would seem to be of an almost textbook quality for consideration by an independent body dedicated to public interest disclosures. Once his department refused to take action on his claims, those bodies to which he then appealed were either not suitable or lacked jurisdiction.

One could well ask therefore: what use were those so-called independent bodies? Who was going to bring the Mines Department to account for its failure to enforce its own legislation? The answer should be: the Parliament itself. Let the record show that while the Queensland Government claimed a fundamental change in attitude and commitment to environmental management by the mining industry the industry has not been subjected to prosecution for breaches of the relevant acts of Parliament.

The Senate committee noted Jim Leggate's wide experience in the mining sector and 'considers him to be an honourable and credible witness'.